Scotia - Coal Mine of Doom

Other Books by Eddie Nickels

Marine Corps Draftee:
A Vietnam Era Draftee's Personal Experiences of Parris Island and Infantry Training Regiment

Six Years to Live:
An Odyssey of Life, Death, and Adversity

Garfield versus Marshall:
The Civil War Battles and Skirmishes in the Mountains of Southeastern Kentucky and Southwestern Virginia

SCOTIA - COAL MINE OF DOOM

THE TRAGIC SCOTIA MINE EXPLOSIONS OF MARCH 9 AND 11, 1976.

EDDIE NICKELS

SCOTIA - COAL MINE OF DOOM

EDDIE NICKELS

ISBN 978-0-9886933-3-3

For Photos/ Illustrations see pages 269-284

Contents

Acknowledgements

The author of a non-fiction book cannot write a book of this genre without the help and understanding of at least a few, if not many, other people helping bear the burden of research, document copying, and technical know-how. My grandson, Dylan Nickels, provided help with all the aforementioned duties and served as my photographer as well. Dylan and I spent several days and many hours driving around the area, gathering needed material for the book. I could always count on him to help me on a moment's notice.

 For his help I am very grateful and thankful that he was always willing to "go the extra mile" to help me in proceeding with the book. Without his help, it would have taken me much longer to complete the manuscript.

For permission to use his maps and other material, I'm very grateful to Benjamin Gish, Editor of _The Mountain Eagle_, Whitesburg, Kentucky. Thanks to Ben, a good map of the mine area where the two Scotia explosions took place enriches the story of what happened and where it happened. _The Mountain Eagle's_ coverage of the two explosions in 1976 and the aftermath was, thorough, factual, and comprehensive.

Thanks to the staff of the Harry M. Caudill Library, in Whitesburg, Kentucky, for their help in my research of source limited Scotia material.

I wish also to express my thanks to retired Scotia Miner Steve Brock, who provided a photo of the last four remaining original Scotia Employees who retired in 2014. They were the last of a long line of former Scotia Miners.

Thanks to other former Scotia miners who I contacted during my research for the book. You helped to jog my memory on some important facts that I had forgotten. Bennett Adams provided additional info on the names of some of the Scotia motormen.

Lastly, I would like to say that one of the most important reasons I decided to write this book was to honor the memories of those 26 men who lost their lives at Scotia and their families who suffered unimaginable pain and heartache beginning March 9 and 11, 1976. Those 26 men and their families will always live in the hearts and minds of their former Scotia co-workers, who suffered and grieved along with them.

FOREWORD

Coal mining has long been considered one of the most dangerous vocations in America, and rightfully so. After all, how many children have a dream of one day growing up to become an underground coal miner? Still, many young men grow up to not only become coal miners, but to also enjoy the benefits associated with producing the energy needs of our country.

Even though the mining of coal has been in somewhat of a slump for a few years due to pollution concerns, men and women still labor as coal miners all over the world and in America, and are proud of their contribution to their respective nation's energy needs.

The men and women who were employed at Scotia Coal Company from the beginning of the Company's operations in 1962 until the end of the Scotia name in 1991 also felt pride in their work. They were doing a necessary job, were receiving good pay and benefits, and were treated fair by their bosses and Company officials when occasional differences and work related issues needed to be addressed.

Many of the issues that needed to be settled involved safety in the No.1, or "bottom" mine which was mining the seam of coal called the Imboden Seam, named after Confederate General John D. Imboden, who developed that particular seam after he settled in Washington County, Virginia, a few years after the Civil War ended.

The Imboden Seam was located under the Big Black Mountain Range of the Cumberland Mountains, and was below the water drainage, which tends to make underground coal mines emit heavy concentrations of methane gas.

The Scotia bottom mine liberated methane in the range of 200,000 to 500,000 cubic feet of methane per 24 hour period, and was considered the "gassiest' mine in Eastern Kentucky. The most active amounts of methane produced were at the mining faces. This amount of methane to be swept from the mine's working faces is relatively unimportant and easily controlled providing that enough proper ventilation measures were taken to keep the methane concentration below ignition levels.

A few mines in neighboring Virginia liberated an even greater amount of methane than Scotia, and still managed to mine coal efficiently and safely and to keep the methane gas below explosive levels through proper ventilation methods.

The Federal Mine Health and Safety Act (of 1969) described adequate ventilation as a minimum of 9,000 cubic feet of air per minute passing over the last open cross-cut at the face of a mine. The Kentucky Department of Mines and Minerals however, ruled that due to Scotia's high rate of methane liberation, 16,000 cubic feet per minute would be required. Scotia has been reported as having produced only about 10,000 cubic feet per minute of air at best in the bottom mine.

When Scotia's 2 Southeast Mains Section reached a point where their continuous miner's cutting head couldn't reach the top of the coal because the coal was higher that the 10ft reach of the cutting head, Scotia's management decided to move the section's equipment outby the section a distance of 1,800 ft. and start a new section in lower height coal.

This move necessitated the producing of coal from the new section (designated 2 Left off 2 Southeast Mains) without taking the necessary time to construct overcasts to properly divert the fresh air into the new section and the old section at the same time.

The unexpected idling of the 2 SEM Section caused Scotia's management to have to make a decision to stop production all-together, spread the crew out between other work crews, have a reduction of their work force, or quickly begin another section and continue producing coal with the crew from the idled section. They chose the latter course, which turned out to be the worst choice they could have possibly chosen, not only because of the illegalities involved, but because of the destruction and devastation that would be set off by this wrong and hasty decision.

My purpose in writing the story of the tragic happenings at Scotia is not to point fingers of blame at anyone or any institution, but merely to tell the story of what happened before, during, and after the explosions at Scotia Coal Company on March 9 and 11 1976, from the perspective of someone who witnessed a large part of it.

Introduction

Confederate Brigadier General John D. Imboden could have been accused of being partly to blame for the two terrible explosions that destroyed the lives of 15 coal miners on March 9, 1976, and of destroying the lives of 8 more miners and 3 federal inspectors two days later on March 11, 1976.

Of course General Imboden wasn't around when these men were killed, but without him, the coal seam they were mining might never have been developed for mining. In fact, the seam of coal that Scotia mined at the time of the explosions was the Imboden Seam of coal, named after General Imboden because of the important part he had played in its development.

With the end of the war, General Imboden had settled in Richmond, Virginia and resumed his law practice that he had given up at the outbreak of the war. During the later years of his life, he resided in Washington County, Virginia, where he pioneered the coal mining resources of the area. He died in Damascus, Virginia in 1895, and is buried in Hollywood Cemetery, in Richmond, Virginia.

Without his work of developing the seam of coal named after him, there might not have been a Scotia Coal Company, or any other company for that matter, mining coal in that particular seam of coal. But the coal was too valuable to ignore once it was discovered. Typically, the height of the Imboden coal is 6 to 7 feet thick and the coal is an excellent metallurgical coal for steel making.

The high quality of the coal championed by General Imboden caught the eye and ear of Gordon Bonnyman, President of Blue Diamond Coal Company and son of the Founder of Blue Diamond Coal, Alexander Bonnyman Jr. Gordon Bonnyman had taken over the Company after the death of his father in 1953 and as President, continued the success the Company had enjoyed since their founding in 1916.

In 1962, Gordon Bonnyman and the Blue Diamond Coal Company leased (or bought) a boundary of coal lying deep under the Black Mountain Range of the Cumberland Mountains, located In Letcher County, Kentucky, and Wise County, Virginia. The newly formed subsidiary of Blue Diamond was named Scotia Coal Company, which would be mining the coal of the Imboden seam. The coal had to be reached through a series of slope entries, instead of a traditional drift mine.

From the beginning, Scotia became known as a "gassy" mine, due to the high concentration of methane which the roof, ribs, and coal emitted constantly. This was due to the fact that the Imboden seam of coal was so deep underground that it was well below the water table, and any coal mine below the water table tends to emit higher concentrations of methane than would a mine located above the water table. Scotia eventually, in 1972 and 1973, started two more mines on its property located much higher up on Black Mountain, and they had few problems, if any, with high methane concentrations at the upper mines.

While Scotia had the gassiest mine in Letcher County, and reportable in all of Eastern Kentucky, there were a few mines in Western Virginia that had much higher concentrations of gas in their mine atmosphere than did the Scotia No.1 Mine. The Scotia Mine liberated in the range of 200,000 to 500,000 cubic feet of methane per 24 hours, with the most active production being at the faces where coal was being produced. The amount of methane liberated is not important if proper ventilation is adequate to sweep the methane out of the mine.

When the 2 Southeast Mains Section in the No.1 Imboden Mine had been driven about 3,800 feet from the Northeast Main/2 Southeast Mains intersection, the 7 ft high coal changed into a height of 10-11 ft coal. The continuous miner they were using to drive the section didn't have enough reach with the miner head to cut the coal at such height. A new continuous miner was put on order that would be able to reach the coal in the heading of 2 Southeast Mains, but that took time, and time was money.

The decision was then made by management to stop mining in 2 Southeast Mains, drop back outby the heading for 1,800 ft. and start another section off in the solid block of coal located in the 2 Southeast Mains return entry. The equipment was moved back the 1,800 ft and soon the new 2 Left off -2 Southeast Mains Section was producing coal on the day shift and the second shift by the first week of February, 1976.

The only problem was that in order to start a new section required that a set of overcasts be built to separate the air flow to direct fresh air to the new section. In the case of the new 2 Left Section, this meant that if the air was shared, neither section would be able to receive sufficient air to keep methane concentrations below an explosive level. Also, a new Ventilation Plan would be needed to be approved by state and federal officials for the new section to mine the first block of coal. Neither of these conditions was completed when the new section began producing coal.

The overcasts were not built when coal was produced on 2 Left and the Ventilation Plan wasn't even submitted until March 1st 1976. The evening before the first explosion, a federal inspector measured just 8,092 cubic feet per minute of air sweeping the working face and shut the 2 Left Section down until sufficient air was directed on section to meet the 9,000 cubic feet of air per minute that was required to sweep across the working face. Two hours later he measured 10,472 feet per minute. Where did this extra air come from, when the ventilation was so bad on that section that one miner of six years experience said after the explosion of March 9, "There's not enough air in there. There's never been enough air in there". This was one of the questions that investigators had following the explosions at Scotia.

For an explosion to happen, three things are necessary and must come together simultaneously.

- Fuel (methane)
- A source of ignition (open flame or arc)
- Oxygen

On March 9, 1976, 2 Southeast Mains unfortunately had this deadly combination in the atmosphere on section;

A. The poor ventilation allowed methane amounts to increase to the 5-15 % needed for an explosion.

B. A source of ignition was present on 2 SEM when a load of rails and two locomotives arrived on section, with one locomotive equipped with a compressor that created an arc when it kicked on.

C. oxygen levels only had to be at 12% or higher to allow an explosion.

Everything needed for an explosion came together just right and at just the right time to allow an explosion to happen, and so it did. Not once, but twice in a period of 60 hours, the Scotia Imboden Seam No.1 Mine was racked by deadly explosions.

This book tells the story of Scotia and the two tragedies that changed Mine Safety laws and 26 families' lives forever.

Author's Note

I decided to write this book about the deaths of 23 miners and 3 federal inspectors in the Scotia Coal Mine explosions after waiting many years for someone else to tackle the job, but since time is moving so fast for me, and the memories are fading even faster, I felt that it was now or never if I wanted to see the job finished. I also felt compelled to write it just so the truth of what happened could be told from the perspective of a Scotia Coal Miner who had been an eye witness to some of the events. There was not a little hesitation on my part to write about the explosions because I felt some people might think I would possibly be too biased for one side or the other in telling the whole story because of my 17 years and 3 months of employment at Scotia. Some others who know me well know that I will always tell it like is and like it happened, to the best of my ability, without inflating the facts or figures involved in the story.

I have told the facts as I have found them no matter what they were found to be during my research, and even when I differed with the investigators, which was very seldom, I explained my reason for doing so.

One situation where we differed was with the official findings of the (then) Mine Enforcement and Safety Administration, (MESA) now called the Mine Health and Safety Administration, (MHSA) when they gave their conclusions as to what caused the second explosion. The different belief I hold about the cause is based on the fact that I too was in the area of the explosions before they were cleaned up and recovered, as a member of the Fresh Air Crew, who followed the Rescue Teams after their explorations during the recovery of the mine. This gave me an excellent opportunity to observe and study the area, equipment, and places involved in the explosions for myself.

In some instances where I felt that my own experience would enrich or confirm the facts in which I was personally involved, I relate what I saw or did as a member of the Fresh Air Crew, but for the most part I tried to tell the story from a general prospective and without speculation on my part.

I felt also that the story of Scotia's beginning, the lead-up to the tragic explosions, and the end of Scotia mining at Ovenfork, Kentucky in 1991, would be necessary to be told in some detail in order to tell the complete story of the now defunct Scotia Coal Company.

My main purpose has been to tell the story of who, what, when, where, and why, as it pertains to Scotia Coal Company and the two devastating explosions that became part of Scotia's history that can never be erased.

It's very important from a historical perspective to tell the facts as an eyewitness and a Scotia Employees Association member experienced them while they are fresh enough for him to remember. May we always honor and never forget the 26 men who lost their lives those many years ago on March 9 and 11, 1976.

Glossary

Bore-Hole—A hole drilled with a drill or rotary tool to provide access to underground working sections of a mine.

Bottom—The floor in an underground mine.

Brattice—A temporary partition in an underground mine consisting of fire-resistant cloth to direct the flow of air into the working face.

Colliery—a coal mine and its buildings and equipment

Command Center—Any work area established directing response to a mine emergency.

Crosscut—A cut through a block of coal to allow access of mining equipment and the passage of air.

Curtain—A piece or sheet of (usually) fire resistant material used to direct fresh air to the working face.

Entry—A passageway about 20 ft. wide that has been mined of coal and connected to crosscuts about every 80-100 feet.

Fresh Air Base—An underground station in the intake airway established by rescue teams during rescue and recovery efforts.

Gob—Waste material produced in coal mining, such as clay, shale, etc.

Inby—In a direction toward the working face of a coal mine.

Outby—In a direction toward the outside of a coal mine.

Overcast—An enclosed airway constructed to provide a means for one air current to cross another.

Panel—A compartment of a coal mine separated from other working places by a large block or several pillars of coal.

Recovery—The restoration of a whole or a part of a coal mine that has suffered damage because of roof falls, fires, explosions, water or other cause.

Regulator—An adjustable partial obstruction in an airway.

Rescue Team —A team of miners trained to work under dangerous conditions while wearing breathing apparatuses for rescue and recovery operations.

Rib—The walls or sides of a mined entry or entries in an underground coal mine.

Roof—The rock immediately above a coal seam.

Seal—The securing of an opening or break against the seeping or escaping of air or noxious gases from a contaminated area of the mine by building concrete barriers and sealing with mine sealant or grout.

Shaft—A vertical opening through the strata that is or may be used in connection with the mining of coal, for the purpose of ventilation or drainage, or for hoisting men, coal, or other material.

Slope—An inclined passage driven from the surface down through the strata to provide access to the mine workings.

Stopping—A wall of concrete blocks and cement or mortar used to seal or close off crosscuts to prevent air from short-circuiting, so as to maintain ventilation to the working faces.

Working Face—The place where coal is extracted from the face in a heading or crosscut.

Scotia-Coal Mine of Doom

CHAPTER ONE

Coal's Global Impact

The history of coal production for use as a fuel, iron ore smelting, and to power the industrial revolution is a recent one as it pertains to the United States, but older nations knew of coal's qualities long before the founding of America.

The early inhabitants of China during the Stone Age period around six thousand years ago also found another interesting use for coal. They used it to make trinkets for ornaments because they liked how the shiny coal made them look. Somewhere around three thousand five hundred years ago the Chinese started using coal mainly for heating purposes. About 100 years before the birth of Christ the Chinese began producing iron by using charcoal made from coal.

The British were introduced to the many uses of coal by the invading Romans, who conquered Britain around 55 B.C. and stayed around until 400 A.D. They called this strange black mineral "agate." Like the early Chinese, they too used this soft mineral to make jewelry and trinkets to send home to their friends and kinfolk in Rome. *

It wasn't long before the Roman soldiers discovered that the shiny black mineral had pretty good burning qualities too. They then began using coal to heat their forts and living quarters, making occupational life in Britain just a little more comfortable for the homesick soldiers. There's no evidential proof that the British themselves used coal for heating purpos-

---

* *Coal, A Human History*, Barbara Freese Penguin Books, U.S.A.,2003

es during this period of time. Another seven hundred plus years would pass before the British started using coal as a heating fuel.

In the late 1100's the writers of that period began to make mention of the British using coal as a fuel. Their name for the mineral was "sea coal." No one knows where the name originated, but the fact that most coal was shipped or moved by water was likely a good guess of the origin of the name. England had plenty of waterways and shoreline to accommodate the movement of coal to market, which made for cheaper production and shipping costs than those associated with moving coal by land over poorly constructed and maintained public roads.

By the 1200's the town of Newcastle in England was an important coal producing town located about 300 miles from London. Newcastle's proximity to the Tyne River allowed for the shipping of coal to London much cheaper that would be the case if the coal was shipped by land. As a result, coal produced in the coalfields of Newcastle was shipped to London in the years 1257-1259 for the construction of the famed Westminster Abby. [+]

In the early 1700's the first steam engine water pump was installed in an English mine to pump water out of the mine. Flooding had been a problem in mines since men first began mining underground seams of coal, especially those coal seams located below the water table. This one engine could do the work of fifty horses and saved mine operators large sums of money when the cost of buying and maintaining fifty horses was figured in the equation. The only drawback to the stem powered engines was that they used huge amounts of coal to keep them working. Luckily, the very fact of being located inside the coal mine assured a plentiful supply of fuel to operate the useful pumps.

In the 1700 and 1800's, the production methods having allowed for the fairly cheap production of coal for fuel and iron making, the British were enjoying the fruits of the industrial revolution and their plentiful supply of cheap coal to drive their world commerce ambitions. Without coal, none of this commercial success and worldwide influence would have been possible for Britain. By the middle 1800's Britain was leading the world in the production of coal and was producing more coal than the rest of the world combined.

While Britain and China had long been using coal to fuel their industries and homes and to literally save lives by providing an energy source

---

[+] ibid

to keep the citizens of their countries warm in the cold winters, other nations had also began to discover the many advantages of having coal as a natural resource. All of Europe and indeed established nations and a relatively recently settled country was beginning to discover that their own fledgling country had abundant supplies of coal with which to supply their industrial needs for a source of cheap and abundant fuel which was just what that nation needed to become a great industrial power.

That recently settled country was in what was then considered the New World but had not yet fought their war for independence that would establish them as a new player on the world scene. This land that would become the Unites States of America was just beginning to discover that the commodity that was then powering other nation's industrial capacity was also available here.

Coal was first discovered by Huguenot settlers at Manikin, on the James River near what is now Richmond, Virginia in 1673-1674. They too noticed that the black mineral was easily obtained from the outcroppings on the riversides. One can imagine that liberal use of the mineral was made during the cold winter months by early settlers of that region.

The first significant use of the James River outcrop coal deposits was in 1702 when blacksmiths needed fuel to power their forges. The mines eventually needed to go deeper to obtain coal and in 1810 several vertical shafts were in operation. In that same year the first recorded mine explosion occurred.

As coal mines went deeper into the coal seams, several new mining hazards become known. Occupational dangers included roof falls, rib rolls, the breathing of debilitating coal dust, and also dangerous gases made their appearance.

Methane (chemical symbol CH_4) is a highly flammable gas that is found in coal mines due to emanations from the coal seam and from carbonaceous shale rock. This gas is most dangerous of exploding when the atmosphere where it is present contains 5-15% of methane and when 12% or more oxygen is present. It then requires an ignition source of 1200° F to explode the mixture of air and gas. The presence of methane and oxygen in an explosive mixture is often known by the term "fire damp." Methane is also the main ingredient in natural gas used as an energy source.

Another hazard common to coal mines is that of "blackdamp." This dangerous condition is caused by an atmosphere that is deficient in oxygen. This deficiency happens most often when ventilation is poor or when an explosion or fire has depleted the oxygen level. This is the condition that one often encounters when he or she enters old works of the mine or goes into an abandoned mine and is overcome, which causes unconsciousness and often death of the individual.

"Firedamp" is the name for the atmosphere following an explosion in a coal mine. Gases that are present or deficient after the initial blast are: carbon dioxide, carbon monoxide, decreased oxygen, nitrogen, hydrogen, and smoke. The presence of these combinations of gases can be, and are often, fatal to those who encounter them after an explosion.

Some means of detection of the presence of at least one on these dangerous gases became a priority in the early years of commercial coal operations. The explosive qualities haven been proven by the first record mine explosion in 1810, one of the scientists and inventors of those early days of mining finally hit on a solution. A man by the name of Sir Humphrey tinkered with the problem and came up with the first flame safety lamp. This device used the height and color of the flame in the device to measure the amount of methane present in the mine atmosphere.

This lessened the danger of methane being present in explosive quantities but didn't eliminate the problem completely. The period from 1810 through 1875 saw 19 different coal mines and 4 metal and nonmetal mines with documented explosions which caused 5 or more deaths with each explosive disaster. From 1875 through 1900 the number of disasters rose to 101 coal mines and 17 metal and nonmetal mines, for a total of 118 deadly explosions resulting in five or more deaths. In comparison, the years from 1976 to 2010 (including the Scotia twin disasters) the number of documented mine disasters dropped to 18 coal mines and one metal or nonmetal mine with 5 or more deaths occurring.

The flame safety lamp served its purpose for many years but was finally phased out in the early 1970's and the methane monitors that are still in use today replaced them. The methane monitors are much easier to use and are safer and more reliable than the old useful but outdated flame safety lamp. Miners commonly call these methane testers "spotters." The most common detectors in use are those that can detect methane that is present in the 0.1 to 5% range. They operate on the "Wheatstone bridge" principle which makes use of electrically heated filaments that burn the methane and measure the heat output. The heat is then translated into percentages on the direct reading dials.

Another methane detector with a higher detection range than the most commonly used "5%" detectors is the Riken methane indicator. This detector was mainly carried by the Federal Mine Enforcement Safety Administration inspectors during the Scotia explosions. It has (or had) the capability to measure methane up to 100 percentage points, which is incredible. Those carried by Scotia employees (including the writer) were the MSA or National/ Drager brands which measured up to 5% of any methane present in the atmosphere. Thus, the presence of a methane "feeder" would have been undetectable with our Scotia detectors we carried.

Two early explorers of Kentucky are credited with the first mention of the availability of coal in the yet to be explored wilderness country. Thomas Walker came through the Cumberland Gap in April 1750 to explore the territory for the Loyal Land Company. Walker did as others had done for centuries, he pulled some coal from the river bank to heat his campfire and perhaps to cook his wild game he killed along the way.

The other early explorer was Christopher Gist, a surveyor, who was the first known European to traverse through the storied Pound Gap in the Cumberland Mountains. He came as an employee of the Ohio Land Company, who having a land grant from the King of England, hired Gist to explore their territory and mark their lands.

He set out on his journey in October, 1750, and on April 1st, 1751 he made this entry in his Journal:

Monday April 1,---Set out the same Course about 20 M. Part of the way we went along a Path up the side of a little Creek, at the head of which was a gap in the Mountains, then our path went down another Creel to a Lick where Blocks of Coal about 8 to 10 In: square lay upon the surface of the Ground, here we killed a Bear and emcamped.[±]

This details his trek up the North Fork of the Kentucky River and through the Pound Gap. Both he and Thomas walker had mentioned the coal they happened upon during their travels, which ironically took place only one year apart.

Between the years of 1779 and 1812 settlers from the east, west, and south began making their appearance in larger numbers into the untamed lands of Eastern Kentucky and the region that would, in 1842, become known as Letcher County. After that date migration into the mountains of the Cumberland Plateau slowed to a trickle.

The commercial development of coal in Kentucky was slow to appear in the 1800's and it was in 1843 before the production figure for the whole state reached 100,000 tons. Just a few years later in 1885 the first land

---

[±] Johnson, J. Stoddard, *First Explorations of Kentucky*, John P. Morton & Co., 1898

speculator and coal reserves buyer, W.J. Horsley, came to Letcher County to hopefully acquire rights to coal seams. He was aided and guided by the former Confederate Colonel, Logan H.N. Salyer, originally from Scott County Virginia.± (Salyer is also a distant cousin of this writer.)

Within a couple of years (beginning in 1887) other speculators and coal buyers were seen throughout the area for the next 20 years trying to urge land owners to sell the rights to their coal for as little as 50 cents an acre. Some succumbed to the offer and sold their rights because they never expected the buyers to be able to mine their property in a thousand years. They couldn't foresee the future when mechanization and new ways of mining would make the impossible possible.

In 1900 the first commercial coal mine in Eastern Kentucky was opened in Betsy Layne, Floyd County Kentucky. Following their example was a commercial mining enterprise which opened in Letcher County the same year. From the year 1900 and extending into 1905 was the "hey day" of broad form coal leases being drawn up in Letcher County and other Eastern Kentucky counties.

In 1820 the very first mine to operate commercially opened in Muhlenberg County in Western Kentucky. It produced only 328 tons of coal that first year. In 1879 coal production for the whole state reached 1,000,000 tons for the first time ever.

One of the first strikes of a working coal mine (if not the first) occurred in Western Kentucky in 1886-1887 when the miners accused the owner of the mine of giving them short weight on their tonnage mined. It was not uncommon in those early days of mining for the owners to try to persuade their weight check men to short weight the cars of coal brought out of the mine. In addition, some companies paid their men by the "long ton", which required them to mine 2,200 lb to count as a ton, while the owner sold the coal by the "short ton" which was 2,000lb. It didn't take long for the company to gain a ton of coal on the backs of the poor working miners.

With the increase of coal production in Kentucky and the nation in the first part of the 20th century came an increase in mining disasters and fatalities. In 1909 there were 20 coal mine disasters in the United States that resulted in the deaths of five or more miners. The next year (1910) saw the greatest number of disasters when metal and nonmetal mines

---

± Cornett, Terry, *History of Letcher County*, State-Wide Printing, 1967

were counted together. That terrible year brought a total of 25 mine disasters; 19 coal, and 6 metal/nonmetal mine disasters.

With the increased production, not only were mining accidents increasing, but the technological advances were coming quickly. The coal industry, especially the larger operations, began to take advantage of electricity and rail transportation to employ electric track motors to haul the coal from the loading point to the outside. These electric motors were widely in use by the end of the first decade of the 20th century.

The 1,583 tons of coal produced in 1889 by the first commercial mine in Letcher County, Kentucky was just a drop in the bucket compared with the fact that over 588,000,000 tons of coal has been produced in Letcher County as of 2005.

The years between 1900-1910 saw an increase of small "dog hole" mine openings that mined small amounts of coal for use as fuel locally and some small commercial ventures that struggled to stay afloat for lack of adequate transportation to ship their coal. Small amounts were moved by wagon over, for the most part, atrocious roads that were best described as wagon paths. Some idea of road conditions at that period of time in Whitesburg and surrounding communities can only be imagined by the testimony of one of those men, a merchant that traveled the road from the Poor Fork section of the south side of Pine Mountain:

"I used to have to haul my goods by wagon over some of the worst roads you ever saw between here and Whitesburg. I would leave here on Poor Fork before daylight and would travel over the mountain through Scuttle Hole Gap, then up Cowan to Lewis Wholesale Company which would take the better part of the day to reach. I would then load my wagon with as many goods as possible before starting back home. If by chance it had rained that day I would usually have to hire a team of horses from a man in Whitesburg to pull me up the muddy street to the top of the hill there. You would about sink up to the hubs the mud would be so deep. The man kept a team of horses for that very purpose. If I was lucky, I would get back to Poor Fork before morning. Sometimes I didn't make it."

The roads (if one could call them by that name) had seen very little if any improvement since the Civil War period (1861-1865). Captain Edward O. Guerrant, Adjutant of General Humphrey Marshall, and who spent some time in Letcher County during those years, said this about the roads in the lower part of Letcher County:

Near Whitesburg
Letcher Co. Ky.
February 7, 62

    Dear Father After nearly a week's riding over the worst roads(or rather NO roads)I ever saw, I arrived last night at Col. Jno Williams Regiment encamped some seven miles from here on a creek called Colly.[*]

---

[*] Edward O. Guerrant, <u>Bluegrass Confederate,</u> Louisiana State University Press, 1999.

CHAPTER TWO

The Railroad Arrives

With the coming of the railroad to Eastern Kentucky and Letcher County in 1912 coal production was about to undergo a drastic change for the coal mines of the region. While coal production in the county had been meager due to lack of good transportation options in the past, the newly installed rail lines provided relatively cheap means to ship coal quickly and easily to factories in the north and steel mills in the south, and also to electric utilities all over the nation and the world.

As early as 1851 a railroad company proposed a road that would have linked Winchester, Kentucky to Abington, Virginia but the corporation that was trying to raise capital for the construction was unable to even start the project.

It was only when the large corporations started to expand their operations in the eastern Kentucky coal fields that the railroads finally decided to extend their lines into Letcher, Harlan, and other counties whose coal seams had barely been touched heretofore. It took a couple of years for the track layers to reach the terminus for the Lexington and Eastern Railroad at McRoberts in northern Letcher County, while nearly at the same time the L and N Railroad reached Harlan County's rich coal fields.

During the building of these railroads by dozens of small contractors the construction crews had endured frightful conditions while trying to negotiate the many streams, rivers, and mountains of sandstone rock that had to be blasted little by little, making progress frustrating, difficult, and very dangerous. Many of these men lost their lives while building the

9

road. It was because of their hard work and dedication that better transportation and a cheaper and faster way to ship coal to market enabled many of the poor farmers and laborers of the region to earn a decent day's pay as a coal miner.

The laborers that built the railroad through the mountains earned the "princely" sum of $1.50 a day. Most of them were black men from the southern states, but many mountaineers were also employed as the lines advanced through the mountains. They were glad to get the work.

Now that the railroads had finally made their appearance the large corporations soon followed them into the mountains with building plans of their own. Large corporations with important sounding names such as; The Elkhorn Coal Corporation, International Harvester Corporation, Inland Steel Corporation, United States Coal and Coke Corporation, and the Virginia Iron, Coal and Coke Company, started building coal mining camps at a feverish pitch.

Before long these new camps and towns sprang up like wild dandelions throughout Letcher, Perry, and Harlan Counties. Names like Chip, Seco, Mayking, Four Mile, Glo, Carbon Glow, Kona, Scuddy, Sassafras, Happy, and Apex became household names with the residents of these communities often living in company owned houses.

These towns were usually named after the corporation "big shots" or after their wives, daughters, or girlfriends. Fleming, McRoberts, Lynch, Jenkins, Dunham, Haymond, and Wayland were named after executives employed by these companies. The town of Jenkins for instance, was practically nothing but a few scattered primitive houses among the trees when the Consolidation Coal Company built the complete town, including dozens and dozens of nice houses for their employees to live in. They even built a power plant to power the town, bringing in the boilers for the plant by way of teams of oxen, which they used to haul the boilers across the Cumberland Mountain Range through the Pound Gap.

A total of thirty-seven large coal camps were built in Letcher County by the beginning of 1930, but when the small camps are included, a total of at least fifty-seven coal camps were constructed by both large and small coal companies between the years of 1910-1930.

In order to provide enough manpower to work so many new start-up mines in Eastern Kentucky and other coal producing states, it was necessary to scour hills and hollows for those men willing to risk their lives in such a dangerous profession. Many of the laborers that toiled on the newly built railroads stayed in the mountains to work in the mines. The knowledge that they had acquired about handling dynamite and blasting rocks and boulders apart to make way for the railroad would come in handy for the former rail layers.

Even with the many local residents and railroad workers who now became underground coal miners, not enough willing men were available to adequately work the mines without going elsewhere for them and that is exactly what the mine owners often had to do. Somehow the word spread that miners were needed in the newly constructed coalfields and many cotton pickers and farm workers from Alabama, Tennessee, Mississippi, Arkansas, and other southern states caught the freight trains and coal trains as they headed north into Kentucky for loads of black gold. There are many instances of black and white potential coal miners who left their homes in the south with little or no money, hoping to get a job in the coal fields.

Even the slight national depression of 1921-1922 had very little effect on the coal mines and those seeking work in them usually succeeded in their quest. The three or four dollars a day they could usually earn as coal miners sure beat the $1.50 they made for building the railroad and the work wasn't much harder or more dangerous than they had experienced when laying rails and blasting rock for a living. Those who had come from the south were usually completely without a job when they left home and $3.00 a day in script or real money sure seemed like a good deal to them.

If by chance there were not enough adult men to be found, convinced, or coaxed to work the mines, another manpower source was available right under the mine owners' noses if they chose to use it. That source was a little bit controversial, but what the heck, they thought, we need workers and even young boys can help us mine coal in some manner. This was a problem that mine managers could easily solve, so they did. They began hiring boys as young as 8-10 years of age to work in the mines.

Since the boys were unable to do much heavy lifting or keep up with a grown man when shoveling coal, there were other jobs that the boys could handle. They could easily carry supplies to the miners at the face of the mine, open and close ventilation doors for men bringing loaded coal cars to the surface, pick slate and slag from the coal, and feed and care for the ponies that some mines used to pull the loaded coal cars.

These chores were necessary to the production of coal and someone had to do them, so why not use boys instead of adult men who could be better utilized in actually producing coal at the face, was their thinking.

Many of these boy miners were used as "driver boys," handling or driving ponies and mules to the face and picking up the loaded cars of coal and bringing them outside to dump into the tipple. Some of these animals never saw the light of day again, spending their lives in makeshift corrals inside the mine and saving time and money of having to hire some man or boy to feed and care for them on the outside of the mine.

Some pony drivers treated the animals decently and humanely, even going so far as to threaten to quit if the driver wasn't allowed to feed the ponies before taking them inside the mine.

In the late 1930's an incident occurred which will illustrate an example of a caring pony driver: This particular driver always arrived at the truck mine where he was employed at least a half-hour earlier than the production crew so he could feed and water the two ponies he used to haul the coal cars in and out of the mine. When he began to feed and care for the animals his boss pulled up and said, "You don't have time for that this morning son, just hitch the ponies up and take'm on in the mine, I've got coal on the bottom and cars loaded, ready to be pulled out!" Without missing a beat the pony driver looked up at his boss and said, " Mister I'm not moving these ponies until I get them fed and watered. If you're in that big a hurry to kill these ponies I'll just quit right now and walk off this hill! You'll kill them if they're not watered and fed before sending them in there." Everything got very quiet and all that could be heard was the animals chomping and chewing their sweet feed as the boss stared at the driver. After a pause the boss walked up to the driver, put his arm around his shoulder and said, "Ed, go ahead and feed and water them, the coal can wait, I don't want you to kill the ponies, you're in the right!" With that, the driver finished taking care of his ponies and kept his job.

One of our subject's co-workers told me about that event after the former miner had passed away. That incident was typical of how he treated people and animals all his life. I might mention here that he was 14 or 15 years old when this happened. He, like his dad before him, was a boy "driver" who had quit school and went to work in the mines.

In the 1920's the increased presence of the "big boy" corporations and companies and so many more miners were at work that the United Mine Workers of America began to try to organize some of the workers but for the most part their efforts were spurned by the mine workers. They were making good wages and their working conditions were on the whole satisfactory, making organizing for the union a fairly tough sell.

12

With so many miners employed it's no wonder that the U.M.W.A. would set their sights on adding to their membership rolls. There were grievances against the mine owners in those days but because the nation was still trying to come out of the slight depression of the early 20's the miners were just satisfied to have a job and didn't want to "rock the boat."

To counter the organizing attempt by the U.M.W.A. some companies hired mine guards either locally or through private agencies. The object was to keep the union organizers far away from the miners in order to prevent any chance of collusion between the two groups.

Sometimes even the governors of states could be persuaded by mine operators to provide National Guard troops to protect and preserve the peace for an area where the organizing drives were resulting in strikes, work stoppages, or unruly picket lines. Harlan County in 1939 and Letcher County in 1959 are two instances where troops were sent to keep the peace in the coalfields.

The largely unsuccessful efforts of the union organizing drives of the 1920's changed to more positive results with the onset of the "Great Depression" years of the early 1930's.Mine operators had attempted in the intervening years to thwart the organizing efforts of the U.M.W.A. by encouraging miners to form their own union as a last resort. One such union was the Progressive Mine Workers , which was endorsed by some operators, and which managed to have some success with their organizing efforts in the depressed coal fields of the early 30's.

Their success was short-lived though and by the middle years of the 30's decade the P.M.W. was gone from the scene. The depression that had such a terrible stranglehold on the nation caused thousands of coal jobs to disappear, with many companies leaving the coal fields, selling their equipment, and in most cases selling their company-built homes to their former miners at much reduced prices. Not much union organizing can be done when there are few miners left to organize, although the few mines operating during this period were mostly the larger ones who had signed union contracts in the years before the depression had fully taken hold.

With war threatening on the horizon at the beginning of the 1940's the familiar "boom or bust" legacy of the coal mining industry was in the boom category at long last. Experienced coal miners had lain down their coal shovels and carbide lamps in the last years of the depression and had exchanged them for hammers, nails, and dirt shovels as they went to work for the government sponsored Works Progress Administration (W.P.A.) or the more military-like Civilian Conservation Corps. (C.C.C.) The difference in the two organizations was slight since both provided needed employment unemployed Americans that were desperate for work of any kind. The W.P.A. workers were for the most part above the military age, while the C.C.C. provided jobs for military age young men in a somewhat disciplined military environment.

The C.C.C. also provided camps for their workers, while the W.P.A. men usually resided at home and worked on local projects. Both groups of men provided much needed labor on the infrastructure throughout the country repairing bridges and roads, working to preserve the parks and forests, planting trees, etc. When war actually began for America on December 7, 1941, many of the C.C.C. and W.P.A. workers easily transitioned to the military side of government employment. Those who didn't volunteer eventually found themselves drafted.

When the coal boom hit, dozens of small 'dog-holes' sprang up around the mountains. Plenty of work was again available for those men who had not yet volunteered or been drafted, but most of the available workers were older workers who had started their mining careers in the 20's or 30's. Their generation had worked the mines when wages were about three or four dollars a day at most, but the shortage of workers now had driven miner's wages to Eight, nine, even ten dollars a day, which was very tempting to those who were just coming out of the terrible depression years.

Suddenly, many potential small truck mine operators were busily scrambling to lease seams of coal and to procure the necessary equipment needed to scratch out a few tons of coal a day they could produce for the quickly expanding war industry. A couple of homemade rail cars, a breast auger, shovels, picks, a small fan for ventilation, a power source for the fan, and a few miners, experienced or not, and the hiring of a bulldozer and operator to uncover the coal seam was sufficient to begin a small mining venture. A small loading tipple to dump the mined coal into was also essential, providing the rough lumber could be procured with which to construct it.

One of these small operators with which the writer was acquainted with in later years described some of the draw-backs to making a profit during this boom cycle:

"I went into business for myself after years of working for the other man, thinking that maybe I could be a rich man in a few years. I did

make good money at first but with so many truck mines in competition with me I found that most or some of them could undercut me because they were mining coal on contract with the bigger mines. I just couldn't compete with them on my small profit margin. It got so bad that many weeks there would be nothing left for my salary after paying my men for their week's work. I made sure they were paid first, then I would have to go home and charge my groceries for a few weeks. I finally had to close it down. My men were members of the U.M.W.A."

By the late 40's another mining "bust" had taken hold in the coalfields again and the coal operators found themselves in a depressed coal market again. Most utilities and factories had stockpiles of coal on the ground and had no need for large amounts of coal because of the slowdown in the economy. The coal mining boom that had seen the rise of so many truck mines during the war years was pretty much over by the middle 50's and would never reach those heights again, even though a few truck mines were still opening and operating into the 1970's.

Letcher County had its share of truck mine operators through the years, helping to provide employment to thousands of workers. The peak year for coal mine employment in the county was in 1949 when 9,114 full time miners were employed. This was the equivalent to almost one-quarter of the county's total population at that time.

The Letcher County *Mountain Eagle* of November 21st 1946, brought the good news for the county that the Louisville and Nashville (L&N) Railroad had been granted permission to extend the railroad from Blackey, Kentucky to a point 25 miles up Rockhouse Creek. The writer of the article in the *Mountain Eagle* said this: *The building of this railroad will be the greatest move forward for Letcher County in more than a decade. The new road will mean new life and new hope for Letcher County.* When the former Lexington and Eastern Railroad had extended its track from Jackson in Breathitt County in 1912 the coal rich area of Rockhouse Creek had not yet garnered much attention from coal speculators or coal buyers.

The same newspaper of the same date mentioned that all coal mines in Letcher County were then closed because of the labor dispute between the U.S. Secretary of Labor and United Mine Workers boss John L. Lewis. Evidently some mines were still in operation despite friction between the two factions because note was made elsewhere in the paper that '*the new coal tipple under construction at Hemphill is nearly finished.*'

At the same time of the announcement of the new railroad spur being built up Rockhouse Creek, Consolidation Coal Company was explaining how it intended to finance the sale of their houses they owned in Burdine, Dunham, Jenkins, and McRoberts. Those buyers who could not come up with the cash for a house could take advantage of a down payment and installment payments, with the tenants interested in buying a "double house" and living there the longest given the first opportunity to buy the entire structure. Some of these homes were advertised for sale by Consolidated Coal Company for as little as $100.00 a room!

The large stockpiles of coal factories and other coal-burning industries had accumulated in their storage and stockpiles became a factor during the last two years of the 40's and into the 50's. The high demand for consumer goods that followed the end of World War II encouraged many entrepreneurs to enter the coal market to supply the needed fuel to enable factories to produce those goods. As stockpiles grew the corresponding demand for coal to add to those stocks lessened.

In 1948 the nation again found itself confronting a slow- down in the economy that would more correctly be called a mini-depression. It was a familiar theme to the old coal-mining adage of a boom and bust cycle. It now entered the phase of the cycle known as a bust.

CHAPTER THREE

The Lean Years

The large corporations had become aware even before the end of the war in 1945 that the need for so many miners to work the coal mines would be unnecessary in just a few years. Mechanization of the mines was a foregone conclusion after the war and innovation had began changing coal mining techniques of the industry.

No longer would horses, mules, and ponies be needed to pull the homemade wooden coal cars to the surface with their small capacity beds. The surplus war material and scrap iron could now be melted down and utilized to manufacture all- steel, (except for the tires) 26,000 lb shuttle cars that could haul 5-10 ton of coal at a time to the dumping point where a large "feeder" made of steel conveyed the coal and crushed it and any rock with it, then dumped it slowly onto a new conveyer belt reaching to the outside stockpile. The coal loading crews were replaced with one machine, a steel monster about 20 foot in length that loaded more coal in a couple of hours into the shuttle cars than ten men could in a shift or more.

These machines were powered by 440 volts of electricity which was possibly produced by the very coal they were mining. Even the conveyor belts transporting the coal were new innovations that were revolutionizing the coal industry in the first half of the 1950's.

Another innovation that changed coal mining for the better was the introduction of the roof bolt introduced in 1956. The old method of supporting the mine roof by the use of timbers with cap boards or "wedges" to tighten them was one that had been in use ever since mining underground was begun. Sometimes miners who worked at the coal face worked without setting props at all for a period of time, making accidents and deaths an invariably frequent occurrence.

These steel roof bolts, ranging in size from around 24" in length to as long as ten or more feet would do a much better job than a timber and a cap wedge could ever do. A roof bolting machine using resin glue sticks that hold the layers of overhead rock and slate tighter than cement can install 12 to 20 resin bolts in a 20ft. cut of coal much faster than a crew of five men could carry, measure, saw, and set 20 timbers in a cut. This is probable an unfair comparison since 20 timbers could never be set in a cut of coal without blocking the next cut from being available to cut. I use this analogy as an illustration only to show the proficiency of bolting the top instead of timbering it.

Using steel bolts to secure the roof improves the safety of the miners tremendously. Timbers decrease the vision and mobility of the miners and will noticeably take weight and sag slightly when the roof gives a few inches as time goes by. With steel bolts the roof will usually hold until "retreat mining" is utilized and the supporting blocks of coal are removed. Then, the whole idea is to let the worked out section fall in to relieve the pressure on the remaining blocks of coal.

Anticipating the need for fewer coal miners as mining techniques and new machinery made its appearance, the larger corporations began divesting of their surplus property, such as houses they had built and other business they had started in order to entice workers to their newly built company towns and coal camps. The coal company businesses ranged from barber shops and beauty parlors to movie houses, ice houses, company stores, and recreation centers.

In early 1947 the Federal Government enacted a mining law entitled:

Safety Standards for Bituminous Coal and Lignite Mines Act.

Shortly thereafter, In May, 1947, the _Mountain Eagle_ mentioned the closing of 48 more truck mines for 'failure to obey safety regulations.' A Senior State Inspector ordered the mines closed after the United Mine Workers of America released a statement in which it said, "All truck operations are violating the laws." No doubt the truck mines were struggling to make a profit in the period after the war, especially 1948 and later when the economy was faltering.

At one point in the early 50's coal was being mined that brought the mine owners only $3.75 a ton at the tipple ramps, while wages sank in some cases to $5.00 per eight hour shift for non-union miners, which included most of the truck miners. Union miners were then receiving $15.00 or better at the time, plus help with their health care bills. Most of the truck miners were on their own after they received their $5.00 per day salaries. Plenty of truck mines were still operating at this time and in fact made up about 12% of the coal production tonnage in eastern Kentucky at least into the early 1960's.

One example of a typical truck mine operation involves the writer of these words and his own coal mining father. The year was 1954 and very few trains of loaded coal gondolas were leaving the Wayland, Kentucky railhead for market. It wasn't always that way, as it seemed as if a smoke belching steam powered unit train went by the Glo, Kentucky coal camp we lived in every day for awhile after we moved there. I, like most youngsters, was captivated by the loaded trains with the whistling steam engine sounding its steam whistle as it went over the crossing leading to our house in the camp. The engineer and the conductor on the deck of the caboose never failed to wave at the youngsters of the camp, including myself, as it went past with the white and black smoke blanketing the nearby houses with soot as it crawled by.

My dad had a job with a nearby truck mine and worked at least five days a week for awhile but I noticed that eventually he stayed home lots of days and I soon learned that his work place only worked two or three days a week at most during that particular school year. We barely had enough to eat most days, an extra piece of light bread being our only snack through the day. I heard my parents once in a discussion saying, "five dollars a day doesn't go very far." Our only break in routine was when once a week a neighbor lady, who had no children of her own, would go to the Wayland commissary to grocery shop and never failed to bring myself and four younger siblings a small bag of toffee candy. To this day I get sick when I think of toffee candy, but back then I was grateful to get any sweets at all, even if it wasn't really very sweet.

When an older cousin visited us during that time I begged dad to take my cousin and myself with him to the mine that he worked at. He worked on the night shift when he worked at all. One cold evening he surprised us both by actually taking us to work with him.

We were excited to be going with him and couldn't wait until the night came, but like all things in nature it eventually arrived. As we went up the steep hill to the truck mine, our anticipation grew and grew, only to be met with disappointment when we saw the small mine openings and the low rock we would be going under. The height was no more than 48 inches and probably not even that high. Another miner pulled in behind us and he and dad helped us get into an empty coal car that was probably a homemade shuttle car, while warning us to keep our fingers out of the pinch points. I was too excited and scared to know what they meant but just lay in the bottom of that car like they instructed. Their carbide lamps were lit and off we went with the motor whining on the machine. We hadn't gotten far before I felt a big jolt and sure enough pinched one of my fingers in the crack on the bottom of the contraption. I was afraid to tell dad I had pinched my finger, figuring he would say, "I told you so." So I kept my mouth shut while my finger throbbed with pain. Luckily I didn't lose it, but I have the scar to show for it today.

Dad and his buddy drilled 8 or 10 holes in the coal face of three or four entries after they had prepared them with a 'breast drill' which was unbelievably hard work. Then they packed the holes with dynamite after inserting blasting caps in the ends of some of the sticks of dynamite. They then finally lit the fuse and hurriedly we all loaded up and headed outside to await the roar of the blast. It soon came and we headed home after an exciting experience I will always treasure the rest of my life, having spent a night in a truck mine with my dad. The experience showed me how hard coal miners had to labor for their $5.00 pay at that time, and I never again had a desire to go back there with dad. I believe that was why he allowed two excited young boys such as we were to go inside a mine with him. It was a good lesson learned, one that would not be possible to teach youngsters in this day of strict mine regulations.

As early as 1947 a group of prominent Whitesburg "movers and shakers" met with some representatives of the United Mine Workers of America to discuss the possibility of building a hospital in or around Whitesburg. The meeting was held at the Daniel Boone Hotel and both sides agreed that Whitesburg was the logical place to build one. A year prior to the meeting in Whitesburg the U.M.W.A. announced plans to build a hospital to serve the miners and their families in the Big Sandy and Hazard coalfields but no location for the hospital was announced or disclosed at the time. The U.M.W.A. assigned a special committee representing the miners of District 30 the task of raising half a million dollars for the projected project.

In 1954-1955 work was begun on the U.M.W.A.'s Whitesburg Memorial Hospital, located on the Tunnel Hill farm that had belonged to Willie Lucas. In March, 1956, the hospital opened for business, its 90 beds and over 100 employees a welcome addition to the people of Letcher County and adjoining counties during those years.

At the same time that Whitesburg welcomed their new hospital, the U.M.W.A. were planning or were already building hospitals in McDowell in Floyd County, Harlan in Harlan County, Middlesboro in Bell County, and Hazard in Perry County.

At the time these hospitals were built there were already small hospitals or clinics serving several coal mining towns that offered some medical services but the new hospitals gave a quantity and quality of medical services that the smaller medical facilities couldn't possible match with their limited facilities and limited medical personnel. Jenkins, Whitaker, Benham, Lynch, and Fleming were some of the towns that had some medical facility in their community, such as a clinic or a small hospital.

Even as the U.M.W.A. was adding new hospitals to provide much improved medical facilities for the miners and their families, the exodus of able bodied former miners from the region to the factories of the North continued to thin the population of Eastern Kentucky. The slow-down in the economy that began in 1948 and continued to around 1954 convinced hundreds of families to head north to Detroit, Toledo, Dayton, Cincinnati, and many other northern cities to try to find work, preferably in an auto factory or other job that would pay more than the $8.00 they might earn as a truck mine employee, providing they could find a job with such a mine. The need for coal loaders dried up with the advent of modern machinery that had replaced hundreds of miners, especially those with no skills or little education.

Almost every family in the coal mining region had at least one and usually more family members who loaded their old Chevy or Ford with their meager belongings and headed north or sometimes turned south in search of a better life. My own close family members were no exception, with my own dad, several uncles, and dozens of cousins who left Kentucky to seek their fortunes in other states. Most are still there, with their extended family members probably now reaching into the hundreds and who are now permanently ensconced as productive citizens of many other states. Thankfully, my dad was one of those mountain people who decided life in the city of Detroit wasn't for everyone and came back home in 1952 after a working a few months in an automobile factory. He had been one of those miners that had been displaced by new machines and a depressed economy in the coalfields. By the early years of the 1960's the population of the Eastern Kentucky coalfields had decreased by at least 25% and the high schools and colleges still to this day see their graduates take their diplomas to other states to seek employment.

In 1956 the Federal Government began handing out commodities to those miners and others who had lost their jobs in the coal slump. The families who couldn't or wouldn't leave the area for jobs in other industries found themselves depending on the government for a large part of their daily food needs. Each family would get surplus food that the government had bought from farmers as part of a program to keep prices high enough to keep farmers from having to sell their crops at a loss and going out of business. This food was distributed at a central location of each county and was distributed according to family size. Items handed out would sometimes include canned beef, powdered eggs, cheese, lard, flour, powdered milk, and several other nutritious food items.

Without help from the government many families would have starved during those days and many people look back on some of the food items they received as some of the best they had seen before or since.

Not very much work in the coalfields was available during those days and jobs that were available were usually part-time jobs only. I remember knowing and observing several men who would leave our community each day in the morning to travel to Whitesburg and nearby places to try to pick up a few hours work so as to earn a few extra dollars for food for their families.

The U .M.W.A. had always been an important factor in the coal fields but the slow demise of the truck mines as a rich recruiting area and the decreased need for men in the larger mines had caused the coal fields of Eastern Kentucky to be poor pickings as the latter half of the 1950's rolled around. With coal mining employment shrinking and with the remaining truck mines not making enough profit to pay union scale wages while competing with the big boys for scarce coal orders, trouble in the coalfields would again erupt in the coal fields.

Some few of the truck mines in the Eastern Kentucky coalfields were still unionized as the latter half of the 50's approached, but there was no way they could pay union scale wages and still be competitive with the large corporations that could out produce the truck mines with their outdated (for the most part) mining methods. Some of the truck mines were still using the same homemade machinery they had utilized in the late 40's. In case of point, at least one truck mine operator was still using ponies in and around the mine in the middle 50's (to the author's knowledge) and there were probably many more still using them at that time.

Truck mine owners' inability to pay union scale wages or even contribute a few cents per ton into the U.M.W.A. Workers' Welfare and Retirement fund which was established in 1947 by the U.M.W.A. to provide benefits to disabled union miners had been a point of contention for union leaders for years. Even though they were aware that the small mines were not adhering to the contract's provisions the U.M.W.A. mostly ignored the disparity of wage and benefit contributions between the big mines and the unionized truck mines.

This disparity in the coalfields came to a head in 1959 when the U.M.W.A. miners came out on strike and picketed the truck mines (both union and non-union) in an effort to force compliance with the contract provisions that had been ignored for so long, and which caused such pay disparity between the small and large union mines.

Kentucky's governor called out the National Guard to keep the peace and to quell the violence that had broken out in various places between the union pickets and (mostly) truck mine employees whose workplaces were shut down by the pickets.

The National Guards' presence did manage to tone down the violence which had taken place before they had been called out, and the burnings, fights on the pick lines, and destruction in general mostly stopped. There had even been a few violent deaths in strike related incidents before arrival of the Guard.

This writer was present every day of the National Guards' occupation of the Whitesburg gymnasium where they (a Somerset, Kentucky unit) were quartered, as were countless other young boys who thought it was an exciting time to be alive, especially to be able to see first- hand their equipment, weapons, and uniforms that young boys admired so much in that day and time.

I remember one time of hearing multiple shots of gunfire, followed by a few bursts of rapid firing which was obviously from a machine gun of some kind or other. I was in the company of several other boys, engaged in building a cabin on top of one of the ridges that surrounded Whitesburg when we heard the firing of those guns, prompting one boy to exclaim, "Wonder who they just killed?" In our minds the firing had to have come from a gun battle between the soldiers and the strikers. We just knew that a violent battle had broken out somewhere, which troubled us greatly at the time, since most of our group of boys had at least one family member involved in coal mining, as a union man or as a truck mine miner who was crossing the picket lines to get to work every day. In our young and adventurous minds there was no way that the soldiers were just target practicing as we later heard from our parents. My friends probably thought the same thing I did at the time, that they just told us that to keep us from being scared or traumatized by what we had heard.

Eventually the presence of the soldiers brought an uneasy peace to the coalfields and they were withdrawn for good. The violence had subsided but nothing much was settled, except that the truck miners went back to work on their terms, with most of them ending their affiliation with the U.M.W.A. What they had subtly did for years they now did openly; that is they mined coal on their own terms without paying union wages or into the United Mine Workers Welfare Fund. Most truck mines went back to work as non-union mines and paid their miners what they could afford to pay, not what they were told they must pay in the contract they had previously mostly ignored anyway.

When their strike failed to bring the truck mines into line, the U.M.W.A. ceased to be the force in the Eastern Kentucky coalfields they once were, and by the early 60's they had all but conceded the fact that non-union mines were here to stay. Even at that, there would still be some unrest during the next decade of coal mining in the Cumberland Mountains of Eastern Kentucky.

CHAPTER FOUR

Scotia Coal Company

Alexander Bonnyman Sr. was born in Edinburgh, Scotland in 1866, just one year after the American Civil War had ended. His father chose to settle in Lexington, Kentucky, where Alexander earned a scholarship to the prestigious University of Kentucky to study civil engineering. Even though he had completed three years of engineering study, his father had other plans for him and entered him in the Edinburgh, Scotland Medical School and advised him that he would be expected to leave by boat next month for Edinburgh. Alexander argued that he didn't want to be a doctor but instead had his heart set on being an engineer. After a big blow-up argument his father informed him that he was ending his support for him at home, so Alexander had to drop out of engineer school at the University and go to work.

After finding employment building railroads in Georgia and Alabama, Alexander met his future wife, Frances Berry, through her brother with whom he worked on the railroad. Because he was a Catholic and she had been raised as an Episcopalian, her family disapproved of the wedding but she decided to convert to Catholicism and marry Alexander despite the disapproval of her family.

Alexander Sr.'s success and skill as an engineer allowed him to work his way up and to secure positions as general manager and chief engineer with various companies in the South, prompting him to move his family to Knoxville, Tennessee in 1912. Just four years later, in 1916, he started the Blue Diamond Coal Company which under his leadership eventually grew to thirteen mines located in Tennessee, Virginia, and Kentucky.

He opened his first mine in Leatherwood, Kentucky, which was near Hazard, and his abilities as an engineer and general manager caused his business to become a very successful venture.

Alexander Bonnyman Sr. managed his coal empire with considerable skill and when he died in 1953 his son Gordon took over as President of Blue Diamond Coal Company. Gordon Bonnyman served in that capacity until 1992 when Blue Diamond entered in bankruptcy proceedings. In 1998 the heretofore successful company ceased to exist as a moving force in the coal fields and sold their operations to the James River Coal Company.

One of the few blights on the record of a string of successful ventures Blue Diamond Coal had enjoyed since their founding involved the Hellier coal camp in Pike County, Kentucky. In the 1950's Hellier Coal and Coke Company sold its holdings to the Blue Diamond Coal Company, which included the coal reserves, tipples, and equipment. After a few years of operation and with many years of coal reserves still remaining, Blue Diamond in 1960 suddenly sold out to Bethlehem Steel Corporation.

Bethlehem didn't want any responsibilities for the town of Hellier, its inhabitants, or even the coal mining shops and tipples on that side of the mountain, but instead wanted to mine from the other side of the mountain. The tipples and mine buildings were then torn down by an outside company and all the equipment, rails, and machinery was withdrawn from the mines. What had been a vibrant mining community (Hellier) became almost deserted and hopeless, with the remaining population having for all intents and purposes lost its means of livelihood.

In 1961-1962 Blue Diamond Coal Company, headquartered at that time at 6205 Kingston Pike, Knoxville Tennessee, acquired the Scotia property, including the coal reserves from the Imboden seam of coal and the B and C seam veins of the Elkhorn coal seam. The first coal seam is considered a "gassy" seam, and the latter two, being above the water table, are considered non-gassy seams. Any seam of coal located below the drainage is susceptible to ample amounts of methane seeping from the seam of coal and out of the cracks in the shale rock deposits.

The top corporate officers of the Blue Diamond organization (at the time) including the two wholly owned affiliates of Leatherwood and Scotia, were Joseph W. Hoffman, president; Gordon Bonnyman, board chairman; and R.H. Watson, vice president for operations. Blue Diamond was the selling agent for the Company's six coal brands; Leatherwood, Blue Diamond Brand, Royal Scott, Starfire, Mayflower, and Tennessee Group. The Royal Scott came from Scotia's Imboden seam.

Some controversy still lingers about where the operators of the Scotia Mine got the idea to name their new mine <u>Scotia</u>. I believe I can shed some light on that subject. The founder of Blue Diamond Coal Company, Alexander Bonneyman Sr. and his father Alexander were from Edinburgh, Scotland originally, as has been mentioned at the beginning of this chapter. The word Scotia is an old poetic name for Scotland and the second meaning of the word Scotia is <u>darkness.</u> When one thinks of the Bonny-man Scottish roots and combine that with the fact that coal mining is done in almost total darkness, it's easy to understand how the combination of words have the double meaning of the name <u>Scotia.</u> The name for the company is especially relevant because though Alexander Sr. was raised as an American boy, he was always deeply proud of his Scottish heritage.

Papers were filed by the parent company of Scotia Coal Company, (Blue Diamond Coal Company,) on May 1st, 1962 and the official start date of Scotia was July, 1962. Much preparation was still needed before the full production of coal began in 1963, including hiring a company to erect the large coal preparation plant, including the tipple, conveyors, and large concrete basins for the Scotia mine. The company chosen to do the work was Mcnally Pittsburg Company of Wellston, Ohio.

In 1962-1963 the Louisville and Nashville (L&N) railroad extended a branch line of their railroad from the Poor Fork Branch in Cumberland, Kentucky for over 14 miles to serve the Scotia Coal Company mining complex. The coal which would travel over this line for the next 29 years would for the most part be the Royal Scott brand of high quality metallurgical coal for steel making but there would also be thousands of tons shipped from Scotia for electricity producing power plants.

The topography of the Black Mountain which is a part of the Cumberland Mountains, is of course mountainous, with the cover over the #1 (Imboden) Mine ranging from just inches to 2,000 ft., with the coal seam averaging from 6 to 7 ft thick, but a few inches lower in some areas and a few ft higher in a few areas of the mine. The immediate rock encountered when mining is anywhere from a few inches to 8ft of shale, which is commonly known by coal miners as "draw rock." Over the shale rock the roof is mostly sandstone but in some areas the sandstone is often embedded with thin streaks of shale, which tends to weaken the roof. The thicker shale encountered often separates from the sandstone causing roof falls which can result in injuries or death of the miners.

Because of this tendency of the shale rock to be of a wet variety because of water seepage from the draw rock in the Imboden seam, occasional draw rock falls near the slope entrance , especially between the roof bolts, would occur and have to be cleaned up and bolted again. This writer had occasion several times to help put new bolts in the roof after such a fall had occurred. This occurred frequently after the mine explosions and we were often engaged in cleaning up the South Main slope entry and making it safe to travel again. Several times we had to have the mine repair shop to cut 12ft length roof jacks in order to have them long enough to reach the top of the roof. The jacks had to be installed upside down in order to tighten the heads of the jacks. We also had to use 72 inch roof bolts (or longer) to enable the bolts to anchor in solid sandstone strata.

One Scotia miner recalled the reaction of at least one newly hired miner as the mantrip proceeded up South Main to the new man's assigned section:

"We were just barely at the foot of the slope when we passed by an open break where a large rock fall had occurred and left the ceiling height about 15 to 20ft high. As the new guy shined his light on the high ceiling and then as his cap light focused on the fallen drawrock lying all around the entry, he shouted for the mantrip operator to stop the bus. Applying the brakes the vehicle came to a stop as the mantrip operator stared at the man and asked, "What's the matter?" The new man replied, "Take me back outside or let me off, I'm not working in a place with top this bad!" According to the miner telling the story, the mantrip proceeded on to the section and the boss called outside for a ride to be sent for the newly hired man.

The man's career as a Scotia miner was a short one. The loose rock visible in the open breaks as one proceeded up South Mains could be intimidating to those who weren't used to it for sure.

One reason, if not the main reason that Blue Diamond Mining decided that the time was right to expand their operations in Kentucky by starting the Scotia Mine was because by 1962 the United Mine Workers of America had for all intents and purposes pulled out of the Eastern Coalfields after their inability to force truck mines to pay their employees' union dues and wages. In the fall of 1962 union leaders began canceling membership and Welfare cards of those miners whose employees were behind in their payments into the union fund. Most truck mines were union in name only, having pleaded inability to pay their employees' Welfare dues for some time, which caused the strikes and labor problems of 1959-60.

Also in the fall of 1962 the U.M.W.A. made an announcement that they would close four of their recently built Miners' Memorial hospitals as of June 30, 1963 unless some other organization agreed to 'take over the reins' of the hospitals' operations. The four hospitals they decided to do away with were the ones that were in the region they were abandoning, that is, the Southeastern Kentucky area. The hospitals to be closed were at Hazard, Middlesboro, McDowell, and Whitesburg. Thankfully, they were all picked up by other organizations and continue to this day to provide excellent medical facilities for their cities and counties.

No doubt the directors of the Blue Diamond Coal company thought that when the U.M.W.A. pulled out in 1962 it might be a good time to start another operation (Scotia) to go along with their much bigger and older Leatherwood mining operations located near Hazard, Kentucky. With the U.M.W.A. now gone there would be less potential for labor unrest in the coalfields of Eastern Kentucky and among the workforce of the Blue Diamond Coal Company. If the Blue Diamond directors were feeling relieved that feeling wouldn't last long.

Upon the opening of Scotia in 1962 the Southern Labor Union was certified as the bargaining agent of the employees of this Blue Diamond Coal Company subsidiary. The abandoning by the U.M.W.A. of any organizing efforts in the area worked to the advantage of the owners of Scotia as they were able to avoid any labor troubles during the opening of their mine and could use the lessened possibility of labor troubles as a selling point in marketing their coal.

The three years following the Scotia mine opening were mostly uneventful as the facilities needed for successful coal mining were completed little by little. A repair shop was constructed, along with a modern bathhouse containing hangers for the miners to change into their mining clothes and put on their mining belts with all the paraphernalia a miner has to carry. The miner's battery powered lamp was buckled on one side of the belt, his self rescuer on the other (which protected the user for approximately one hour from the effects of carbon monoxide, but did not provide oxygen.) Various other items could be hung from the belt, such as a flame safety lamp, tools, etc.

A very useful and handy piece of equipment that was attached to every miner's belt was a small piece of metal, about 1 inch x 3 inches in size and which had each the belt owner's individual employee number stamped on it. Each miner also was provided an extra piece of like metal also stamped with his man number to keep on a wooden board, called a "check-board" where he would hang his employee number tag on the "In" side of the board when entering the mine for any reason. When he came back outside he took his tag from the "In" board and switched it to the "Out" side of the board.

This simple procedure enabled one to quickly assess who was inside or outside the mine should a tragedy occur. Forgetting to check in when going inside the mine or to check out when coming out was a violation of federal, state, and company rules, but one which, like all other rules, was violated from time to time, as all coal miners are human and subject to forgetfulness. One can imagine the confusion that would arise if a section of men are trapped or missing and a miner who forgot to tag in his employee number on the board is inside the mine but his tag says he is outside. That circumstance would be devastating to a family that had a loved one missing or unaccounted for, and not knowing whether their loved one is involved in the tragedy or safe outside the mine.

When the Scotia mine first opened its #1 Mine and began mining the Imboden seam and advanced into the mine, they were advancing at a fairly steep angle, as the coal seam slopes downward for the first 1,000 ft. or so. When the bottom of the slope was reached the coal seam leveled out with very few hills or elevations in the contour of the coal and rock for the next four miles or so making the advancement much easier.

When the coal had been extracted to the bottom of the slope and had advanced further into the mine the miners were taken into and brought out of the mine by means of an open mantrip connected to a steel rope which was hooked to an electric motor to lower the mantrip to the bottom of the slope and to bring the men out at the end of the shift. As the mine was advanced even further another less steep entry portal was opened just below the bathhouse and track was installed from the outside supply yard and office to allow the men to travel to the sections straight from the bathhouse. A runaway side switch was installed halfway down the slope of the new opening to allow any track motor or mantrip to be stopped by a solid block of coal instead of having to ride the runaway vehicle all the way to the bottom of the slope. Right at the foot of the slope was a fair sized curve which a vehicle coming down the slope had to contend with and one can imagine the devastation which could be caused when two 8 ton track motors attached to 3 or 4 cars of supplies or a load of rails on rail trucks lost their traction and hurled down the slope. Of course a man-trip full of miners flying down the slope could be even more devastating.

As one who brought many heavy loads of supplies down that slope and made many, many trips with loaded mantrips, I can attest to feeling a little scared when easing down that slope while praying that my rail sanders were working correctly and that I could keep control of the track vehicle I was driving. I imagine all motormen that had occasion to travel that slope felt as I did about it. I never trusted the runaway side switch because hitting the solid coal rib at 50 m.p.h. or so didn't appeal much to me and besides the slope of the mine caused one side of the runaway to be higher than the other which could cause injuries if the vehicle hit the coal rib and jumped the track. Of course it's expected that all coal mining jobs are dangerous and the dangers must be taken into consideration when seeking employment as a coal miner.

Since the 1962 opening of the Scotia Mine, Blue Diamond had had very few labor disputes at either their large Leatherwood Mining complex in Perry County nor their Scotia Mine by the beginning of 1965. Most of the problems that had occurred during this period were those having to deal with individuals concerning work and safety problems that occur occasionally in any large organization.

That period of few labor related problems began to change in the latter few months of 1964. Blue Diamond closed their Leatherwood mine for several months and when they reopened in December, 1964, they did so as a non-union mine. The following month, January 11, 1965, 70 pickets appeared at the mine and they were later joined by 21 other pickets who had at first went back to work without a contract but later decided to join the picket line.

Scotia labor relations had also suffered few problems with management since the opening of the mine but this was about to change big time. The U.M.W.A. decided to try their dormant recruitment efforts once again in the area that had all but abandoned in 1963. They opened an organizing drive at Scotia in September, 1965. Even though the Southern Labor Union was still the Scotia employees bargaining agent when the U.M.W.A. recruiting effort began, many miners were receptive to the promises of the U.M.W.A. union organizers. At least one hundred and eleven of the one hundred and thirty employees then working at Scotia put their signatures on union cards designating the United Mine Workers of America as their bargaining agent.

Shortly thereafter an election was held by the employees and the count showed that 83 voted for U.M.W.A. representation, 44 voted for the Southern Labor Union, and one miner voted to have no union representation at all. With the election results favoring the U.M.W.A. the National Labor Relations Board (NLRB) certified the U.M.W.A. as the bargaining agent for the Scotia employees in March, 1966 and negotiations began in early May with the company. Talks proceeded slowly between the two parties and after a few weeks of negotiations talks broke down when the company representatives claimed the U.M.W.A. was invading management rights by refusing to allow the use of diesel equipment in the mine. (Years later, in the 1980's, the company began using diesel shuttle cars in the Scotia #1 or "bottom" mine with the approval of the Scotia Employees Union and Federal and State Inspectors. The author was one of the operators of the diesel shuttle cars at that time and found them to be perfectly safe to operate as long as the frequent carbon monoxide, carbon dioxide, and hydrogen sulfide monitoring and testing was done in accordance with the requirements.)

The talks having broken down, on June 1st, 1966, the Scotia miners came out on strike although the negotiations continued. Blue Diamond decided to hire strike breakers to work the mines and on July 15th 42 of the Scotia miners crossed the U.M.W. picket lines and returned to work. In the following days and weeks more workers crossed the picket lines and went back to work, escorted across the lines by Letcher County Sheriff's deputies and Kentucky State Troopers.

Tragedy struck the Scotia mine in October, 1966, when Clifford Baker, a 53 year old miner from Whitesburg lost his life in a rock fall after his regular shift had ended and he returned to the face to mark and measure the coal cut for the next shift. The rest of the crew were on the mantrip waiting for him to join them and after a period of time, one of the miners returned to check on him and discovered the tragic accident.

One interesting incident during the strike was related to me and others in the 1970's by a miner who was had crossed the picket line to go back to work;

"Some of us got together in one of our cars as we started to work that day, figuring there was strength in numbers when we crossed the picket lines. We went up Pine Mountain and as we reached the top we were stopped by a picket line across the road there. We never expected to see strikers so far from the mine entrance, but there they were. They were U.M.W.A. picketers who were waiting for us on top of the damn

mountain and though we tried to resist as best we could we all got a good thrashing that day and were sent packing back the way we had come. When they pulled me out of the car, I tried to make light of the situation by sayin, as I took my cap off and rubbed the top of my bald head, "you men wouldn't beat up an old bald headed man, would you?" They would and did. Obviously they didn't have a sense of humor. That's the worse day I had as a picket line crosser, although we crossed the line many days after that with the law protecting us."

In December, 1966, the NLRB denied the U.M.W.A.'s claim of unfair labor practices by the Scotia mine owners. In June, 1967, the NLRB issued their final denial of the U. M.W.A. claim. A few weeks later the company signed a contract with the newly formed Scotia Employees Association. The U.M.W.A.'s effort had failed but the picket lines weren't gone for good, as the U.M. W.A. set up picket lines several times during the remaining years of the active mining at the Scotia mine. Sometimes when the U.M.W.A. was on strike during negotiations with their own employers they would set up picket lines at the Scotia mine openings in hopes that doing so would help their own cause. As far as I know, there were never any attempts to organize Scotia employees during their picketing. Actually, since Scotia workers had their own independent union, The Scotia Employees Association, certified by the NLRB, the miners felt an obligation to ignore the pickets and cross the lines to work.

Sadly, one month after the U.M.W.A,'s failure to organize the Scotia workers, anther Scotia miner lost his life on July 27,1967, in the Imboden #1 mine. Leslie Caudill, a continuous miner operator, was killed when a rock fall covered him and his mining machine while cutting a cut of coal from the mine working face. When the roof started falling he had jumped under the miner boom for protection but the rock covered up the boom also crushing Caudill.

Sometimes crossing the picket lines would result in a set of tires on your vehicle being ruined by running over "jacknails" which had been strewn across the mine entrance road in hopes of discouraging one from crossing the line. Several incidents of this nature occurred over the years at times when Scotia was being picketed

During the last month of the strike against Scotia by the U.M.W.A. the local union members (Local Union 1435) ran an advertisement requesting that; "no coal miner seek employment with this company."

CHAPTER FIVE

Coal Boom

After the labor problems of the 60's the management of the Scotia Coal Company must have felt a little shell-shocked , especially when the first couple of years of their new operation had been without labor strife and work stoppages, only to see the next three years (1965-1967) dominated by strikes and unrest in the labor force.

With their labor problems settled, the next few months were uneventful for the Scotia miners and managers but in November, 1968 an event happened that would once again remind everyone how dangerous coal mining could be.

Around 5:15 a.m. on November 20, 1968, a powerful explosion ripped through the Consolidation Coal Company No. 9 Mine in Farmington, West Virginia. At the time of the explosion, 99 men were underground on the midnight to 8:00 a.m. shift. During the following days, 21 men managed to escape; but on November 30, 1968, after repeated explosions and uncontrolled fires, rescuers were forced to seal the mine, entombing 78 miners inside the mine.

Once again, public attention was aroused and with the issues of mine health and safety the topic of debate, the 91st Congress enacted the Federal Coal Mine Health and Safety Act of 1969. This was the most stringent coal mine safety act to that date. For the first time surface mines were included in the act which among other regulations instilled criminal penalties for willful violations and provided compensation for totally disabled miners who had been diagnosed with pneumoconiosis, more commonly known as "black lung."

Several previous laws had been enacted covering most coal mines but this was the first time that criminal penalties were threatened against those that ignored mining laws as had been through the years. This law finally "had some teeth in it."

Beginning in the latter years of the nineteenth century the Federal Government finally came to the conclusion that coal mines, metal mines, and non-metal mines needed to have some control over their mining procedures, especially when it came to ensuring the safety of the miners. With this in mind the U.S. Congress passed the first mining regulations in 1891 and have continued to make changes and pass new regulations every few years. The major coal mining safety regulations enacted are:

1891- The first Federal Mine Safety Statute passed.

1910- Bureau of Mines Created

1941- Right of entry granted to Federal Inspectors.

1947-Safety Standards for Bituminous Coal and Lignite Mines

1952-Federal Coal Mine Safety Act passed.

1961-Study Authorized to Examine Hazards in Metal/Non-Metal Mines

1966-Federal Coal Mine Safety Act

1966-Federal Metal and Non-Metal Mine Safety Act

1969-Federal Coal Mine Health and Safety Act

1973-Mining Enforcement and Safety Administration created. (MESA)

1977-Mine Safety and Health Administration created. (MSHA)

2006Mine Improvement and New Emergency Response Act (Miner Act) passed.

The 1969 Federal Coal Mine Health and Safety Act was created as a result of the Farmington, West Virginia coal mine disaster in 1968, and the 1977 Mine Safety and Health Administration act (MSHA) was created because of the Scotia mining disasters in 1976.

The years 1969-1970 saw no labor unrest at Scotia due to signing the contract with the new union now representing the Scotia miners, "The Scotia Employees Association." This is the organization that would represent the employees of Scotia Coal Company until the then Arch Coal, Inc. owned company, Cumberland River Coal Company, idled their two operating complexes in Wise County, Virginia and Letcher County Kentucky on July 21, 2014. Speaking with first- hand knowledge I can attest to the fact that both Blue Diamond Coal Company and Arch Inc. always seemed to bargain with the Scotia Miners' union in good faith and treated the hourly employees with respect. As a member of that particular union for over 17 years I have seen a couple of times when senior members of the Blue Diamond Coal Company management would come to the picket line and make a case for settling a strike. We always listened and treated them with respect even as they us did like-wise.

After the 1969 Federal Coal mine Health and Safety Act was passed, the inspections at Scotia became a little more stringent. The Farmington explosion in 1968 where 78 men lost their lives was still fresh in the minds of all those involved in mining which made everyone more cautious of the many hazards involved in coalmining. Despite the caution, deaths still occurred occasionally. On August 4,[th] 1970, miner Billy Whitaker of Whitesburg was killed while working on the beltline at Scotia.

After every major mine disaster it seemed that the Federal Government and coal mining States reacted by passing a new, more stringent series of mining laws. The worst mining disaster in U.S. history, the Monongah, West Virginia explosion of Monongah Nos. 6 and 8 Mines in 1907 resulted in the deaths of 362 men who were underground at the time of the explosion. Four others escaped or were rescued. As a result of this disaster, the Bureau of Mines was created in 1910.

Another tragic mine explosion that resulted in multiple lives lost was the Nos. 15 and 16 Mines of the Finley Coal Company of Hyden, Leslie County, Kentucky, where 38 miners were killed on December, 30, 1970. This incident did not result in another Federal Mining Act, likely because the 1969 law had barely had time to take effect when the Finley Coal Company incident occurred.

Scotia Coal Company Summary of Violations, 1970

Total number of violations issued	79
Total number of closure orders issued	6
Total number of 104(a) closure orders issued, (imminent danger)	5
Total number of violations and closure orders,	85

The violations and closures listed above are for the period from May, 1970 to December 31, 1970. *Source: Mine Enforcement Administration, U.S. Department of Interior.*

In 1971, Scotia management decided to open the "B seam" of coal, located east of, and about one half mile higher on Black Mountain than the portals of the #1 Imboden Mine, which was mining 2,000 below the mountain. The B seam was commonly known as the Elkhorn Seam and was substantially lower in height than the #1 "Bottom" mine. Where the #1 Mine Imboden coal averaged from 6ft. to even 10 ft. in a few places, the B Seam probably averaged no more that 42 in., and in some places even a little lower. There was very little drawrock in this coal and this accounts for the low ceiling height. Those miners that had been accustomed to the more than adequate height of the Bottom Mine were shocked when they found themselves transferred to the B Seam following a lay-off or transfer as the years went by.

A few months after opening the B seam (also known as the Middle Taggart Mine) Scotia opened another seam of coal, the "C" Seam or the Upper Taggart Mine. This mine was located higher up on the mountain than the B Seam and the coal was higher, averaging about 55 inches in height and around 6-8 inches of drawrock above the coal. Usually the coal and drawrock extraction allowed a 6ft. tall miner to be able to walk upright but having to hold his or her head to one side, which is more uncomfortable than having a lower height where you walk more stooped over at the waist. Many Scotia miners preferred to work in the C Seam if they had a choice because the greater height of the #1 Mine had draw backs of its own; that is, the methane problem, the thick drawrock that had a tendency to drop from between the roof bolts, and the dangerous ribs of coal that also had a tendency to "take weight" and separate from the solid coal during mining and fall into the entries. There's very little chance of survival when a large slab of 24 inch slate rock falls on you when it rolls from loose ribs of coal. Even if one is fortunate enough to survive such an occurrence, serious injury is nearly always suffered when hit by a large rib roll.

If the C Seam, (or Upper Taggart) was many miners' choice to work, the B Seam (Middle Taggart) was the least favorite. Both new mine openings were above the drainage table which assured that little or no methane gas would seep from the coal or loose rock, which the miners knew and appreciated, but the low height of the Middle Taggart coal was difficult to endure by miners who were very tall, very big, or very old. Only fit and smaller miners could scurry around the sections with comparative ease. The only advantage for working in this mine was that the rock when falling did not have very far to fall and wouldn't hurt too badly if it was a small rock. On the other hand, a rock no bigger than your fist could easily kill or badly injure you when falling from 10-20 heights often encountered in the #1 mine, especially when working around the old works that have suffered large rock falls and been re-bolted.

The Bottom Mine (#1 Scotia) was also many miners' choice to work, especially those miners that had started their Scotia career working in that mine. They were more than willing to accept the bad points of the mine to be able to stand up and walk around just about anywhere in the mine. There were few places in the whole #1 Mine where one couldn't do so but one particular low ceiling in 2 Southeast Mains would come to play a large part in the second explosion at the mouth of Southeast Mains, which will be discussed in a later chapter. Most of those miners who worked in the Bottom Mine recovery efforts after the two terrible explosions of March 9 and 11, 1976, would come to prefer to work in the Bottom Mine instead of the two upper mines at Scotia. (The author is one of those former recovery workers who came from the upper mines and spent the rest of his coal mining career in the Bottom Mine.)

The management of Blue Diamond Coal Co. and Scotia appeared to be almost clairvoyant when they decided to open the B and C Seams of coal in 1971-72. In 1973, a war in the Middle East, the Arab-Israeli War, disrupted the oil flow between that region and the U.S. because of the oil embargo imposed on the U.S. by the Arab oil rich countries. Arab members of the Organization of Petroleum Exporting Countries, (OPEC) imposed a total oil embargo against the U.S. in retaliation for the U.S. decision to resupply the Israeli military. This embargo was eventually extended to other countries that supplied Israel. In the U.S. cars had to wait in long lines to buy gas providing gas stations has any gas at all. Some stations went days or weeks without any gas deliveries. The embargo was ended in March, 1974 when negotiations between Israel and Syria provided the impetus for all parties to lift the embargo.

Those who witnessed those days will likely never again take for granted that there will always be endless supplies of gasoline and other kinds of energy, such as natural gas, propane, and even wood. Sometimes people almost panicked when they had sat in a long line for two or three hours, only to have the station run out before they reached the pump. This happened frequently during that time of scarce gasoline and hardly anyone was immune from the stress of trying to find fuel for their cars, trucks, and commercial vehicles.

Sometimes people would top their tanks off by going from station to station and buying the limit allowed, usually ten gallons or less, until they managed to fill their tanks. This had the effect of making the product even more scarce than it would have been if everyone just bought the gas they needed. Even today, if every vehicle owner in America decided to fill their tanks to the brim of every vehicle, a shortage of gasoline would probably be the result.

One case in point from a personal perspective will give the flavor of those times. I was employed as a traveling salesman for a wholesale grocery company in those days and was in a customer's place of business when a woman pulled up to the gas pump. The embargo had ended a few days before and gas was now available in most businesses that sold it. The store owner went to the pump to get the woman's gasoline, but he had been gone only a minute or two when he returned, cursing as he came through the door. "Can you believe that?" he exclaimed as he walked behind the store counter. "That lady's tank took just 25 cents to fill up. I wish she would waste somebody else's time instead of mine!" His frustration was understood when you realize that dozens of others in that community had probably been by to top off their tanks in the same way. Fear does strange things to people and there was plenty of fear in those days.

The Arab oil embargo had the effect of creating a greater demand for energy of all kinds, especially for the coal industry. The fear that the embargo might last for years had the effect of causing most utilities and steel manufacturing plants to increase their orders for coal, even if it was going into their stockpiles for storage. They expected coal prices to rise and they weren't disappointed in their expectations.

The Middle Taggart mine was completely developed and running at least two sections when the minor coal boom started in 1973 but the Upper Taggart mine had just one section mining coal and were just a few breaks in from the portal. It would be early 1975 before another section was started in that mine. Both mines were running conventional sections, that is they were not using the more productive and modern continuous miners to cut the coal from the face, but were instead using coal cutting machines which undercut the coal before it was blasted from the face using blasting powder. The following is an example of how a conventional coal mining section works to get the coal from the face area:

After the cutting machine undercuts the coal a large electric rubber wheeled coal drilling machine then drills 6-10 holes to a depth of 10-15 ft. in the undercut coal , then the operator and his helper inserts 6-10 sticks of powder into each hole, inserting a blasting cap into the first stick that goes into the hole. Each blasting cap in each hole is then wired by series and the two ends of the wire are connected to the wires leading to a battery detonator. The operator of the drill then backs his machine up to get away from the blast. The next step is to connect the two detonator wires to the wires leading to the sticks of powder. The shot-firing crew then gets behind a pillar of coal and shouts as loud as they can, "Fire! Fire! Fire! The detonator button is then pushed by the drilling machine operator or his helper and the coal is blasted onto the mine bottom where the loading machine can scoop it up and load it into the shuttle cars.

This is basically how a conventional mining section works to mine the coal. A mining section that has a continuous miner to cut the coal is much more productive because that machine eliminates the need for a coal loading machine, a cutting machine, and a coal drill. That one machine, the continuous miner, does the work of three machines and does it much more efficiently and more productively.

On July 14, 1973, a new contract agreement was signed between the Scotia Coal Company of Partridge, Ky. and the Scotia Employees Association, Inc. of Millstone Ky. The contract guaranteed a $3.00 per day raise, (the first raise to begin 7-14-73, the next raise on 11-1- 73, the next 11-1-74, and the last raise (of the contract) on 11-1-75) for the Scotia Employees Association (S.E.A.) members over the next three years beginning July, 14, 1973, and ending July 14, 1976. The contract was signed by Freddie Maggard, Superintendent of Scotia Coal Company, and by Douglass Roberts, President, S.E.A., J.B. Holbrook, Secretary, S.E.A., Denver Sturgill, Robert Couch, and Paul Cornett, Mine Committeemen, S.E.A.

The highest pay scale and dates they took effect in the contract were as follows:

7-14-73	11-1-73	11-1-74	11-1-75
$ 45.00	$ 48.00	$ 51.00	$ 54.00

In the winter of 1973-74 Arab (OPEC) oil embargo was at its worst and the deficiency in the supply of heating oil was beginning to affect the U.S. in every region of the country. Coal was about the only fuel abundantly available and the demand for it was increasing as the winter months wore on.

The increasing demand for coal resulted in a hiring bonanza for the unemployed coal miners all over the nation, especially in the Eastern Kentucky coalfields. Just like the coal booms of the past, entrepreneurs from all over came to Eastern Kentucky to buy or lease a suitable seam of coal for strip mining or deep mining. One of those who saw a future for increased coal sales during this time was an individual named Claude Canada, who was said to have migrated to Pike County with a Chevrolet El Camino and $10,000 to invest in starting a coal mine, and managed to make a fortune in just a few years. There were many others who took a similar relatively small amount of money and made a small fortune in the coal business during the early 70's.

Just like in the earlier coal booms, used mining equipment was at a premium with so many small operators opening up new mine portals all over the mountains. Not only equipment, but experienced coal miners became a scarce commodity in the early months of 1974. Some older miners who had retired from mining or had quit the mines for various reasons were going back into the mines in droves. Money was no object in securing the labor of those experienced miners. Where $45.00 for an 8 hour shift had been a good wage for a miner before the boom started, sometimes even an offer of $100.00 a shift wasn't enough to entice an experienced miner back underground. ($100.00 would be equal to $512.46 in today's currency.) With these wages it's easy to understand how so many former miners made the decision to go back into the mines at that time.

During that winter I was still employed as a traveling salesman and saw first-hand how tempting such an offer can be when one of the business owners I had been calling on for over six years surprised me one morning with the news that he had been offered $100.00 a day to "shoot coal" in a small truck mine and that he had accepted the offer. He said he thought he had gotten out of the mines for good but the offer was "too good to pass up." I myself was making less than $40.00 a day in a job I loved, but I then for the first time began thinking about whether I should "go for the money "and change careers, even though I had never before given one thought to being a coal miner before money became such an important factor in the decision.

CHAPTER SIX

YELLOW HAT

B ecause of the expanding coal boom and an increasing positive out-look for the coal industry, the giant conglomerate W.R. Grace flirted with the possibility of buying the Blue Diamond Coal Company in early 1974. Despite the interest shown by W.R. Grace the merger didn't go through. Blue Diamond went as far as to quote an asking price of 33 million dollars for their assets, which would have included their large Leatherwood Mining complex in Perry County and the Scotia Coal Company in Letcher County. When the merger failed to go through Blue Diamond continued as an independent company with their head-quarters in Knoxville, Tennessee.

I was familiar with the Scotia mining complex, as I had been passing by the entrance to the mine for years and could easily observe the L&N trains as they were being loaded with coal pouring from the large tipple that sat astride the tracks. I would also take notice of an old wrecked and abandoned black van that was sitting near the road just outside the entrance to the Scotia Mine. Interestingly enough, the van had many small round holes in the side of it that were clearly bullet holes. Every time I passed by the van I would wonder if the bullet holes were left over from a violent gun battle between Scotia workers and the U.M.W.A. pickets of the latter 1960's, or were they there because of drive by shootings over the years? After all, almost every rural road sign had a bullet hole or two as if some rural cowboy is staking his claim or marking his spot with the holes.

Whatever the cause, the sight of the holes always reminded me of the labor problems that coal mining always seemed to invite over the years, and I had made up my mind to stay out of the mines if at all possible.

That reluctance to even entertain the notion of becoming a coal miner began to weaken somewhat in the early summer of 1974 when my brother Jimmy submitted his application to Scotia Coal Company and was hired in a short time. He had been working for the same company as I, but decided to go into coal mining because of the better pay. The fact that many inexperienced miners were being hired was an incentive to others who saw a chance to improve their lives by leaving their minimum wage jobs while other employment was available.

Most young men who were seeking jobs in the coal industry were well aware that coal mining had always been a boom or bust proposition. You either prospered as a miner some of the time and at other times you went bust. The bust side of the equation was the one that kept many good men and woman out of the coal industry altogether. Not many people were willing to work at a vocation where a few months or even a few years would bring a bust where they would lose everything they had accumulated during the boom times.

But this time seemed different to them. The oil embargo had brought home to even the young generation that good times and bad times were a fact of life and the present coal boom was here now and it was time to take advantage of it, and many did, some entering the mines in their 30's and 40's for the first time. Besides, the Vietnam War was winding down and many veterans were returning home and looking for jobs wherever they could find them and $45.00 or more a day sure sounded better to them than the $78.00 per month they received as new recruits during most of that war.

Scotia was taking applications but even the coal boom was no guarantee of being hired the first time you went to their office. In fact, many potential miners would put in an application and be told by the staff to check back occasionally with them. Some applicants would submit an application today and would return tomorrow and every day until either they were hired or they became tired of making the trip to the office. Some were even hired the same day, mostly those with prior experience, although many were going into the mines for the first time.

Doubtless, there were even a few women who turned in their applications for employment at Scotia during this time. A woman had first gone to work in a U.S. coal mine in 1973. By 1980, of 255,888 U.S. coal miners,

15,252 were women. The fact that woman were once considered to be bad luck in a coal mine had probably contributed to their late appearance as coal miners as much as any prejudicial fears.

Many utilities that had been using oil to power their generators during the Arab oil embargo now began to switch over to America's most abundant fuel, coal. America's coal reserves were the "ace in the hole" we were holding that now began pouring out the coal our nation needed to beat the embargo. Every ton of coal produced would save roughly one barrel of oil which would produce about 22 gallons of gasoline and eleven gallons of other gasoline derivatives. The phrase "The Saudi Arabia of Coal" was coined to describe the U.S. coal industry for the first time, which apply described the ability of the coal industry to supply the coal needed as an alternative fuel during the oil crisis.

The coal industry's share of electric generation in America grew from about 46% to nearly 56% during the 1970's. During the same period 70 new nuclear generation stations went into service, without which coal would have had an even greater market. During this same period and into the early 80's about 10,000 megawatts (mw) of new coal fired capacity was added to the power grid each year.

The increase in the use of coal to power those new power plants led coal producers to hire about 45,000 new coal miners in 1974 alone. The fact that many of those new hires were younger than those already working as coal miners caused the average age of coal miners to drop from 45 years of age to 35 years of age in the five years from 1970 to 1975.

With so many of my generation choosing to seek employment in the coal mines and earning good money when successfully landing a job there, including my younger brother, I was susceptible to the temptation of the "more money" lure. Like many other young potential miners I was well aware of the boom and bust cycle of coal mining that had been the norm since the dawn of coal mining in the U.S. Despite my misgivings and with the urging of my brother I decided to apply at Scotia Coal Co., where he and many other inexperienced miners had managed to get a job with them in the summer of 1974. My intention was to put in my application around the last week of August, since I had scheduled my vacation with my employer, Lewis Wholesale Company, around that time. I had come to the conclusion to try the mines after much thought and informed Jimmy that I had made up my mind to apply the end of August. He mentioned to me that he would put in a good word for me at the mine office if I wanted him to and I assured him it would be alright with me.

The only potential cog in the wheel was the fact that by the time my vacation rolled around I had pretty much changed my mind. I had thought it over carefully in the weeks since I had told Jimmy to go ahead and put in a good word for me and had come to the conclusion that while the money was better in the mines, I loved my (then) current job with the Wholesale and had been told that I was in line for a move up in the company very soon.

I regretted having asked Jimmy to put in a good word for me since I had changed my mind, but in order to not let him down, I decided I would wait until the last day of my vacation to put in my application at the Scotia main office at the mine. I was aware then that virtually all inexperienced miners had to show up day after day for weeks after submitting their application before the staff at Scotia considered hiring them. I felt confident in the fact that I traveled so far from the Scotia Mine each day that I would have an excuse not to have to stop to check on my application. I was also aware that Jimmy had been hired almost immediately, so I knew there might be a chance that could happen but the possibility was remote at best to my way of thinking.

On August 3rd, 1974, I loaded my three kids up, and with my wife Wanda, we left Colson, and traveling through Camp Branch, Thornton, Mayking, and Ermine, we continued up the north side of Pine Mountain on U.S. 119, past the Ovenfork Post Office, then on to Partridge where we came to the entrance of Scotia Mine. The black van with the bullet holes was the first thing my wife saw as we pulled into the entrance and on across the one lane concrete bridge. As we jolted along the unpaved road my wife asked, "Did you see those bullet holes in that old van sitting beside the road?" She was very apprehensive about me working in the mines since she had bad memories about the time her dad was covered up in a rock fall when she was a young girl. I had already explained that I was just putting my application in because I had gotten Jimmy to put in a good word for me and I was doing this to not let him down.

As we passed the small guard shack sitting about 500 yards from the entrance I answered her question with the words I had told her when we left home, " Don't worry about me working in the coal mine, I told you I was just doing this because I didn't want to let Jimmy down. There's not a chance they'll want a salesman as a coal miner, and even if they offer me a job I'll turn it down." "Well I hope you would, I've got enough worries without worrying about you in a coal mining job!"

We drove on up the steep hill which was very rough with large gravel mixed in with the abundant mud for traction. As we proceeded down the other side and rounded a large curve the whole mining complex lay before our eyes and it was huge for sure. We first passed a small trailer which I learned later was the safety trailer, then across a set of railroad tracks which were in their apex of a large curve that started as a straight line from the supply yard and which was the means by which supplies and men were hauled into and out of the mine. As we crossed the tracks we noticed the rails led down a steep incline cut into the steep cliff that made me wonder how in the world does anything traveling on rails manage to get up that steep incline? This was my first glance at the slope entrance which would become so familiar to me over the next seventeen years and three months.

I pulled in front of the supply shed with pallets of rock dust stacked under the shed. To our right was a large building which I learned later was the miners' bathhouse. There were no women miners at that time working for Scotia to the best of my knowledge, but this would change in just a short time.

I made mention earlier in this chapter that women first started working as miners in the U.S. in 1973. In my career at Scotia Coal Co. as a miner I worked with several women miners and always found them to be as hard workers as the men and always did their jobs without complaint. All the men who they worked with treated them with the upmost respect. There might have been exceptions to this but I personally know of none.

Opening the door of my '69 Chevy station wagon I got out and proceeded into the one story office building which was a part of the supply house and machine repair facilities. The first door on the right was the secretary's office and as I entered I stood out like a sore thumb with my dress pants, polo shirt, and dress shoes. Several men with their mining clothes, hats, lights and adorned with assorted paraphernalia hanging from their mining belts were going in and out of the hallway as I entered. A few others in civvies were standing around outside the doorway. I found out later that these were men who came by often, some every day, to check on their applications.

The lady in the office asked if she could help me and I stated that I was there to put in an application for employment. Handing me one, she advised me to find a seat in the hall in order to fill out the app.

Like all applications, they had the usual personal and work history questions. When I came to the one that asked my mining experience I jotted down the word "none." As I did so I was thinking that no experience meant no job after I had witnessed the men waiting outside the door who had come by to check on their apps.

Several others were also filling out applications as I did, and one by one we finished them and handed them to Rhoda, the secretary, I had first talked to in the office. As I handed her the sheet of paper she said, "We'll take a look at your application and get back with you in a few days." Well, I thought, as I thanked her and walked out the office door, that's that. I'll never hear from them again and that's o.k. with me. I've done what I promised Jimmy I would do by coming by and putting in my application. I can go back to the job I love and do the work I love doing while feeling good that I didn't let Jimmy down. I have to confess that I didn't once mention to the secretary that Jimmy was my brother who was already employed here and had said he might put in a good word for me. I made sure I neglected to do that because if I did I just might be hired as a coal miner, which I didn't want or need at this time.

I walked across the set of rails next to the mine office and strode to my car where my family was patiently waiting on me to return. The area was alive with activity as forklifts were busily loading mining supplies, such as creosol timbers, bags of rock dust and five gallon cans of oil into supply cars. When first pulling into the yard I was somewhat fearful of one of the forklifts running into my station wagon, which I had just purchased from one of my customers in Pike County.

I had almost reached my car when I heard a woman's voice shout loudly, "Hey!" I quickly turned my head to see if I had entered into forbidden territory among the supplies or the mine property, but as I looked back I saw the secretary, Rhoda, waving at me to come back as she again shouted, "Come back here, I want to talk to you!" As I turned around to walk back, I was thinking that maybe I had screwed up my application and the lady probably needed another one filled out. What else could it be? After all, few words were spoken by me the whole time I was in the building. I purposely hadn't mentioned that I wanted or needed a job because of course I really didn't want or need a coal mining job. I already had a job where I drove a company car and just carried a pen and a clip-

board with a sales kit and price list. What job could be easier or more sa-
tisfying than that? I had merely come by to fill out the app and turn it in,
thus meeting my obligation to Jimmy, and that was that.

As I passed by the men still waiting outside the office they were now
staring at me because I had been summoned back to the office. Like me,
they were wondering why. I can imagine they were thinking; what's this
dandy doing here with his dress shoes and duds on, is he a salesman or
might he possible be trying to get a job here? Say it ain't so, might have
been their thinking as I entered the door of the office once again.

As I walked in the office Rhoda was smiling at me and exclaimed,
"We've been waiting for you, I didn't notice the name on the application
until you left the office!" With those words my heart sank, as she continued, "Your brother came by here and put in a good word for you a few
weeks back and I was beginning to think you had changed your mind and
wasn't coming!" I gave her a weak smile without replying. "Wait right
here while I take your application to the Superintendent's (Freddie Maggard) office. He might want to hire you today." The large lump in my
throat made it difficult for me to do more than grunt a barely audible,
"O.K."

She headed through the hallway with my application in her hand.
While she was gone my head was spinning as I tried to absorb what was
happening. Surely they weren't going to hire me here, I thought. How
could they hire an inexperienced underground miner the first day he
comes by to submit an application? What about all the talk I had heard
that it takes weeks or months to get on here, even with mining experience? It just wouldn't be right to hire me on the first visit and when that
lady comes back that's basically what she'll tell me. I'll just tell her, "thank
you," and then leave, then call back in a week saying, "I'm sorry, but I
have changed my mind." That's it, that's how I'll get out of this unbelieva-
ble situation. Jimmy will understand, I'm sure of it. He knows I have a
good job with good benefits and that management there likes my work
and has big plans for me. He'll understand completely and I can stay out
of the mines and still have my dignity.

With all these thoughts running through my mind, I barely noticed
Rhoda's return to the office after being gone about five minutes. Still
grinning as she stepped into the office from the hallway she looked at me
and exclaimed excitedly, "He hired you!" With those words no one but me
knows how close I came to blacking out and hitting that gray concrete
floor. Even today the memory is still as fresh in my mind as it were yes-

48

terday. I had rolled the dice and lost. I had assumed that no one is hired on the first visit, because that is what I had heard ever since the coal boom had surfaced. So much for assuming anything is remotely similar to what you have heard. My goose was cooked. My train had left the station. I was doomed. I was a coal miner. What would have delighted an experienced underground unemployed coal miner had become a nightmare for me, swooping down on me like a vulture in the night.

I was barely hearing the words as Rhoda was explaining some 'need to know points' about working there. I do remember her telling me that I was assigned to the Bottom Mine (Imboden #1 Mine) on the second shift (3:00 p.m. until 11:00 p.m.) and that my start date would be September 3rd, 1974, as that would give me time to give my present employer a short notice. She mentioned that the mine would be idled for the Labor Day Holiday on Sept. 2nd. She gave me a self rescuer and some instructions on its use in case of fire or explosion on a section, while explaining that the self rescuer was used for filtering out carbon monoxide but didn't contain oxygen in itself. The need to buy a mining belt to carry the self- rescuer, cap light and other gear was also explained. I was instructed to buy a good mining hat and to paint it yellow, which was required of all inexperienced miners and which had to be kept painted yellow until I had a year's experience as a miner under my belt.

When she finished her instructions and I had filled out the paperwork she had presented for my signature, she asked, "Now, do you have any questions?" I had been thinking about the shift that they assigned me and knew Jimmy was on the same shift, but was working at the Middle Taggart B Seam. I knew if I kept my word and took the job we could ride together across Pine Mountain and also ride the nearly one mile to the B Seam if I could get assigned there instead of the Bottom Mine. With nothing to lose but my dignity I looked at Rhoda and said, "I have one question, would it be possible for me to be assigned to the Middle Taggart Mine so my brother Jimmy and I could ride together? She quickly answered, "Sure, I can handle that. Instead of reporting to the Bottom Mine on Sept. 2nd, just report to the B Seam and they'll assign you to a section." I thanked her and went out the door still in mild shock and dreading to tell the family the news, especially Wanda, who had been waiting patiently in the car. Our three children would likely not understand much about the change nor the dangers involved in going into coal mining.

As I opened the car door and sat down, Wanda asked, "What did that woman call you back for?" "Wanda, I said in a whisper, they hired me."

"They did what?" "That's right, they hired me. I didn't have a chance to say no!" She looked stunned by my words.

"You know I won't let you work in the mines, I thought you said no one was hired on the first day they tried to get a mining job!" I felt and probably looked shell-shocked as I explained what happened and how I felt an obligation to Jimmy to keep my word. I don't even remember driving home that day, as my thoughts were absorbed about I was going to get out of this situation.

By the following Monday I had made up my mind to keep my word and take the mining job for two reasons, one; I would be making $43.46 an eight hour shift, about $10.00 more than my sales job, and two; I was keeping my word to Jimmy when I let him speak to the Scotia management personnel for me. Besides, the benefits at the mine were a little better, especially the fact that we would have full health insurance coverage with no co-pays or deductibles, which made changing jobs much easier for us to accept.

Monday August, 29, 1974, was a day I dreaded because my employers at the Wholesale Company had always treated me kindly and with respect, and had given me a raise every year I worked for them. They never once questioned my judgment in any matter involving our customers and never said one harsh word during the almost eight years I was employed by them. They were an old, established business that had been in business since 1890, since the business was first started by their father. It's not easy to leave a company that had maintained the highest degree of integrity in their business dealings over so many years, and Lewis Wholesale Company, of Whitesburg, Letcher County, Kentucky was that kind of business and more.

When I asked the three owners for a quick meeting when I arrived at the office at 6:a.m., the four of us gathered in the back office and I informed them that I would regretfully be leaving the company after Labor Day, as I had accepted a job, after much deliberation on the subject, with a coal company and that I wanted to thank them for the kindness they had shown me in all the years I had been with them. As I expected, they were surprised by my announcement and one owner asked, "Have you made up your mind for sure yet?" I assured him that I had spent the weekend talking it over with my wife and other members of the family and since I had made some promises to others (my brother) I was a man of my word, and would have to keep it.

The eldest of the owners was the one that always made the final decisions and he asked me to hang around the office a few minutes before leaving on my regular Monday sales route. I got my sales materials together while waiting, wondering if they were trying to decide whether to either fire me now or allow me to work until Labor Day weekend.

In a few minutes they came back to the front office and asked me to step outside onto the loading dock. One of the owners began the conversation, saying, "We've talked it over and want you to know that we appreciate the job you have done for us over the years and that we really hate to lose you. We want you to know that if money is the reason you're leaving, we have decided to offer you a raise now and another one at the beginning of next year. Of course we also understand that you might have other reasons for leaving, and if so, we want you to know that we'll accept your decision and there won't be any hard feelings."

I studied hard for a moment and replied, "I really appreciate your offer of the two raises and I've appreciated the bonuses and raises you gave me at times through the years, but no, it's not the money at all, although the new job will result in a little more money. The main thing is that I have given my word to people that helped me get the job and I need to keep my word, even though I actually had a change of mind after I made the promise. I've always kept my word when I promised something, as I have with this company through the years."

I think we were all nearly tearing up after out talk, because they were like family to me and I had been in some of their homes several times on business and they always made me feel completely at home with them. I don't think I've ever regretted leaving a job and the owners of a company as much as I did that company that day.

The next few days went by fast, as I had the unpleasant responsibility of telling all my customers in Letcher, Knott, and Pike Counties in Kentucky, and Wise County, Virginia, that I was making my last visit to their store. All of them understood the choice I was making, as some of their own families had recently decided to enter the mines because of the coal boom and high wages being offered.

The high wages being offered by the truck mines had not extended to the larger mines, mainly because they were under contract with unions and had negotiated the contracts years before. The Scotia Mine had signed their contract with the Scotia Employees Association in July, 1973, and the contract pay scale was locked in until July, 1976. That explains why that while some truck miners were receiving $100.00 for an eight hour shift, I would be receiving $46.46 for an eight hour shift. The good news was that all overtime worked after an eight hour shift was compensated at one and one-half times the regular hourly rate.

On Tuesday September 2nd, I drove across Pine Mountain with a lot of apprehension for what lay ahead on my first day in my new mining job. I wondered what it would be like, since I hadn't been inside a mine since I was seven years old and dad had shown me and my cousin Paul Yonts the truck mine he worked in. I had talked to dad over the weekend and he gave me some pointers about roof conditions and other hazards in the mine and brother Jimmy had also filled me in with some do's and don'ts of mining.

As I drove down the south side of the steep Pine Mountain, (second highest mountain in Kentucky at a little over 2,400 ft. elevation) I could see the Black Mountain Range in the near distance. The wide valley (about one mile broad) between the two mountain ranges was always as beautiful as any valley in the Shenandoah Valley in Virginia to me. It seemed a little foreboding this day as it loomed in the distance, knowing that I would be inside that mountain shortly. A sudden feeling of regret swept through my body as I felt like I was about to enter a world that was out of my element. Would I be able to stand the rigors of coal mining? Would I feel claustrophobic in the mine? Would I be able to keep up with the experienced miners? These questions and more were in my mind as I drove to work that day.

Arriving at the entrance to the mine I drove past the guard shack without being stopped and noticed that the guard was familiar to me. I had met him in a Hazard medical clinic just a few days ago when I took the physical for my Scotia employment. At the time I didn't ask what he would be doing at the mine, so I was a little surprised to see him working as a security guard. I never asked his name and never learned it, but saw him nearly every day at the guard shack over the next seventeen years and three months.

Scotia had a large parking lot for the workers located above the slope entrance which had a metal walking bridge spanning the cut-through leading down the slope. I parked my car there and walked down the steep pathway and crossed the deep cut via the bridge for the first time, but which I would cross thousands of times in the coming years. I entered the bath house and entered the large room with a ceiling height of about 25-30 ft. and noticed dozens of small baskets in which the personal possessions of the miners were stored while they were inside the mine. The baskets were raised and lowered by a chain and pulley system. A series of low benches were aligned on the concrete floor to provide a place to sit while talking or to lay one's gear on while lowering and raising the basket of clothing and gear. After raising the basket to the top of the ceiling a lock was inserted into the chain link near the bottom, there-by securing one's belongings from theft or disturbance.

Having worn the clothes from home that I intended wearing in the mine, I didn't select an empty basket just yet to hang my clothes. I wanted to check everything out before making a decision as to whether I wanted to bathe at the mine after work or were my mining clothes home and bathe there. Since my brother Jimmy had been going straight home from work, I chose that route at first, since we would be riding together. Later on down the road a few months, we decided to bathe at the mine bathhouse for convenience and continued to do so for the rest of our years spent at Scotia.

After checking the bathhouse out I went back across the bridge and climbed the hill to my car, where I was to meet Jimmy so we could ride to the B Seam together. I was glad we were able to work on the same shift and the same mine, as that made the transition from salesman to coal miner a little easier for me.

I made sure I arrived early that first day, which gave me time to not only check the bathhouse out, but to observe nearly the whole mining complex from the vantage point of the hill that had been graded off to make the large parking lot. From here I observed the 100,000 lb capacity railroad gondolas (gons is the familiar abbreviation commonly used) being slowly moved along the rails by a blue colored yard locomotive as they were being loaded with clean coal from the tipple chute, which loaded a car in just a few minutes. This was a view I was destined to see many times, but it would usually be a couple of L&N locomotives pulling a 100 car unit train under the loading chute for a steel mill or a power utility. I never tired of watching this process because it helped me to realize that coal mining was very important to our nation's economy and helped motivate me to do my very best to help produce as much coal as I could. That statement might sound like a cliché but I was always aware that our jobs depended on producing enough coal to keep us working. That's very important when one has a family to support as most of us did.

Although many miners felt as I did and did their best to produce as much coal as they could, the dirty little secret is that there is always a few in every crowd that believes the exact opposite, that is, they believe that one shouldn't go beyond the limits of their job to help the company no matter what the consequences might be. Fortunately there were but few miners that felt this way at Scotia.

When Jimmy arrived at the parking lot I loaded my new mining belt, yellow mining hat, and lunch bucket into his car and we drove up the hill which led to the B Seam. I wasn't particularly nervous by that time but still felt uneasy about my situation. We passed a few loaded coal trucks coming off the hill as we ascended and was behind one as we went up. This was the method by which the coal being mined at the B seam was transported to the large stockpile near the tipple. I would come to be used to sharing the Scotia roads with loaded trucks, not only coal trucks, but also massive Uke trucks weighing almost 300 tons and capable of hauling around 400 tons a load were engaged hauling waste rock from the tipple to somewhere on the mountain to scatter around. If one met one of those monsters on the road it was best to pull over and give them the road.

As we arrived in the B Seam parking lot I took in the scenes around me and the mine office and portals were visible to me for the first time. The mine had four low entries, with a large fan pulling the air from the mine in entry #4. There were mine supplies on the yard and a few cars and trucks parked around the lot. The fan was roaring and making talk difficult if not impossible so we gathered our gear and walked into the mine office where Jimmy introduced me to the Mine foreman. After the introduction and the foreman welcomed me, he assigned me to the same section as my brother was on, the One Left section.

We went into the lighthouse where I selected a cap lamp and buckled it on my new light leather belt. The belt and new hat that I had painted yellow to signify an inexperienced miner stood out like a sore thumb in the lighthouse where several miners were waiting on the benches to go inside. I felt all eyes on me and I feel confident in saying that some of them were thinking of what the odds were that I wouldn't be able to hack coal mining. If so they wouldn't be the first to feel that way, as I had been told by a friend or two that I'd never make it as a coal miner, I was too used to carrying a pencil and clipboard around for a living. Standing in that lighthouse that day I was beginning to think they had been right in their prediction.

At exactly 2:30 p.m. (the 2 upper seams of Scotia started 30 minutes earlier than the Bottom Mine as I discovered that day) the one-left boss, Sonny Cornett, shouted, "Loadem up boys!' We proceeded to the set of steel tracks leading into the mine where an electric track motor of about 6 ton was hooked to two low mantrips made of steel. I stood there for a moment wondering how in Heaven's name I or anyone else was going to be able to insert ourselves into that small of a space. Watching as the men began sliding into the contraception, I noticed that one of the men was a very large man and I thought that I would watch him and see how he did it. He managed to get his over 6ft and maybe 250lb body into the mantrip which gave me some hope but just to be sure I waited until four others got in and I lay down next to the entrance opening of the mantrip. When loaded, we somehow managed to get a whole crew of 10 men in the contraption.

As the motorman swung his trolley pole around and connected it to the power (trolly) wire hanging above the track we left the outside and went through the thick rubber belt ventilation curtain and my eyes beheld the inside of a very, very, low ceiling mine. I shined my cap light against the ceiling of the mine and saw that the roof was barely above the low hanging power line that our motor's trolley pole was connected to. The height of the mine was no more than 36-42 inches, if that. I lay there and watched the pillars of coal as we advanced into the mine and thinking what in the world have I gotten myself into? Maybe my friends were right, maybe I wouldn't make it as a miner. I then remembered that I had made it through the rigors of Parris Island and if I could survive that hellish place I could survive anything. That thought braced me for whatever might come next no matter how rough it might be. Besides, I had no other place to go to earn a living, as I had quit my job and there was no turning back now.

CHAPTER SEVEN

COAL MINING MAN

When we reached the end of the track the boss cautioned me to watch the roof as I went towards the section and to take my time getting there, as the roof was very low. I was in full agreement with him as I could do no more than squat on my knees as I contemplated my next move. As I squatted in the loose coal and rock dust I saw the other miners quickly duck walking up the entry towards where the working section was. I already knew from what Jimmy told me that the section was about 30 or more breaks from the end of the track, which meant at least 2,400 ft or more. As I began my duck walk towards the section I was heartened to see that the big miner I had watched struggling while outside as he got into the mantrip, was beside me and having the same problem trying to make progress towards the face of One Left section. I had already been informed that the big man was always the last on section every day. I was fairly confident that he would no longer hold that honor after today.

I had gone no more than 25 yards before I had to sit down and rest a spell. That's when my walking buddy informed me that "It takes a while to get your leg muscles conditioned to have to squat to walk. You'll be as sore as the dickens by the time we leave here tonight." I thanked him but in my heart I could see a situation where I'd be lucky to reach the working face by tonight. We rested a few minutes and started again, with my having to alternate from my squatting position occasionally to actually getting on my knees and "walking" awhile. Several times I had to crawl in order to keep up with the other man, whom by this time I was beginning to respect to no end. He was having as rough a time as me but he was still pushing along with me bringing up the rear a few feet behind him. I was struggling to just breathe as I crawled along. I was sure paying for my lack of activity over the past few years.

Eventually my new equally sweating friend and I reached the section after what seemed like several hours and an equal number of miles had passed, but what was probably only 20-30 minutes after we had exited the mantrip at the end of the track. I'll admit that one question I had in my mind as I labored to the section was a simple one which had probably been asked before. Why don't they just install a few more 60 lb steel rails and bring us all the way to the section? I didn't want to appear like the fool that I apparently was, so I never asked that question.

When I and my buddy reached the section we took a long drink of liquid we carried in our dinner buckets (his was water, mine was orange juice) and I sort of revived after I cooled off and wiped the sweat from my eyes. The boss was grinning as he spoke to me, "See there, that wasn't too bad a walk was it?" I gave him a weak grin as I held my light in his eyes. I later found out that one doesn't hold their cap light in another miner's eyes. You blind him by doing this and it's the first sign of an inexperienced miner.

As he shielded his eyes with his arm he told me to follow him, which I did but I had much trouble keeping up with him. He took me to a big machine with a revolving set of heads with steel teeth and informed me that this was what was called a "feeder" and my job was to shovel up the coal the shuttle cars spilt while dumping on the feeder. The feeder conveyed and dumped the crushed coal and rock on the belt.

It was so noisy that I barely could hear him, even though he was nearly hollering at me. I shook my light O.K. and he bent over and walked away without having to duck walk as I had. I envied him and hoped that I might be able to do that someday, that is if I showed up for work tomorrow. I had my doubts at that moment.

As I looked around I began to wonder if those shuttle cars actually managed to dump any coal into the feeder at all, as most of it seemed to be piled in the last few feet leading to the feeder. In a few minutes the first car pulled onto the feeder and turned the car's conveyor on and dumped most of his load into the iron monster. He left about one-haft ton for me to shovel from the front and sides of the feeder. I had that #4 shovel smoking for a few minutes but that didn't last long. I couldn't keep up with the mess the shuttle cars were making and it took me just a few minutes to ask another stupid question of myself. Why don't they use one of those large scoop machines I saw at the mine office the other day to clean this mess up? Since that first day until this one I don't know if they even had a scoop on section or whether they were just testing me.

About an hour into the shift I shoveled up a shovelful of coal and as I slung the coal I heard someone yelling loudly, then a tremendous "BOOMMMMM" reverberated through the air and the whole mine shook and vibrated. I saw a flash of bright red fire from the working face of the same entry I was in. I threw my shovel through the air and my hat and cap light were blown off my head by the concussion from the blast as I fell onto the pile of coal I was shoveling. I was nearly traumatized as I lay with my face in the coal pile. Oh Lord, I thought. My first day in the mine and it's blown up. Help me Jesus!

I lay there in the coal pile until I could get my senses back and eventually managed to get my cap light back on my head. Looking towards the face where the fire and explosion had originated I could only hope no one was hurt as I whispered a prayer that everyone had escaped the blast. The coal and rock dust finally settled enough to where I could see lights a hear voices and I knew that help was already there and since I didn't know where I was or what I should do, I decided to wait where I was until someone came for me.

In a few minutes I heard a shuttle car coming towards the feeder. As the driver dumped his load of coal he said, "Let's go to the dinner hole and eat dinner!" I looked at him as I thought; go to the dinner hole? The section has experienced an explosion and all he can think about is dinner? I shined my light in his eyes and said, "What about that big explosion a few minutes ago? Was anybody hurt in that?" "What explosion,?" he asked. "That big blast a while ago, was anyone hurt?" He grinned and exclaimed, "That weren't no explosion, that was the coal drill man putting off a shot!"

That's how I found out I was assigned to a conventional section that used coal drills and dynamite to extract the coal from the face instead of a continuous mining machine. It would have been nice if someone had warned me of a pending shot being put off in the same entry only a few yards away from where I was working my fanny off trying to keep the feeder clean. I lost all my pride, dignity, and some of my faith in humanity that day.

When I got to the area where the 7,200 volt power box was located every miner sitting there had their eyes on me. I was sweating like I never had and very thirsty, since I hadn't had anything to drink since I drank the orange juice when I first came on the section. I had slight indigestion after drinking the juice and no doubt I would never bring that item inside to drink again. Water is the drink to have when coal mining.

Several of the men wanted to know if I had been scared when the shot was put off earlier. "Nah, I said. It surprised me a little but I knew what it was, so I was ready for it." There it was, my fist lie as a coal miner, but no way could I have the other men thinking (maybe I should say knowing)I was weak. Sonny Cornett, the section foreman, asked how I was doing at the feeder and I assured him I was doing fine as I finished the quart jar of orange juice I had opened when I first arrived on the section. That was my second lie in the first five minutes at the dinner hole.

One didn't have to worry about lying down to rest at the dinner hole because there was not enough height to sit up comfortably and drink from a quart glass jar, so I had a good excuse to recline and I took full advantage of it. I wondered if I could live until quitting time or if I would die of heat exhaustion. Even though the mine temperature averaged 50 degrees on the inside, I felt as though I was sitting in an oven after shoveling the feeder over the last three hours.

I was too tired to eat my peanut butter crackers, so I unwrapped the large chunk of raw cabbage I had brought for lunch. I had been a confirmed vegetarian since 1968, so cabbage was my main fare. I assure you that was the worst mistake I made that first day. As soon as I went back to the feeder after lunch and started shoveling, I felt fire in the belly and pain in the esophagus. My whole system was on fire but I had to endure it until quitting time somehow, which I managed to accomplish, but barely.

At 9:45 p.m. Sonny came by the feeder and told me to go to the dinner hole and rest awhile before we walked out to the mantrip. He didn't have to tell me twice, as I had been ready to go since I got on section. I followed him to the dinner hole and found the other men were already there and ready to go. We all left the section at the same time but once again my walking buddy and I were the last ones to reach the end of the track where the mantrip was waiting on us. I believe I made a little better time leaving than I had coming, although I was in bad shape and could barely stand when we reached the outside.

After Jimmy and I got our cap lights hooked into the charger in the lighthouse, he looked at me and said, "Eddie, It'll get easier in a few days after the soreness is gone." I was shocked to hear that the soreness might last a few days. In actuality, he was trying to let me down easy, as the soreness lasted two weeks or more.

When I got home that night Wanda met me at the door and as I went in the house she took one look at me and said, "I'll bet you're wore out!" "Wore out won't come near enough to explain how I feel," I replied. She had supper prepared and I managed to eat a little even though I was still feeling the effects of that stalk of cabbage that I thought would be a good idea for a snack when I left home at noon that day.

I slept soundly that night but upon getting out of bed I discovered the soreness had intensified instead of felling better. We drove to Tunnel Hill to visit my parents in the morning to fill then in on my first day in the mines. Both my parents (Ed and Nell) had been against my changing jobs, as had my wife, but in the end I made the decision on my own. At least I could say that I always keep my word. Going up and down their many steps was a chore because of my sore leg muscles everyone had a good laugh at me as I held onto the banister and pulled myself up the steps. I tried to make light of my first day's work when telling everyone of my es-capades but in my heart I was dreading returning back to the mine that evening. I was glad that I had been taught to not be a "quitter" because that thought passed through my mind but I was determined to do what-ever it took to prove that I could hack the mines.

The next couple of days were just about a carbon copy of the first day, with my shuttle car driving friend and I faithfully bringing up the rear as we unloaded from the mantrip at the end of the track and walked to the section. The only change was that I managed to get even more sore than I was at the end of my first shift, which I thought would be impossible.

I was learning a little more each day about coal mining and finally managed to visit the coal face the third day on the job and watch the coal being loaded into the shuttle cars. My main job was as on the first day though; shoveling around the feeder. I did manage to wander around the feeder and shovel the tailpiece of the beltline and finally saw the crushed coal as it fell onto the belt and began the journey to the outside stockpile.

Those two 18 SC shuttle cars kept me busy most of the time shoveling up the coal that fell off their loaded sides as they dumped their loads of coal. That fact hadn't changed from my first day on the job. I suspected at first that they were pulling a fast one on me by keeping me so busy but I learned that the coal spilling from the sides of the cars was a common oc-currence and couldn't be helped.

After three days on the job I managed to become used to the blasting of the coal from the face by the coal drill crew and barely flinched when they put off a shot. I didn't envy them, as I knew they had a dangerous and dirty job that someone had to do. I watched them at their work which caused me to think back to the time my dad had taken me into the mine in Floyd County, Kentucky with him. I now felt more respect than ever for him because he had to do his drilling of the shot holes with an old fashioned breast auger. I watched as the big coal drilling machine on our section pulled up to the face of the coal and drilled eight twelve ft. deep holes in the coal in just a few minutes. The coal drill man and his helper then inserted the powder into the holes and tamped each hole with a long wooden round pole and in a few minutes had it wired and ready to shoot. Oh how those shot firers of years past would have enjoyed having the use of an electric powered coal drill!

On Friday, September 5th, I drove my own vehicle to work because I had to go by the mine office to turn in some paperwork concerning my health insurance and tax withholding information. It turned out that I made the right choice when I drove my own vehicle because when I drove to the B Seam I was approached by my section boss, Sonny Cornett, who said he wanted to speak to me for a minute.

He said that he had orders to send a utility man from his section to the New Taggart Mine in the C Seam immediately, and since I was the youngest in seniority and had just started working for him, I was the lucky designee. He also mentioned that he was concerned about having two brothers on the same section because of the possibility of losing two people from the same family in case of accident. His explanation made sense at the time but I've wondered since if choosing me was mainly because I knew how to do absolutely nothing on his section but shovel coal. Of course having been on section for only three days was barely enough time to even know how many pieces of machinery were on section, much less how to operate one of them. Regardless of the reason, it turns out that he did me a great favor by sending me to New Taggart.

The new C Seam Mine was called by management the New Taggart Mine or the Upper Taggart Mine. The miners who worked the mine gave it a new name, the 'New Tygart' Mine. In conversation with other miners over the years I never heard it referred to by any of them as the New Taggart, C Seam Mine or Upper Taggart Mine. It was usually called the 'New Tygart Mine.' So with that in mine I will refer to it hereafter either as the New Tygart or New Taggart Mine.

Some explanation is in order also about the B Seam mine where I first worked. The proper name for this mine was, The 'Middle Taggart Mine.' Some called it Old Tygart Mine. To make the distinction easier for the reader, I will refer to it as the B Seam Mine. To the miners of Scotia, the names of New Tygart and the B Seam would become the familiar ones used in conversation through the years.

After talking with Sonny, I drove off the B Seam hill and turned up the dirt road leading to the New Tygart Mine which was of course unfamiliar to me as this was my first trip up it. I passed several coal trucks hauling coal to the stockpile on the main yard. Like the B Seam Mine, the new mine had a large area where coal was being stockpiled and one had to circle back around it to reach the parking lot. As I parked my car I noticed that the beltline coming out of the mine had a walkway that had to be crossed to reach the mine office. There was nothing else located on the parking side of the belt except for the mine fan and the one mine entry that the fan was in.

After crossing over the walkway I went into the mine office where the foreman was talking to another miner and reported to him. He shook my hand and told me he was glad to have me because he had been doing without a utility man since the mine had opened. He motioned with his hand towards a door leading into the lighthouse in the other large room of the building as he spoke again, "Grab a cap light from the lighthouse and we'll head inside in a few minutes." I went through the door where he had motioned and found myself in a large room of about 20'x30' dimension, with a large laminated board on one wall being the only item in the room except for a couple of wooden benches where 5 or 6 miners were sitting and talking among themselves.

"Are you our new utility man?" asked one miner. "Yeah, I guess I'm the lucky one," I replied. Have you just started?" another one inquired. "No, this is my fourth day, I've been working at the B Seam." "Well ole buddy, you'll like this mine, it's a lot higher that that B Seam back-breaker. I worked there a while before I came up here and it's as much different as daylight and dark!" I grinned as I answered, "I'm glad to hear that, I've got half-inch furrows in my back from trying to tear the heads off roof bolts in the ceiling on One Left section!" That brought a laugh and a little hint of acceptance from the other miners, which was what I had hoped to achieve by the comment. My roof bolt comment was accurate, as

I had been brought to my knees several times by trying to raise my back a little and instead catching the head of a roof bolt in my back, which was a fight I couldn't possibly win.

After grabbing a cap light from an adjoining smaller room, I sat with the other men for a few minutes until the boss came out of his office while motioning and shouting, "Let's go boys, what're you waitin' on, payday?" We grabbed our dinner buckets and followed him out the door. Mine was the traditional black painted pail, but a couple of the miners had the old type with the round lid and in which drinking water could be stored in the bottom of the pail. I noticed that the two miners that appeared to be the oldest were the ones with older type dinner pails. It turned out that they were actually the two miners who had the most mining experience among us that day. Throughout my mining career at Scotia, miners that carried that type dinner bucket were the ones with years of coal mining under their belts. There was probably no particular reason for it but it was an interesting fact. One reason could have been that just maybe their dads had carried those types of pails or maybe they just simply liked the fact that water could be stored in the bottom. Every individual coal miner has his reasons for his behavior, just like people the world over.

As our crew of ten men came of the building I noticed that there were no rails outside anywhere leading into the mine. I didn't ask, but it was obvious that none had been installed yet, meaning that we were walking into the mine. I thought to myself, here we go again, I'll have to duck walk into the mine. As we parted the ventilation curtain just inside the portal I was pleasantly surprised to find that the height of the mine entry was just about 6ft with a few lower spots occasionally as we traveled down a sloping, wet, and slick entryway towards the face. The miner who told me about this roof being higher than that at the B Seam wasn't joking. I found that even with my height I could walk comfortably down the entry without having to bend over continuously. I was elated to find out that I would be able to reach the section at the same time as the other men. I had felt ashamed to be one of the last on section at the B Seam.

After we had traveled down the incline about ten breaks (around 800 ft) the mine leveled out considerably and the top got a little lower, averaging around 65 inches in height. I had to hold my head sideways, which was a little uncomfortable but which was an unspeakable improvement from where I had come.

We continued on for another four breaks and came to the 7200 vote power box which, like the one at the B Seam was the unofficial dinner hole. I was a little surprised to see everyone sit on the power box and have a snack while the boss was gone to the face to check for possible methane gas and loose drawrock. The power box setting wasn't done by my first section at the B Seam, but the reason was obvious. The roof was too low to allow anyone to sit on the box there.

When the boss returned everyone closed their dinner buckets and headed to the face to start loading coal. The boss kept me there at the power box and as we sat there he explained to me that ours was the only working section at New Tygart at the present but when we advance a few more breaks another crew and more equipment would be added. He also informed me that as his only utility man, he was making me his supply man also. My job would be to make as many trips as needed during a shift to the outside and back with a load of rock dust, 5 gallon cans of hydraulic oil, roof bolts, dynamite, and blasting caps by means of a wheeled electric "Julie car," which he would show me how to operate. I can handle that, I thought. He explained further, "As my utility man, you have to be a 'jack of all trades,' which means you have to keep the feeder clean, the entries clear of coal so the loader can get to a cut of coal, and help the coal drill operator in your spare time. On top of that you'll be my flunky runner, I can't be both outside and in here at the same time so I'll depend on you to help me out sometimes. Lastly you'll have to help the bolting machine operators catch up if they get behind. The cutting machine operator doesn't need to wait while they bolt a place. If you do all this we'll keep a nice little house here! One last thing, when you bring the supplies in, take them to the face and scatter the rock dust and load the bolts and sticks of glue on the bolt machines and put the dynamite and caps in the containers on the coal drill."

With those words of admonition he jumped down from the power box (he had short legs) and told me to follow him. We went over to the next break, the #3 entry, where a 440 amp charger was located. A large open topped 4 wheeled vehicle was connected to the charger and was receiving a charge of electricity. This was obviously the Julie car he had told me about. The next hour or so was spent in learning how to connect the car to the charger and how to service the vehicle in my free time. After all that he expected me to do, I couldn't possibly imagine at the moment when I would have any free time to help on section.

Over the next few days I discovered that even with all the things I was expected to do, I managed to stay ahead of the machine operators and also find some time to help them occasionally. The higher roof of the mine made all the difference in the world and the work seemed much easier than what I had experienced at the B Seam.

The nine other miners (counting the boss) were for the most part good men that tried their best to run as much coal as they could and do it safely. Methane gas wasn't a problem at all and while I'm sure the boss checked occasionally, I never heard him say anything about finding any pockets of methane. It's highly doubtful that he did, because we were high above the water table which plagued the Imboden #1 Mine.

One of the machine operators didn't like the fact that the coal drill operator would catch up to him and just sit around and wait on him to finish his job. The one who was caught up and relaxing would catcall and kid with the one who was hurrying to complete his job. One day the jesting and ribbing got out of hand and one pulled a knife on the other and chased him all over the section, whether in jest or not was not known, but the rest of the crew urged the knifeman to put it down, which he eventually did. This could have easily ended tragically but thankfully ended peacefully. I was told later by one of the miners that alcohol had likely played a part in the incident.

Just as our section foreman had told me, he spent a good deal of his time outside in the mine office nearly every day after he came inside the mine and checked the section out. I assume he was fire bossing the mine each day while we were waiting on him and eating our snack at the dinner hole. Usually, after we started running coal he and I would hop into the Julie car and drive outside to get supplies. If we had enough supplies to do for most of the shift, he and I worked around the supply yard, cleaning up and straightening up the pallets of supplies. We had no fork lift, so everything had to be done by hand which took a good amount of time.

When we finished loading our supplies we would head back inside to unload, then he would check the faces and check with the men to see how the coal running was coming. In fact we could tell how the crew was doing by the coal going into the stockpile. We had an excellent view of the whole New Tygart complex from the hill beside the mine office. If coal was coming over the belt we worked outside until we finished loading the Julie car with supplies and had the yard straightened up. If the coal stopped flowing over the beltline he was instantly on the mine office phone to the section to check on what was wrong. Sometimes he would head back inside and leave me to finish up the job by myself, then I'd head back inside with my load of supplies. Of course I still had to keep my shoveling up on the inside and keep the section rock dusted after every cut of coal. Being young and fit during that time I was mostly able to keep up my work.

We hardly ever had visitors to come by the mine. Occasionally Charles Kirk, the Scotia Safety Inspector, the security guard, or sometimes a Scotia Company official would make an appearance outside the mine but other than that our one working section was left alone. Even the Federal and State Mine Inspectors usually came by when the day shift was working but for the most part left us alone. We still had no steel rails laid to enable us to have a track motor or mantrip to provide transportation for us at this time.

After I had been at New Tygart about two months an unusual situation developed. The boss showed up one evening as our crew was preparing to walk inside to the section and told us to go on in that he would be in later. That had never happened before but we followed his orders and went on in the mine and did our jobs as if he was there with us. I was cleaning up around the dinner hole an hour or two later and heard the mine phone page us. One or two other miners were around the phone and I don't remember which one of us answered it, but I do remember us getting the word that a different boss would be inside to supervise us shortly. After the new boss showed up he informed us that our foreman had been fired and escorted off the property for some reason or other. We learned that the security guard had made a trip to the mine shortly after we came inside and he ended up calling a Company official with his concerns, whatever they were, and as a result our boss was fired. Any reason given here for the firing would only be speculation because the rumors flew fast and furious without the true facts being known. The foreman was a salary man that had no union protection and could be fired for any reason or no reason at the company's discretion. Our Scotia Employees Union could also not protect a new miner from being fired in the first 30 days of his employment. Some few were fired before they got their 30 days in for various reasons, usually proper ones.

In a few days our new boss, Jack Begley, made his appearance at the mine. Jack was the type of boss that could get along with anyone. He ended up being one of my favorites. As long as you worked hard and kept busy he kept out of the way and never raised his voice to anyone. He had a good sense of humor even when things went wrong and never asked anyone to do what he wouldn't do himself. This was the first time he had me as a member of his crew. He later left Scotia for awhile, then again came back as a section foreman and I was in his crew as a shuttle car driver.

Once, during his second term as a Scotia foreman he sat down beside me at the dinner hole where I was eating my dinner, looked at me intently with a smile on his face and then said, "Eddie, I'd like to ask you something." "Go ahead Jack." With a mischievous grin he blurted out, "When you first worked for me I always thought you were the best worker I had ever seen in a coal mine.... my question is; what happened?" With that he burst out in loud guffaws of laughter. That was his way of telling me that he thought I still was a pretty good worker even after 10 years or so had passed. At least I think that's what he meant.

On November 1, 1974, Scotia employees received $3.00 per hour raise as per the July, 1973 contract. This brought my hourly pay as a sectional utility man to $49.46 per eight hour shift. This amount would be equal to $245.32 in 2017. Looking at these figures, it's easy to understand why even inexperienced potential coal miners were flocking to the Human Resources Departments of large coal mines seeking employment there.

Jack Begley was transferred to another mine in early 1975, and Veril Boggs was designated our new section foreman. He was also the acting outside mine foreman for New Tygart and had his hands full in that capacity. He continued using me as not only the sectional utility man, but also the supply man for the section. He would often go outside the mine with me on my supply run and help me load the supplies as had my other two bosses. I always appreciated their help and never once complained about it. The union employees and company bosses almost always had very good relationships among themselves. We thought nothing about turning over our piece of equipment for a foreman to run while we broke for lunch. We all wanted the company to succeed in their push to hold down costs in any way we possibly could.

CHAPTER EIGHT

Good Times--Bad Times

The fact that I had to be outside often and for long periods of time as the supply man for our section allowed me to be able to enjoy many beautiful sunsets from the ridge on which New Tygart was situated. With the coal pouring over the belt and onto the stockpile while the fading sunlight at dusk shined directly through the coal, it created an almost perfect scene for a painter or photographer to capture. I never observed the setting sun from that ridge but that I didn't wonder at how God so very much loved and favored his children when he created this beautiful world for them.

Veril Boggs managed to convince the company that we needed some track laid into the mine in order to allow us to save time getting our supplies and men into and out of the mine. The company sent us a load of 60 lb -33ft long steel rails and we spent a weekend and some overtime hours in extending the track all the way to where another section was scheduled to turn right and be designated the One Right section. The single coal production section had advanced quite a ways since I joined them in September when they were only 17 breaks into the mine.

Just a few dozen ft inby where the One Right section would soon be started was a bore hole that had been drilled by a drill rig from the top of the mountain. When we first cut into the seam of coal there we were surprised at the nearly full stream of water pouring from the 4inch bore hole

68

in the mine roof. Eventually, Hargus Maggard, James Miles,and myself drove a wooden wedge into the hole which slowed the water coming through to a tolerable amount. Actually, my role involved more watching than helping as only one man at a time could be involved in holding the wedge, while another used a sledge hammer to drive it in.

Afterwards, nearly every time I operated a motor or other track vehicle past that spot, I would stop and take a long sip of that cold, refreshing water. No mountain stream could have been as cold or tasted any better that that water. I wasn't the only one that enjoyed it, some of the miners would fill their water jugs with water from that hole to take on section. I wish I could personally thank the man that drilled the hole in that mountain. He has no idea how much Scotia miners enjoyed his work.

With the completion of the laying of the rails to our section, the Julie car was made obsolete and we soon drove it outside to be picked up and be used somewhere else. It had served its purpose well over the past months since I had come on board but the time had come for a new mode of transportation.

We soon had a new (or newly reconditioned and painted) bright yellow six ton low seam motor sitting on the track, along with two supply cars and two mantrip cars. The two supply cars were made to haul coal from the mine but the bottoms had been welded to convert them to supply cars. The mantrip cars were of welded steel and were designed to be coupled to and pulled by a track motor, but this was a big improvement over walking to the section which had advanced deep into the mine by this time. Unlike the B Seam motors which were powered by electricity via trolley wire and a trolley pole system, this motor was battery operated, with the two large steel battery cases located in the center of the motor. The operator's deck was large, with room for three or four men to occupy if needed but was comfortable for only the operator and one passenger. The New Tygart Mine was now getting modern, it seemed.

With the addition of the new motor a full time second shift motorman was needed. Since I had been dealing with the supplies and working on the section for almost a year I was glad to be able to see my job made easier with the addition of the track motor. I assumed I would soon be replaced by a classified motorman from another mine but my duties continued as usual and I was made the unofficial motorman by our foreman.

I stayed in this capacity a few weeks before Boggs called me into the mine office one day and said, "Nickels, as of today you're the permanent motorman for the second shift. I'm going to try to get them to send me a utility man to replace you on section and another motorman or utility helper for you on the motor. Is that alright with you?" "Sure, I replied, whatever you say." The only problem was that I took a $1.02 cut in pay per day. That was no problem as I often found a few extra minutes of overtime on my paycheck when a difficult task was completed.

Because we had only one motorman and one motor, the boss continued helping me out with the supply detail and from time to time I still assisted on the section when I got caught up with my supply duties. I often helped the coal drill man with his duties, drilling and shooting coal from the face. I usually prepared the charges in one entry while Abby Boggs was drilling the holes for another set of charges in the next entry. This resulted in my obtaining quite a bit of knowledge about the handling and preparing of the blasting powder and to become acquainted with other safety procedures needed to protect myself and others. This doesn't mean that the use of explosives on a conventional section is error free though. For instance, when visitors come on a section they should always notify the boss and machine operators of their presence and what they will be doing while on section. In one instance an engineer crew on another section (not ours) for some reason either forgot to tell the boss they would be setting spads (markers for following the correct direction of the coal seam to be mined) or either told him and he forgot to pass the word. A cross break had been drilled and the charges had been prepared for blasting and the coal drill crew connected the battery to set the charge off. The battery operator shouted, "Fire, fire, fire," then pushed the firing button. It turned out that the break was almost through into the other cut, and the resulting blast threw chunks of coal into the midst of the engineer crew who were standing directly on the other side in the open break. Other than a few scratches, bruises, and bumps to go along with the shock and humiliation of getting nearly blown up or covered up in a cut of coal, none of the two men were seriously injured.

On June 4,th 1975, I was at the dinner hole on section with the boss when a voice came on the mine phone and called out, "New Tygart," then a slight pause and this time the voice shouted, New Tygart!" Veril was close to the phone so he picked the receiver from the hook and answered, "New Tygart here!" He listened to the person on the other end, then said, "O.K." and hung the phone up. He looked at me blankly and said,"Nickels, that was the mine office. My nephew is hurt bad. His shuttle car rolled back and the canopy caught him in the chest. They want me outside. Keep an eye on things here and holler at the mine office if you need anything.

70

They'll probably send someone up to take charge as soon as they can. You'll have to take me to the outside in the motor."

I took him outside and he left in his vehicle for the main office. I waited around for awhile and sure enough a foreman was sent to boss the rest of the shift. I can't be sure but I believe it was Meryl Rhodes, who I would come to know well. None of the rest of our crew had their certified foreman's certificate. I made up my mind that day to try for my mine foreman papers as soon as I was eligible. An assistant foreman's certificate was available to achieve after three years mining experience. I had been a miner for nine months on that date.

Tragically, Veril Bogg's nephew, Kenneth Boggs, was killed in the shuttle car accident that day. He was standing outside the shuttle car next to the canopy to better see if the car was fully loaded with coal when the car rolled back against him, pinning him against the coal rib. Kenneth had worked on our New Tygart section for awhile and I had gotten to know him fairly well. Our whole section grieved for him and his family.

His was the first death at Scotia since May, 1971, when utility man Dale Cornett was killed by a rib roll. In Cornett's death Federal Investigators faulted management for "failure to detect and take down or adequately support a loose overhanging brow." Scotia was fined $5,500 in the incident.

In Kenneth Bogg's death, MESA's report on the incident criticized Scotia's handling of the installation of cabs and canopies but what fine was assessed if any, is not known by this writer. Federal regulators had been under pressure to install the cabs and canopies on their equipment and were criticized by the Feds for ordering "kit" form or ready-made canopies instead of designing custom made ones. That resulted, according to the Feds, of operators not being able to tell when the car was fully loaded.

Having spent over twelve years as a shuttle car driver, I can vouch for the difficulty of achieving good vision from under a canopy, but that was something I was willing to forego because of the protection the canopies provided the operator. I did once regret having a canopy on my shuttle car when I was assigned again to the B Seam for a short period of time because of a layoff, and my SC 18 canopy caught the 440 cable hanging in front of the 7,200 volt power box, pulling the power boxes into the roadway and knocking the section's power off.

The boss (Bob Childers) was standing nearby when I snagged the power cable and without saying anything to me he slowly picked up the receiver from the mine phone and said, "Hello supply house!" In a few moments they answered and Bob spoke into the receiver, "A shuttle car has moved our power into the middle of the entry and we'll have to shut down while we move the power back." I thought he was remarkably calm for all the destruction I had caused. I had figured he would say, "This fool of a car driver has shut the section down and I'm sending him outside." I was glad when I left that section for the high country again.

Scotia sent another locomotive (motor) to join the one they had furnished us with earlier. This particular motor was smaller in size and tonnage than the other one. This was a five ton battery powered motor that had about as much pulling and pushing power as the six ton one. We had been out of compliance with Federal Regulations while using one motor. The regulations called for a motor to be connected to each end of a man-trip or a group of supply cars when inside the mine.

A new section was started at this time at New Tygart which meant more supplies had to be hauled inside the mine and another motorman would be necessary to operate the new small motor. To fill that position management sent another motorman to work with me by the name of Wayne Morgan. He had been working at the B Seam where he had been running one of their trolley motors. He was just in time, as we had to help get some of the mining equipment inside the mine for the new section they were starting. The new section was opened with a continuous mining machine instead of using a cutting machine, a loader, and a coal drill. The day shift motor crew was assigned the job of getting the continuous miner inside the mine to work the new section, while my buddy and I took in some of the power boxes, a roof bolter and other mining equipment.

When the new section started running coal we were assigned a new mine foreman to be over both working sections. Jerry Herron had been an assistant mine foreman at the B Seam and the New Tygart job was a promotion for him. I and my buddy were now reporting to him and he was keeping our timesheet. I was officially relieved from any connection with my original New Tygart coal production section.

At one point in 1975 the Scotia employees received a $10.00 per shift raise beyond what the contract called for. This brought my pay for an eight hour shift to 58.44. While we never officially received word of why we suddenly got such a large raise beyond what the contract called for, the rumor was that one of our coal contracts was with the government, who required a raise for all employees in order to get the coal contract. I don't know for sure but suspect it might have had something to do with the fact that around that same time Blue Diamond was found guilty of ignoring minimum- wage and safety laws in violation of the Walsh-Healy Public Contracts Act. Whatever the reason for the raise, the extra $10.00 per shift made a big difference in our paychecks.

The importance of having a motor on each end of our two supply cars became crystal clear to me one day as we were pushing two empty supply cars out of the mine toward the outside. For some reason of which I don't now remember, we unloaded our supply cars and headed out of the mine pushing those cars in front of us. We usually not only coupled the cars together but used a safety chain to double secure the couplings. We had a good sized hill to go down and when we went down it that particular day somehow the cars became uncoupled. We were unaware of it because we were in the opposite end where the controls were located. We were unable to raise our heads above the motor to check out the track ahead because there were only two or three inches of clearance between the top of the motor and the mine roof.

I was operating the motor and when I reached the bottom of the big hill I began raising my head to try to peep over the top of the motor to check to see how the two cars were doing. Just as I raised my head a tremendous collision with something on the track threw me backwards and knocked my mining hat off my head, putting my light out and shocking the heck out of me. I thought sure we had collided with another motor or something very big. In my mind's eye I could just see and imagine people lying all around us badly injured. Wayne Morgan was sitting in the deck with me and he was treated about like I was by the collision. When the collision happened my hand was knocked from the controls so we were thankfully protected from the motor accidently moving after the hit.

When the coal and rock dust had settled and the cobwebs were cleared from my head, I slowly climbed from the deck and walked to the front of the motor, which had a headlight before the crash but which was no longer shining. I discovered that one side of my caplight would still burn (it had two bulb controls) so I could see that we had collided with our two supply cars which had in some way become uncoupled as we came down the steep hill and got ahead of us for a little ways, then came back to meet us causing a big collision.

We had called the outside dispatcher at the supply house for the right of way on the track and felt safe in pushing the cars with one motor but hadn't counted on having a collision with our own cars we were pushing. Somehow the two supply cars had stayed on the rails without being wrecked. After coupling the cars again and wrapping our safety chain around the couplings we proceeded slowly to the outside. We had a close call that evening but came out alright in the end.

The same week that Jerry Herron left the B Seam to become the mine foreman at New Tygart my brother Philip or Phil as the family called him, who had been working at Scotia for about six months, left Scotia to attend the Kentucky State Police Academy at Frankfort, Kentucky. He had submitted his application with the State Police before he started working for Scotia and had assumed he wouldn't get called to the Academy after so long a period of time had passed without hearing from them.

Jerry Herron had been Phil's boss at the B Seam. Jerry told me that Phil had been the best belt man he had ever worked around. He said that he had cleaned up his belt head drive the best he had seen it since the mine opened. He asked me to tell Phil that he was welcome at Scotia anytime if he wanted to come back. Phil never came back to Scotia but instead made the choice to make a career of the State Police from which he retired in 1995. After retiring from the Kentucky State Police he took a job with the Whitesburg City Police Department in Whitesburg, Kentucky, and retired from that job just a few weeks before he passed away of lung cancer in 2004.

Herron served as the mine foreman for about six months before he was called to boss at one of Scotia's other mines. He and all the other foremen I had worked for were good at their jobs and the company rewarded all of them with a higher position in the company.

After Herron's departure the company sent Bruce Jones to us for a mine foreman. Bruce was an excellent boss who always had a great working relationship with every employee he ever came into contact with. He never raised his voice to the employees, listened to their ideas and concerns, and when something went wrong (which was frequently) he never blamed anyone else but took the blame himself instead. Bruce Jones was the type of man that you wanted to have watching your back in a combat situation on the battlefield.

Not every incident that occurs among coal miners is of a serious nature. Sometimes a potentially serious event can be used for humor. One such incident occurred when Wayne Morgan and I were preparing to take the section crews inside on the mantrip. As the men were climbing inside the cars, one of the men stumbled against the steel door frame and drew a little blood from above his eye, but only had a scratch to show for it. As he wiped his hand across his face and looked at the smudge of blood on his hand he asked, "Boys, am I hurt bad?" One wag spoke up, "Yeah ole boy, I'm afraid you're not gonna make it!" With those words the man with the barely noticeable scratch passed out cold and hit the ground. A little cold water brought him back around but the men never let the victim forget it. If you had a weakness of some kind, your fellow coal miners would discover it at one time or another. The many humorous nicknames among the miners was a testament to the humor rampant among them.

The motormen were responsible for keeping the rock dusting caught up in the main entry (where the track was located) and on the main beltline. This was quite a chore for those charged with scattering the dust. We had to load a flatcar with as many 40 lb bags of rock dust as it would hold and travel slowly through the main line scattering the dust by hand.

This job was made much easier when the company bought a 2 ton capacity battery operated rock duster. The machine was as large as a track motor or larger and had two large bubble shaped chambers that held one ton in each bubble. As the motor pulled the duster along the track one man stretched a long four inch flexible hose to the area that needed rock dusting and just hit the starter button on the duster and let it fly. The only drawback to the operation was that the bubbles had to be loaded with dust by hand.

The following are some facts on the reasons for rock dusting in a mine:

Mine operators are required to apply rock dust in underground bituminous coal mines to reduce the explosion potential of coal dust and other dust generated during mining operations. Effective and frequent rock dust application is essential to protect miners from the potential of a coal dust explosion, or if one occurs, to reduce its severity.

Where rock dust is required to be applied, it shall be distributed upon the top, floor, and sides of all underground areas of a coal mine and maintained in such quantities that the incombustible content of the combined coal dust, rock dust, and other dust shall be not less than 65 per centum, but the incombustible content in the return air courses shall be no less than 80 per centum. Where methane is present in any ventilating current, the per centum of incombustible content of such combined dust shall be increased 1.0 and 0.4 per centum for each 0.1 per centum of methane where 65 and 80 per centum, respectively, of incombustibles are required. Federal Register/Vol. 76, No. 119/ June 21, 2011

Rock dust is basically a pulverized stone used to cover coal dust and render accumulations of it inert. If methane is present a larger percentage of rock dust is required in order to be in compliance with Federal Regulations. The stone composing rock dust is pulverized limestone, dolomite, gypsum, anhydrite, shale, adobe, or other inert material, preferably light colored *"100 percent of which will pass through a sieve having 20 meshes per linear inch and 70 percent or more which will pass through a sieve having 200 meshes per linear inch, the particles of which when wetted and dried will not cohere to form a cake which will not be dispersed into separate particles by a light blast of air, and which does not contain more than 5 percent of combustible matter or more than a total of 4 percent free and combined silica'...*

I have been specific with the descriptions of rock dust to show how important this item is in coal mining. For example, in 2009 the Federal Safety and Health Administration (MSHA) determined for the period from 1976 through 2001 there were six explosions that resulted in 46 fatalities in which rock dusting conditions and practices in intake air courses contributed to the severity of the explosions. The six explosions are; Scotia Mine in 1976, Adkins Coal Company, No. 11 Mine, in 1981, No. 1 Mine, RFH Coal Company in 1982, South Mountain Coal Company Mine No. 3 in 1992, No. 9 Mine, Day Branch Coal Company in 1994, and Jim Walter Resources, Inc. No. 5 Mine in 2001.

The Federal Register/Vol. 76 No.119, June 21, 2011 says: *The Scotia Mine, Scotia Coal Company, experienced two explosions in 1976, March 9 and March 11. The first explosion, which claimed the lives of 15 miners, resulted from the ignition of a large methane accumulation. Coal dust entered into this explosion, but only to a minor degree. The second explosion, which claimed the lives of eleven miners, started as a methane explosion and coal dust entered into the explosion and aided in the propagation of the explosion. (DOL/MSHA 1993)*

The year of 1976 started out with all sorts of water troubles at my home in Colson. Our water lines froze solid in the first part of the winter and we had been carrying water from Dad's house in buckets and gallon jugs for several weeks by the time the New Year came in. The plastic ¾ inch line ran from the house to an old coal mine located more than 1,500 ft straight up the mountain, making it all but impossible to cover it with dirt to keep it from freezing. This had been our main water source since buying the house in 1973. We had a well drilled but never had any appreciable amount of water to be available from it.

If that wasn't enough to contend with, we suffered a flooded yard, roadway, and a stopped up culvert when a thunderstorm roared through the county. The water looked and acted like a river running down the driveway and down the holler to the highway.

I had to hire the culvert cleaned out with a backhoe and had to replace the septic system because of all the damage. All of it was caused by an abandoned strip mine that had left two silt dams installed above our property which overflowed every time a hard rain came. One good thing resulted from the flood waters; we were able to catch water from a small normally dry holler which was near the house. As long as it was flowing we didn't have to haul water which made life a little easier for us.

Then on January, 21, 1976, my grandmother (Nancy Sexton) passed away while my brother Jimmy and I were working at Scotia. They called us out of the mine and told us what had happened and gave us the rest of the shift off. The night was very cold and I remember huddling around my dad's coal stove in the living room while we discussed our maternal grandmother's death. We had lived nearby her for most of our lives, making her loss much more difficult for the family.

After her funeral, work at the mine settled into a normal routine. The thing most miners were concerned about was the coming contract negotiations for a new contract. The old one was scheduled to expire July 14, 1976.

CHAPTER NINE

A Gassy Mine

Scotia had the reputation of being the gassiest coal mine in the State of Kentucky among State and Federal Mine Inspectors. Although this was a true fact, there were other coal mines that liberated far more cubic feet of gas per 24 hour shift than did the Scotia Mine. The total amount of gas liberated by the #1 Mine was between 200,000 to 500,000 cubic feet per 24 hour shift, with the most active production of methane being at the working faces of the mine.

Methane gas is found in almost all coal mines, along the roof of the mine, in the rises and recesses, in the vicinity of the working faces, in dead ends, and above falls. It's detected by chemical analysis or by use of a portable battery powered methane detector, with the most common detectors being able to accurately measure concentrations of methane over a range of zero to 5 percent. The flame safety lamp can also detect methane but these have been replaced by the explosion proof detectors.

The explosive range of methane is between 5 percent and 15 percent. If the methane concentration is below 5 percent there can be no explosion because the heat, liberated by combustion, is dissipated into surrounding air sufficiently rapid to prevent flame propagation. If the percentage of methane is greater than 15 percent, there can be no explosion because the amount of oxygen present is insufficient for rapid combustion to occur. Also, if the oxygen level is below 12 percent no explosion of a methane- air mixture can occur.

Therefore, for an explosion to happen, the percentage of methane in the atmosphere must be between 5 percent and fifteen percent and the oxygen percentage present must be twelve percent or greater. If the air and methane percentages are present in explosive levels, all that is then required for an explosion is an ignition source. For the ignition to happen, the temperature of the ignition source must reach 1200°F or higher.

The presence of methane causes coal dust to be more easily ignited and the force of the explosion is greater. The presence of coal dust in the air also causes the explosive limit to be reduced. This means that it is possible to have an explosion with less than 5% of methane if coal dust is present in the air. This is the reason why the liberal use of rock dust in a mine is so vitally important.

In the same manner that proper rock dusting helps prevent coal dust from exploding, the proper use of ventilation in a mine controls the buildup of explosive levels of methane. This is vitally important in any coal mine but especially a mine that is known for the large amount of methane it releases each day. Proper ventilation is achieved by using check curtains in the working face to direct the air within two or three feet of where a cut of coal is being mine by a continuous mining machine. This check curtain directs the air from the last open break to the mine face. The open breaks behind the working section are blocked up with 4x6 inch concrete blocks to direct fresh air to the section. This all works together to achieve the minimum 9,000 cubic feet per minute of air directed to where the miner is cutting the coal.

The Federal Coal Mine Health and Safety Act describes adequate ventilation as a minimum of 9,000 cubic feet of air per minute passing over the last open cross-cut at the face of a mine. The Kentucky Department of Mines and Minerals had, however, had ruled that due to Scotia's high liberation of methane, 16,000 cubic feet per minute was required for safety. According to the record, the Scotia Mine at best produced about 10,000 cubic feet of air per minute.

Almost every miner that has been at the face of the mine has seen, heard or been present when the miner is cutting coal in the face area and hits a pocket of one percent methane or better while the miner bits are cutting into rock. When this happens it usually results in a loud bang and a small explosion ensues, but not big enough to do any damage. As a shuttle car operator I have seen it happen a few times. Sometimes the miner operator will back the miner out of the coal to see what's going on, then proceed to take an air reading to make sure the 9,000 cubic feet is present at the face. At other times a miner operator would just keep on cutting the coal. Without good ventilation those small incidents might have resulted in something much bigger.

According to MESA's records during the period May 13, 1970 to March 8, 1976, (the day before the first explosion) 855 notices of safety and health violations were issued to Scotia. In addition, the Scotia mine was ordered closed 110 times during this period. In total, therefore, Scotia was found to have violated the 1969 Coal Mine health and Safety Act some 965 times prior to the March 1976 disaster. Scotia was deemed to have repeatedly deceived MESA inspectors with respect to safety and health problems in the mine.

Of the 110 closure orders issued 39 were for imminent danger, 23 were for failure to abate (terminate) in time, 46 were for unwarrantable failure to comply, and 2 were for accidents. In terms of methane and ventilation conditions at the Scotia mine, MESA Inspectors issued a total of 149 notices of violations but only 23 closure orders; 3 for imminent danger, 2 for failure to abate, and 18 for unwarrantable failure to comply. In almost every case the ventilation closure order was terminated by MESA the same day it was issued.

During the 15 month period immediately prior to the March 9th disaster, Scotia was found to have violated the ventilation standards some 33 separate times, but only 3 Section 104 (c) closure orders were issued, all of which were terminated by MESA the same day they were issued. The following will illustrate MESA's casual policy governing closure orders at the Scotia Mine. This case history is for the 15 month period prior to the explosions at Scotia's #1 Mine. These MSHA enforcement activities deal with respect to Part.301 of MSHA's Ventilation Standards: "Not enough air reaching the face of the mine."

On January 27, 1975 MESA issued a 104 (c) (2) *closure order* for a 75.301 violation; the order was lifted that same day;

On January 30, 1975 MESA issued a *notice* for a 75.301 violation which was terminated the same day;

On February 25, 1975 MESA issued a *notice* for a 75.301 violation which was terminated the same day;

On March 13, 1975 MESA issued a *notice* for a 75.301 violation which was terminated the same day;

On March 19, 1975 MESA issued a 104 (c) (2) *closure order* for a 75.301 violation; the order was terminated the same day;

On April 24, 1975 MESA issued a 104 (c) (2) *closure order* for a 75.301 violation; the order was terminated on the same day;

On May 27, 1975 MESA issued a *notice* for a 75.301 violation which was terminated the same day;

On July 10, 1975 MESA issued a *notice* for a 75.301 violation which was terminated the same day;

On July 28, 1975 MESA issued a *notice* for a 75.301 violation which was terminated on the same day;

On August 25, 1975 MESA issued a *notice* for a 75.301 violation which was terminated on August 27, 1975;

On September 17, 1975 MESA issued a *notice* for a 75.301 violation which was terminated the same day;

On September 29, 1975, MESA issued a *notice* for a 75.301 violation which was terminated on the same day;

On January 13, 1976 MESA issued a *notice* for a 75.301 violation which was terminated the same day;

On January 20, 1976 MESA issued a *notice* for a 75.301 violation which was terminated the same day;

On January 29, 1976 MESA issued a *notice* for a 75.301 violation which was terminated the same day;

On March 8, 1976, the day before the mine exploded, MESA issued *two notices* for two 75.301 violations, which were terminated that same day.

This record of Part 75.301 Ventilation Standards violations is a clear indication that there was something chronically wrong with Scotia's ventilation system. On sixteen different occasions MESA found that insufficient air was reaching the working face of the mine, yet only three 104 (c) closure orders were issued for unwarrantable failure to comply with Part 75.301. MESA could have used its closure authority under its Section 104 (c) powers to interrupt the production of coal at Scotia until it made fundamental changes in its health and safety, particularly its ventilation policies and practices.

MESA's Mine Closure Authority under the 1969 Coal Mine Health and Safety Act of 1969 provided MESA with the authority, under certain circumstances, to effectively close coal mines by issuing orders for the withdrawal of miners. The act provides for the following types of mine orders:

Imminent Danger—Section 104 (a) provides that if an authorized representative of the Secretary of the Interior (MESA) finds that an imminent danger exists in a coal mine he shall forthwith issue an order requiring all persons to be withdrawn immediately from the mine, or affected mine area, until such time that the representative determines that the imminent danger no longer exists.

Failure to Abate—Section 104 (b) provides that whereupon any inspection of a coal mine by an authorized representative of the Secretary finds that there has been a violation of a federal health or safety standard which has not created an imminent danger, the representative shall issue a notice of violation fixing a reasonable time period for its abatement. If the violation has not been abated in the specified time period or possible extension thereof, then the representative shall issue a withdrawal order with respect to those miners affected by the violation. The withdrawal order shall remain effective until such time that it is determined that the violation has been abated.

Unwarrantable Failure to Comply—Section 104 (c) provides for two types of withdrawal orders, Under Section 104 (c) (1) if an authorized representative of the Secretary finds a violation of a health or safety standard which does not pose an imminent danger, but which could cause a mine safety or health hazard, and if he finds that the violation resulted from the unwarrantable failure of the mine operator to comply with the standards, then the inspector shall issue a notice to this effect. If during the same inspection, or any subsequent inspect within 90 days, the inspector finds another violation which resulted from the unwarrantable failure to comply, he is required to issue a withdrawal order. The order remains in effect until such time as the violation is abated.

Section 104 (c) (2) provides that once a withdrawal order under 104 (c) (1) has been issued, additional such orders shall be issued if, upon any subsequent inspection, violations are found similar to those for which the initial 104 (c) (1) order was issued. This order shall remain in effect until such time as an inspection determines the absence of any such similar violations. Following an inspection which determines that no similar violations exist, the provisions of 104 (c) (1) are again applicable. According to the legislative history of the Coal Mine Health and Safety Act, Congress defined "unwarrantable failure of the operator to comply" to mean "the failure of an operator to abate a violation because of a lack of due diligence, or because of indifference or lack of reasonable care, on the operator's part."

Mine Control Following an Accident—Section 103 (f) provides that a federal inspector may issue withdrawal orders following a mine accident to insure the safety of any person in the mine. Except for the imminent danger closure authority, which, under current MESA policy, is applicable only in limited circumstances—the unwarrantable failure provision is the most effective closure tool in controlling the day to day operations of a mine like Scotia, with a demonstrated history of chronic mine safety and health violations.

* Note: Please keep in mind that this chapter deals with Scotia's violations under the 1969 Coal Mine Health and Safety Act. The violation numbers and the mine closure orders listed above (and the following) may or may not differ from the 1977 Mine Safety and Health Act, (MSHA) the 2006 Mine Improvement and New Emergency Response Act, (Miner Act and/or the 2010 Miner Safety and Health Act.

Section 104 (a) of the 1969 Coal Mine Health and Safety Act states:

If, upon any inspection of a coal mine, an authorized representative of the Secretary finds that an imminent danger exists, such representative shall determine the area throughout which danger exists, and thereupon shall issue forthwith an order requiring the operator of the mine or his agent to cause immediately all persons (except certain selected individuals) to be withdrawn from, and to be prohibited from entering, such area until an authorized representative of the Secretary determines that such imminent no longer exists.

The Act defines imminent danger as "the existence of any condition or practice in a coal mine which could reasonably be expected to cause death or serious physical harm before such condition or practice can be abated."

MESA Inspectors had been to the Scotia mine 530 times since the 1969 Federal Coal Mine Health and Safety Law went into effect in 1970. Their visits had resulted in their writing 855 violations of the law and 110 temporary closure orders. By March, 1976 they had settled 650 of those violations. The violations were initially assessed at $204,489, but Scotia's parent company Blue Diamond Coal, persuaded MESA to settle for $78,877, which was a 60 percent discount.

Of the 530 inspections MESA conducted between May, 1970, to February, 1976, 225 inspections were spot inspections, 23 were regular inspections, 113 were special hazard inspections, and 169 were classified as miscellaneous inspections. According to MESA Administrator Robert Barrett;(in 1976) "prior to the explosions (of March, 1976) federal inspectors had spent more than 1,000 man-days inspecting the Scotia mine, issuing 855 notices of violations and 110 closure orders." Other MESA officials testified in hearings held after the explosions that the Scotia mine was the most inspected mine in Eastern Kentucky.

In their report on the explosions in 1976, the staff of the House Committee on Education and Labor, Subcommittee on Labor Standards wondered why after all the MESA inspection activity, notices and closure orders, did the Scotia mine continue to operate as an unsafe and dangerous mine? The answer is, they determined, that the Scotia Coal Company was essentially permitted to ignore the law. They continued, "We are convinced that MESA failed to adequately use its authority to properly enforce the Coal Mine Health and Safety Act at the Scotia Mine."

On September 15, 1975, this memorandum was sent to the MESA District 6 office in Pikeville, Kentucky:

Memorandum
To: Lawrence D. Phillips, Acting District Manager, Pikeville, Ky. Coal Mine Health and Safety District 6.

From: B.A. Taylor
Federal Coal Mine Inspection Supervisor, Field office 6003

Subject: 103.(i) Inspections at the Scotia Mine, Scotia Coal Company, Ovenfork, Letcher Co., Kentucky.

This mine was put under the provisions of 103 (i) while it was in the Norton, Virginia inspection district. (District C) Since the mine has not had the methane liberation, a gas ignition, or an explosion it was evidently brought in because of other hazardous conditions. I feel that the 103 (i) inspections are no longer needed at this mine for the following reasons.

84

1. Management has adopted resin roof bolting as a means to help control the fragile roof conditions at this mine.

2. The total liberation of gas in a 24 hour period was determined during the last health and safety inspection, to be 498,000ft. The required face equipment has been equipped with methane monitors and the tests required by the Act are made with approved methane detectors; this, along with improved face ventilation has reduced this hazard greatly. Very seldom is over 0.2 of one percent detected in the face area.

3. We think that we have had a good improvement in the clean-up and rock dust system.

4. Improvements have been made in the track haulage system by restricting traffic in certain areas and by control of a dispatcher.

5. Daily accident prevention inspections are being made in the areas where accidents have occurred that has caused the frequency rate at this mine to be above the national average.

6. The 103 (i) along with the regular health and safety inspections, the A.P. inspections, electrical inspections, spot inspections, etc, would require three (3) inspectors to be at this mine almost continuously.

I recommend that this mine be taken off the 103 (i) inspection list.

(Signed)
B.A. Taylor
Federal Coal Mine Inspection Supervisor
Whitesburg Field Office

(From The Mountain Eagle, Whitesburg, Kentucky, Thursday, March 18, 1976.

I was present on the day when resin roof bolting was first tried on my section at New Tygart. There's no doubt that resin bolts were a vast improvement over the "bolts alone" method of roof bolting. I was also present when a dispatcher was first used to direct track vehicles in and out of the mine. We (motormen at New Tygart) were skeptical as to why we needed a dispatcher at the supply house to direct our trips when we had just one working section in the mine. Later on, we came to appreciate and understand why one was needed when our mine had more than one section and much increased traffic in the mine.

When the dispatcher system was first started the personnel in the supply house and the maintenance shop were used to answer the calls for the track clearance. A little later the dispatcher's office was installed in a small front room inside the men's bathhouse. This was more than likely changed because a full time dispatcher was needed for safety reasons. The shop and supply personnel had to answer the phone in between their regular jobs and weren't always available to answer the phone in a timely manner. One drawback to the new location was the fact that that when it rained, the dirt road just outside the dispatcher's office was susceptible to becoming very muddy.

Scotia, like other coal operators of the period, was required to submit a complete ventilation and dust control plan to MESA every six months. In May 1774, Scotia failed to file their plan that was then due and that violation was written up by MESA Inspectors. The company then requested extensions for submitting their plan in June, July, August, and September, which were granted. In October they finally submitted their plan which was, by then, five months late.

In January, 1976 Scotia submitted its ventilation plan for the year to MESA which had neither been approved nor denied by March 1st, when Scotia submitted a revised version of their plan. As of the first explosion, March 9th, no action had been taken on the plan. The MSEA Mining Engineer for the Pikeville, Kentucky District Office, R. Keene, later in a hearing told the MESA investigation panel that any delay in approving or denying a ventilation plan in excess of a month or six weeks was unusual. The investigative panel was unable to determine why after nearly 2 and 1/2 months preceding the explosions MESA failed to act on Scotia's proposed ventilation plans.

MESA's procedures for evaluating and reviewing ventilation plans also came under scrutiny during the investigative hearings following the explosions at Scotia. According to MESA mining engineer Keene, ventilation plans are approved on the basis of air quality figures supplied to MESA by the company and then periodically checked by MESA inspectors to determine compliance.

Herschel Potter, Chief of MESA's Division of Safety, told the joint House-Senate investigative panel that the only way to determine the adequacy of a mine's ventilation system would be to conduct a complete ventilation survey, "but there is no way that that inspector making an inspection could have come to that point." The last ventilation survey conducted at the Scotia mine (before the explosions)was in 1974.

One example of where the MESA ventilation plan inspection broke down was when the last "regular" health and safety inspection was conducted prior to the March 9 explosion. During January and February 1976, MESA inspectors spent about eight weeks inspecting the entire Scotia mine but failed to take notice of the fact that coal production had been altered in that section of the mine.

Prior to initiating production in this section, 2 Left Panel off 2 Southeast Main, Scotia, in violation of MESA regulations, failed to notify MESA of its intentions. This section had been producing coal in 2 Southeast Mains heading when the coal had gotten so high that the head of the continuous mining machine couldn't reach high enough to cut the coal and drawrock. A new continuous miner was put on order that could reach the height of the coal but would take months or years to be available. The decision was made to pull the men and equipment out of the heading and move them back approximately 1,800 feet and start a new section which would be called 2 Left Panel off 2 Southeast Mains.

This new section was started around the 1st of February before the building of any ventilation overcasts to properly divert the air into the 2 Southeast Mains section and the 2 Left Panel at the same time. Instead, ventilation was achieved by diverting the fresh intake air from going into the 2 Southeast Mains section and diverted instead into the 2 Left panel section. The diverting of the fresh air was achieved by means of hanging plastic brattice cloth (curtains) across the intake entries. This meant that when the brattice cloth was hung from the roof and wedged tight against the ribs that the fresh air being diverted into 2 Left Panel would be sufficient for mining coal. The heading of 2 Southeast Mains would however, be deprived of most of the air needed to properly ventilate that section. It was a setup that was nothing less than a disaster in the making and these two sections, one idle and one active, would be the scene of devastation and destruction a little more than one week after the last MESA regular inspection ended.

Thus, Scotia violated its ventilation plan by starting the 2 Left Panel before submitting a revised ventilation plan on March 1st, 1976, which had not been acted on by MESA when the explosions happened. When the plan was submitted 2 Left Panel had already been driven four breaks. During the MESA investigations hearings held after the explosions, MESA mining engineer Keene was questioned about this development. According to the hearing transcript:

Question. Should you have been notified that 2 Left was begun?

Keene. This is the requirement of the plan; that the projection be shown on each approved map.

Question. Were you not made aware that they moved into 2 left?

Keene. When I first became aware that they moved into 2 Left was when they submitted the map on March 1st.

Question. However they moved in there roughly around?

Keene. About a month prior to that date. The section was advanced approximately four breaks at that time. (March 1st.)

Question. Did you consider that a violation of the ventilation plan?

Keene. I would.

On March 8th 1976, MESA inspector Cecil Davis showed up at the Scotia Mine to inspect the Scotia mine, specifically the 2 Left Section. Scotia miners who worked on the second shift would later say that the section was tipped off by telephone that Inspector Davis was on his way there. The speculation was that the tip either came from the mine office or if not there at the portal when Davis would have had to announce where he wanted to go.

In any event, according to other miners, foreman Jimmy Williams was warned about the pending inspection. Production was stopped and according to MESA Chief Robert Barrett, "each man on section was assigned a cleaning job, rock dusting, hanging curtains, cleaning up, and tightening ventilation curtains so that when Davis got on section things were in pretty good shape."

When Davis arrived on section he took an air reading at the face between 3:30 and 4:p.m., then wrote up a violation notice for insufficient air. The required minimum amount of air at the face was 9,000 cubic feet per minute. Davis recorded only 8,092. He notified Williams that he was giving him half an hour to abate the violation. At 6:p.m. he again measured the amount of air flowing across the face and found 10,472 cubic feet per minute, which was adequate for producing coal at the face. Inspector Davis at that point terminated the notice he had issued just two hours before.

According to testimony at the MESA investigation hearings, the increase in air flow at the face was allegedly achieved by "robbing air from other sections and diverting it into the 2 Left Panel." According to Meryl Rhodes, who was assistant mine foreman at Scotia at the time, he was aware that management was considering erecting temporary curtains to divert more air from 2 Southeast Mains into the 2 Left Panel.

According to the hearing transcript:

Question. You say that you were not aware of nor were you present when there was discussion regarding the hanging of two checks (curtains) across the straight (of 2Southeast Mains), that is four and five?

Rhodes. The boss asked me about hanging them and I told him not to hang the curtains.

Question. The boss is?

Rhodes. James Williams (the section foreman).

Question. But you were aware that he was (planning to hang the curtains?

Rhodes. He didn't say what particular vicinity he was going to hang the curtains. If he did, I didn't catch it. He was talking about hanging some curtains and you know I thought that is what he was talking about (hanging them to divert air.) I told him not to hang it because of the gas accumulating.

Question. But you knew that he was thinking about it?

Rhodes.

I know he said he had been told to do it but I don't know whether he had or not.

Testimony at the MESA investigation hearings indicates that Williams, with the assistance of other employees did in fact hang the curtain which diverted air into 2 Left Panel from 2 Southeast Mains. Gary Smith, a utility man at Scotia, told the MESA panel that he personally helped Williams hang the curtain which diverted the air into 2 Left Panel. According to the MESA transcript:

Question. Are you aware that he (MESA Inspector Davis) had taken an air reading and it was deficient?

Smith. Yes.

Question. After he took the air reading and let the section foreman (Williams) know that there was a violation, what was done to correct that violation as far as you know?

Smith. We hung block curtains up there (2SEM) in the track (entry) at (entry numbers)four and five.

Question. Were you instructed to do that?

Smith. Yes.

Question. You were instructed to put up two check curtains?

Smith. Yes.

Question. Across four and five----

Smith. Four and five.

Question. In the main?

Smith. Yes.

Question. You were instructed to do this by whom?

Smith. Bird Dog. Jim is his real name.

Question. Mr. Williams?

Smith. Yes.

Question. Was anyone else present when you were hanging these curtains?

Smith. Yes, Hargus Maggard and Jim (Williams), they helped me.

Question. Were there any others who were aware of the fact that you were hanging curtains?

Smith. Not right then.

Question. Later was someone aware of it?

Smith. Yes, Carl Smith and Matnack went and took them down. Roy Matnack.

Question. Mr. Smith, was the inspector aware of what you were doing?

Smith. No.

Question. Was there any reason given to you for hanging those checks?

Smith. We didn't have enough air. That is what Bird Dog (Jim Williams) said. And that was good enough.

MESA Inspector Davis testified that it was not part of his inspection to inspect 2SEM for ventilation or other possible hazardous conditions. According to the MESA hearing transcript:

Question. Are you saying that when you went up the track through the intersection into 2 Left and there was no curtain (air regulator) that it would not have been part of your inspection to have considered the potential trouble spot up the Main (where the explosion occurred)?

Davis. No Sir. Any outby areas, that is not my inspection.

Davis testified that he was a "coal mine health technical specialist, and that his primary job was concerned with the evaluation of respirable dust and noise." According to Davis his assignment on March 8 was "to begin evaluations (respirable dust) of the---all sections of the Scotia, Upper Taggart Mine in the B Seam....this would be a complete <u>health</u> (inspection) of the entire Blue Diamond operations at Oven Fork."

Except for noticing general mine conditions as he traveled to the designated area, the only section Davis inspected was the 2 Left Panel section. He did not go into nor inspect the 2SEM section where the explosion occurred.

Although Davis' main concern was respirable dust conditions in the 2 Left Panel, he did cite Scotia for other violations while he was on 2 Left. The insufficient air violation was already mentioned and the others were; the line curtain used for directing air to the number 5 entry working face of 2 Left was more than 10 feet out from the face; eleven water sprays on the continuous miner in the 2 Left section were inoperable; and the average concentration of respirable dust was 5.2 milligrams per cubic meter of air, which was excessive.

In their 1976 report of the Scotia Mine disaster, the staff of the House Committee on Education and Labor , Subcommittee on Labor Standards, concluded that the record indicates that the inspection of March 8 was conducted by a "coal mine health specialist" whose primary job was to evaluate the respirable dust conditions exclusively on the 2 Left Section, (that he) did not go into the 2SEM section, and therefore could not have been aware of any dangerous conditions in that section. In addition, the record supports the assumption that "something" was wrong with the ventilation in 2SEM including the 2 Left Panel, and that Scotia employees purposefully diverted air from 2SEM into the 2 Left Panel so as to achieve compliance with the Davis violation notice. In this respect, whatever was technically wrong with the ventilation in 2 Left Panel was never corrected, and may have been one of the factors contributing to the March 9th explosion.

CHAPTER TEN

The First Explosion

MESA Inspector Cecil Davis spent eight hours inspecting the 2 Left Panel sections on March 8th. During his inspection he had written four notices of violations, two of which were ventilation violations. Davis however, did not inspect the 2SEM section.

That evening, (the evening of 8-9 March) the third shift fire boss, Charles Fields, conducted a preshift examination of the Scotia mine but failed to inspect the 2SEM section. The 1969 Coal Mine Health and Safety act requires a preshift examination for possible hazardous ventilation, methane, and other conditions within three hours prior to any miner entering an active area of a mine. The Act also requires that such examinations are to be conducted at least once a week in those "idle" areas of a mine in which no one is working.

The morning of March 9th 1976, dawned cold and clear at the foot of Black Mountain as Scotia miners arrived at the mine for their shift of work. At 7:a.m. the section crews, belt men, and brattice men loaded aboard the battery powered mantrip or portal buses and were transported down the steep slope, then inside to their working areas.

A total of 106 men went into the mine to produce coal on the five working sections that morning, 13 of them were in 2 Left Section off 2 Southeast Mains and the mouth of 2 Left and 2Southeast Mains. Virgil Coots, section foreman of the two Left Section, had nine men on 2 Left Section (ten, including Coots) producing coal, 2 men were assigned to build overcasts at the mouth of 2 Left, and one man was manning the belt head drive where the coal from 2 Left Section dumped on the beltline.

The two men that were assigned to build the overcasts were beginning work on the vitally important job of getting the ventilation into compliance by building the overcasts. They were likely sent into the mine that morning because of the insufficient air reading and violation notice that Cecil Davis had cited Scotia with while he was inspecting 2 Left the evening before. When the overcasts were completed, air could be legally diverted into 2 Left Section and 2Southeast Mains Section at the same time. The violation notices had likely given management a sense of urgency to finish the overcasts.

At 7;30 a.m., after all the mantrips had cleared the track, J.P. Feltner, Scotia Underground Construction Foreman, called Richard Combs, General Mine Foreman, and told Combs of his plan to have his motor crew deliver a load of steel rails from 1 Right off 2 East, where they were stored, to 2 Southeast Mains. They had already discussed delivery of the rails after Combs had expressed a need to extend the track in 2 Southeast Mains heading so as to be ready to receive the continuous mining machine that was on order. The plan was to reactivate the 2 Southeast Mains Section as quickly as possible after the new continuous miner arrived on section.

After Feltner informed the motor crew of his plan for them to pick up the rails at 1 Right off 2 East he proceeded to the 2 Left Panel in search of a rail bender and oxygen and acetylene tanks. (These were pieces of equipment needed to install a track switch. The track had been extended into the 2 Left Section in February. The section had advanced a total of 600 feet by March 8.) James Bentley, Scotia's Assistant Mine Foreman for Ventilation was also on 2 Left Section with Feltner while he was there. Feltner stated that he didn't test for methane or take air measurements while he was there, and that he didn't go inby the 2 Left Section.

According to Feltner, there was no check curtain across the track diverting the air into the 2 Left Section when he was there, but he did see a piece of curtain on the mine floor between the No. 2 and 3 entries, near where the check curtain was supposed to be hung. He also stated that he was unaware that the absence of a check curtain at this location caused a short circuit of the air current which was ventilating 2 Southeast Mains.

Feltner then proceeded to the mouth of Northeast Main where he met the motor crew with their load of steel rails. There was a battery charging station located near the switch and the motor crew was engaged in charging the batteries on the No. 6 locomotive. The No. 8 locomotive was operating on only one set of trucks, so both motors were coupled together in order to have enough power to transport the load of rails. The No. 6 locomotive, a 7 ton Goodman that had been manufactured by the Toledo Industries in Toledo, Ohio in 1943, was equipped with an air compressor for the pneumatic braking system and was operated that day by Roy McKnight. According to one Scotia miner the Goodman locomotive was "in pitiful shape." The compressor on this locomotive would "kick on" about every 10-15 minutes in order to build pressure back up in the pneumatic brake system. When it did so, one could actually observe the flash of electricity when it came on. The sound the compressor made when running always reminded this writer of water bubbling out of a container full of that liquid.

The No. 8 locomotive was an 8 ton Westinghouse and was that day operated by Lawrence Peavy. This motor was equipped with a conventional mechanical braking system. While at the Northeast Main switch and after the No. 7 locomotive had received some charge in the batteries, the two locomotives were coupled together and the rail trucks were placed in front of the locomotives. The locomotives and the rails were now situated so that the rails could be pushed up to the 2 Southeast Mains Section and dropped off at the end of the track, allowing the two locomotives to head back to the outside of the mine.

The motor crew left the mouth of Northeast Mains with the load of 33ft long steel rails at about 11:35 a.m., according to Feltner, who watched then head out.(Other accounts say 11: 15a.m. – 11:20 a.m.) The trip to the 2 Southeast Section would normally take about 10-15 minutes for the locomotives to reach the end of the track. The distance was approximately 3,800 feet between the mouth of Northeast Main and the end of the track on 2 Southeast Mains.

If the check curtains were in place as the locomotives went by the 2 Southeast-2 Left Panel intersection it's likely that the load of rails would have torn it down as they went through or perhaps there was no curtain hung there to divert the air into 2 Left Section. We know that the curtain was hung across the track during the previous shift when the 2nd shift foreman, Williams, had his men to hang one there to increase the air flow after a violation had been written By MSEA Inspector Davis. It's notable though, that Coots, the 2 Left day shift section foreman, complained about losing his air just about the time the locomotives would have gone by the 2 Left intersection with 2 Southeast Mains.

The motor crew would have to climb a hill of considerable height to reach the 2 Southeast Main Section, and with myself being one of those motor operators who later drove a locomotive up that hill, I would think that the motor crew that day had to get a good "running go" to reach the top of the hill without having to either stop part way up it, or lose control and the locomotives fly back towards the mouth of the section out of control.

As it turns out, they successfully ascended up the steep hill with their load of rails and parked their locomotives and the rails at the end of the track to uncouple. Their ascension must have been a close call though, as one of the locomotives had skidded one wheel nearly all the distance up the hill after a long piece of steel rope about ¾ inch in diameter was caught under the wheel (truck) as they pushed the load of rails up the steep grade.

After the mine was recovered and before the two locomotives were brought out of the mine, I observed the steel cable, still caught under the wheel of one of the locomotives and I also followed the skid marks on the rail, all the way from the hill to the 2 Southeast Mains Section and came to my own conclusion that the steel cable could be ruled out as the cause of the explosion that day. Others who were with me on that occasion were convinced that the explosion could not have been caused spark from the steel cable, as there was no damage at all to the wheel itself.

When the motor crew left the mouth of Northeast Main for 2 Southeast Mains with the load of rails, Feltner stated that they did not have any gas detecting equipment, such as a methane detector, and that he had never at any time instructed them to make any tests or examinations of 2 Southeast Mains inby 2 Left Section before entering the area. He assumed that the area had been preshift examined because it was on intake air.

According to his testimony at the official hearings, James Bentley made an inspection of the abandoned 2 Left Section off Northeast Main the morning of the explosion. He discovered that a regulator was open about four feet wider than he had originally set it after the section was abandoned. He proceeded to close it to the original position, then walked to the No. 3 belt drive in Northeast Main near the entrance of 3 Southeast Main where a telephone was located.

He first called Lawrence Cohen, section foreman in the Left Panel-Southeast Main and asked him to take an air reading, then call him back. Bentley then called Virgil Coots, section foreman in 2 Left Section off 2 Southeast Main and informed Coots that he had inspected 3 Southeast,

Right Panel Northeast Main, Northeast Main, and 2 Left Section off Northeast Main. He also told Coots about the regulator being open four feet wider than it was supposed to be. He explained to Coots that he had closed it back and that the ventilation on his 2 Left Section off 2 Southeast Mains should now have better and increased ventilation. Bentley then asked Coots how much air did he have on section now and Coots replied, I've just lost my air! I'm not getting any air! I'm coming down to see what the problem is." By "coming down" Coots meant that he was going to walk 600 feet or so to the mouth of 2 Left Section where he had two men working on overcasts to see if they might have removed a stopping or a curtain, which would have short- circuited the section's ventilation.

Approximately two to three minutes later, about 11:30- 11:40a.m. the explosion occurred in the heading of 2Southeast mains. Within seconds the force of the explosion roared out of the 2 Southeast Mains for approximately 3,000 feet and snuffed out the lives of the four men who were in the vicinity of the mouth of 2 Left Panel, including Virgil Coots, the boss, who had gone there to check on his air. The two men building the overcasts and the belt head man were found close by the boss, in the Nos. 1 and No. 2 entries of Southeast Mains near the entrance of 2 Left Section.

Three other victims on section were killed in the explosion and were found along the No. 4 entry of 2 Left Section. Six of the men who were on the section at the time of the explosion survived the blast and actually headed down the return entry to try to reach safety. Later in the year, as a member of the mine recovery crew I would walk down the return where the six men had opened their self-rescuers and threw the lids on the mine floor. This was an emotional moment for myself and the other miners that were on the mine recovery crew, knowing how close those miners were to making it out of the section to fresh air the day of the explosion.

It was obvious to us that the six survivors of the explosion walked or ran to the mouth of the section and seeing the thick smoke and dust in the air, made the decision to return to the section and barricade themselves until help could arrive. What they appeared to be unaware of, was that if they had followed the return entry for another 2,000 feet they could have reached fresh air. No doubt when seeing the thick smoke in the air and the destruction all around them, they would have thought the whole Scotia Mine had blown up. Everyone who worked in the #1 Bottom Mine had heard about all the methane the mine liberated. Their greatest fear was realized with the blast they had just experienced. They might even have seen the bodies of some of the four miners who were killed in the explosion and who were lying nearby where the six men would have come out at the mouth of the section. There's no reason to second guess their decision, every man is told from the beginning of their mining career that if you can't escape, barricade. That's what they did.

When the six surviving miners went back to the section, they selected the No. 5 entry, which had just been started and was only about 18-20 ft. into the coal, to barricade in. They took a 25-30 ft. length of yellow brattice cloth and used large pieces of slate and blocks of coal to weight the bottom of the curtain down and shoveled (maybe with their hands) a line of loose coal on it also. They then tightened the loose ends into the coal and rock, hoping that they had a tight seal.

The only problem was that the blast had disrupted all the ventilation for both the 2 Southeast Mains Section and the 2 Left Section where the men were barricaded. Eventually what little oxygen that was present after the explosion soon disappeared.

The explosion appears to have originated at or very close to where Peavy and McKnight were located with their locomotives in 2 Southeast Mains. The explosion had swept away everything in its path as it roared back down 2 Southeast Mains and through the 2 Left intersection. Some of the power of the blast carried a little ways into the 2 Left Section, but most of the force carried past the intersection and traveled on down the straightaway.

The Section foreman, Virgil Coots, had almost reached the intersection to check on the air when the blast occurred. It's doubtful that either he, the two men building the overcast, or the belt –utility man lived more than a few seconds.

The blast had blackened and charred everything from the heading of 2 Southeast Mains to 1,000 feet or more down the track and past the 2 Left and 2 SEM intersections. Stoppings had been blown out, the battery lids on the locomotives had been blown off, belt structure and belt line was twisted and blackened, and the ribs, roof, and mine bottom were black and charred without any rock dust remaining on the coal. The whole area was a shambles.

When the motor crew had started out from the mouth of Northeast Main with their rails, J.P. Feltner had left at the same time from there and traveled to Southeast Main where he had a crew sitting timbers along the track haulage road, about 800 feet inby the Southeast Main belt drive. A few minutes after his arrival there he said he felt a gust of air moving outby opposite to the normal direction of the air flow. He also noticed rock dust in suspension around the track area. Thinking a crushed stopping had been the cause of the gust of wind and change of air direction, he took his timber crew to investigate. After traveling about 600 feet outby, they noticed that the air flow had returned to its normal direction. When Feltner learned that an explosion had just occurred, he contacted all the active sections in the mine and was able to reach them all except the 2 Left Section he had just came from.

When the explosion occurred, John Hackworth was working at the 2 Southeast Main belt drive which was located in the No. 3 entry of the Left Panel Northeast Main. As the force of the explosion rolled down the 2 Southeast Main track it caught and rolled Hackworth a short distance but without any serious injury to Hackworth.* He then immediately called the dispatcher outside the mine and reported what had happened. He tried, but was unable to reach anyone at the mouth of 2 Left Panel or on the 2 Left Panel Section. He decided to put his self-rescuer and try to see what happened up the 2 Southeast Main track entry, but after traveling approximately 2,200 feet without making contact with anyone he was forced back due to the thick smoke, and poor visibility he encountered. The self rescuer canister that Hackworth and all Scotia miners carried did not provide any oxygen but merely filtered out any carbon monoxide present in the atmosphere. They were advertised as lasting for one hour, but would likely last for a shorter period when breathing heavily, as Hackworth would likely have been doing after walking 2,200 feet or more. The oxygen level was probably lower also after the explosion due to the disrupted ventilation in that area.

That same morning MESA ventilation engineer Rick Keene drove from the MESA District office in Pikeville to the Whitesburg Field office to discuss Scotia's revised mine ventilation plan that was missing some information from the mine map. For instance, the map did not show the quantity of intake air flowing into 2 Southeast Mains. He was discussing Scotia's ventilation plan with Scotia company representatives, explaining his concerns, when the telephone rang. The time was 12:26 p.m. The call was from Scotia. Methane had been ignited, there had been an explosion and somewhere in the vicinity of 2 Southeast Mains and there were 15 men missing and unaccounted for.

---

* John Hackworth would be one of the fatalities in the March 11th explosion.

The First Explosion-March 9, 1976

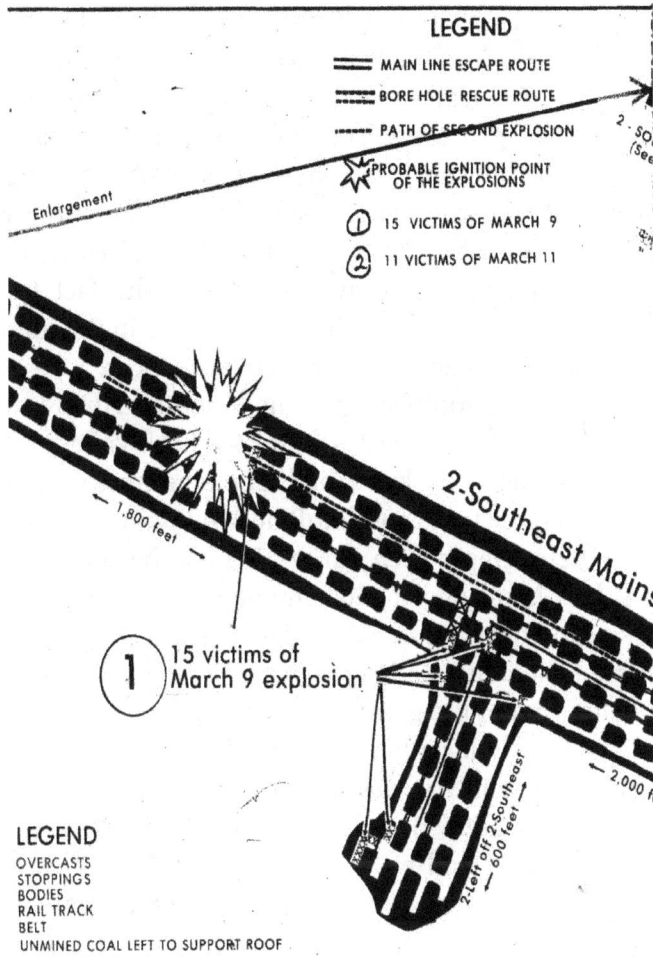

LEGEND

- ☰☰ MAIN LINE ESCAPE ROUTE
- ▥▥ BORE HOLE RESCUE ROUTE
- ▪▪▪▪ PATH OF SECOND EXPLOSION
- ✴ PROBABLE IGNITION POINT OF THE EXPLOSIONS
- ① 15 VICTIMS OF MARCH 9
- ② 11 VICTIMS OF MARCH 11

Enlargement

2 - SO
(See

2-Southeast Mains

← 1,800 feet

① 15 victims of March 9 explosion

2-left off 2-Southeast
← 600 feet →

← 2,000 f

LEGEND

OVERCASTS
STOPPINGS
BODIES
RAIL TRACK
BELT
UNMINED COAL LEFT TO SUPPORT ROOF

The Scotia Mine
Oven Fork, Kentucky
A subsidiary of Blue Diamond Coal Co., Knoxville, Tennessee

untain Eagle 1976

Map courtesy of the *Mountain Eagle* -Whitesburg. Ky.

At the very moment that the Whitesburg, Kentucky MESA Field Office was receiving the telephone call from Scotia informing them of the explosion, I was getting into my station wagon at my home in Colson to go to work on the second shift at New Tygart. It was a little less than 25 miles from my home to Scotia and normally took about 45 minutes to make the trip. I always left home early because of the many problems associated with oversized trucks that often jackknifed on Pine Mountain's atrocious curves on both the Whitesburg and the Eolia side of the mountain. Many times, arriving early for work early resulted in a little extra overtime pay that you could earn if the boss asked you to start work early. I imagine the most urgent reason I always arrived early was the fact that I always wanted to be on time, a trait I acquired when I was in the military, where being late for any reason had unpleasant consequences.

As I eased down the south side of Pine Mountain, the Black Mountain range was looming in my view across the Poor Fork Valley, with its abundant pine trees looking as dark as usual. The pine trees on that mountain always appeared darker that those on Pine Mountain and the cloud cover that day made them appear even darker. If I had been aware at that moment of what had happened in that mountain just 90 minutes ago I'm sure the trees would have seemed even darker to me.

As I crossed the concrete bridge at the Scotia Mine entrance, I noticed in the distance that the guard was standing outside the guard shack. That was unusual as he usually just stood or sat inside and watched the workers coming and going to work.

I rolled my car window down as I approached him as I could tell he was going to stop me. I had never once been stopped before in the one and one-half years I had been an employee of Scotia. I knew something was up as I approached.

"Hello," I called out as I stopped. With a worried look on his face that I'll never forget, he said, I don't think there's gonna be any work today, somethin' has happened in the Bottom Mine. "What Happened?," I asked. "They don't know for sure but they think there might have been an explosion of some kind. Just between me and you, I believe some of the miners might be missing, because they haven't heard from one section yet." His words stunned me and I was nearly speechless. I finally managed to blurt out, "Will they allow us in (to the property) to try to help in some way?" "Yeah, you might want to go on in, I'm sure they'll need all the help they can get,besides they haven't told me to stop anyone yet."

After the conversation with the security guard, and with a heavy heart, I drove to the upper parking lot above the Bottom Mine portal and walked down to the foot bridge, then crossed it to the bath house. I didn't yet know that I would be in and around the bathhouse while witnessing some heartbreaking scenes of the arrival of the missing miners' families at that bathhouse where facilities were opened to them while they were awaiting word on their loved ones fate. I would be there for the next 18 hours while events unfolded.

After receiving the telephone call from Scotia officials that an explosion had occurred there, MESA Inspectors were immediately dispatched from the Whitesburg Field Office and the Pikeville District office. The Pikeville office notified the MESA national office in Arlington, Virginia of the accident. Shortly thereafter, the Norton, Virginia and Pikeville MESA offices notified area mine rescue teams that their services would be needed.

When word was received at 1.00 p.m. in Arlington, Virginia of the tragedy at Scotia, MESA's Mine Emergency Operations Group (MEO) was called into action. MEO arranged for an Air Force airlift of MESA's Mine Rescue Teams and other mine rescue equipment. Their Command /Communications vehicle was deployed and set up as a command base providing invaluable radio and telephone communications. Rowan Drilling supervisory contract personnel were brought to the Scotia site to provide consultation expertise for probe hole drilling. MEO personnel installed over 10,000 feet of gas sampling tube bundles which were connected to continuous gas analysis equipment. Also a down - hole television survey was successfully conducted at the face area of the 2 Southeast Main heading, the possible area of the explosion. In Baltimore, Maryland, MEO logisticians arranged for the purchase and delivery of many items which were necessary for the recovery operations. The Command/Communications vehicle was retained on site control until March 15, 1977.[+]

A little after 1:p.m. MESA Inspectors arrived at the mine and immediately issued a 103.f order, an order providing that a Federal Inspector may issue a withdrawal order following a mine accident to ensure the safety of any person in the mine.

[+] A Historical Summary of MSHA's Mine Emergency Operations Program, by Jeffrey H. Kravitz.

Between 2:00 and 3:00 p.m. Scotia personnel attempted rescue efforts but failed to make any progress. At approximately the same hour (3;00 p.m.)MESA officials Monroe West, Sub-district Manager, Norton, Virginia office, and Bill Clemons of the Pikeville, Kentucky office, an assistant district manager for MESA, arrived at the mine and assumed control of the rescue and recovery operations. Charles Sample, MESA Coal Mine Inspection Supervisor, Harlan, Kentucky office, arrived soon after.

West and Sample went underground to direct rescue operations; Inspector Clemons took charge on the surface just as the first mine rescue teams starting arriving. Some other rescue teams would not arrive until 11:00 p.m. that evening. The Benham Mine Rescue team was the first team on the scene and the U.S. Steel Lynch Mine team and the Westmoreland team arrived soon thereafter.

By 4:00 p.m. some of the rescue teams had completed their preparations to go underground and the first team left the surface from the mine office portal at 4:30 p.m. Five minutes later the second team followed them. Seven teams in total would enter the mine, all wearing breathing apparatus. The Bethlehem Mine Rescue Team (Captain Charles (Charlie) Adams) stayed behind as a back-up team. The teams established the first fresh air base at 5:00 p.m. at the mouth of Northeast Mains and 2 Southeast Mains.

From there they began their slow exploration of the 2 Southeast Mains area, starting from the switch where Construction Foreman Feltner had last saw his motor crew begin their journey to push the steel rails to the end of the track in 2 Southeast Mains. Their progress was necessarily slow, as they were exploring as they walked and had to proceed according to mine rescue tactics and regulations. At that point they didn't know if they were on a rescue mission or a recovery mission, so they all felt a sense of urgency, yet precautions had to be taken for their own safety.

Around 4:00 p.m. members of the missing mens' families and friends began gathering at the Scotia mine entrance to wait and pray that the miners had managed to somehow escape from the force of the explosion. The company designated the company bathhouse for the immediate families to gather to await word on their loved ones that were missing. A telephone and restroom facilities were available there and the wooden benches provided seating, although the benches were not a very good replacement for chairs. The accommodations were crude at best but it was the best that could be provided for them at the moment. Here the families would continue to wait where they at least had some warmth from the cold outside.

They would not have long to wait. At around 1:30 a. m. March, 10, they received the awful news they hadn't wanted to hear. All 15 of the men that had been missing had been found dead. This writer was there in the bathhouse when the word spread through the building.

After establishing the first fresh air base at the Northeast Mains- 2 Southeast Mains intersection, the rescue teams had slowly explored an area five entries wide and 10 entries in length, (about 1,000 ft.) before establishing their second fresh air base . This took them until 9:00 p.m. to accomplish. John Collins, the captain of the National Mines rescue team, told the House- Senate Investigation Committee that "the entire area was charred.....everything was charred from the fresh air base where we started, all the way up to the face." (3,800 ft.) In addition the rescue teams reported that a number of air stoppings had been blown out and the battery lids on the two locomotives had been blown off.

By 9;30 the rescue team had explored another 500 ft. of 2 Southeast Mains and established their third fresh air base. They were now only a little over 1,500 ft from the 2 Left Section. Their progress remained agonizingly slow but it couldn't be helped, due to the hazards they were facing and encountering.

After advancing another 500 feet they established their fourth fresh air base at 10:00 p.m. Here they were joined by some high-ranking officials who had arrived at the mine at 8:30 that evening. MESA Administrator Robert Barrett, Assistant Administrator John Crawford, and R. Peluso, Assistant Administrator Technical Support, were briefed by company and MESA officials, then went immediately underground to see for themselves. When they arrived at the 4th fresh air base that had just been established, they began assisting in the operations to reach the missing miners.

Meanwhile outside the mine and while the recovery operations were still going on, Bill Clemons, Assistant Manager of the Pikeville, Kentucky District Office, arrived at Scotia and assumed responsibility for directing the rescue and recovery operations now going on. He had assumed responsibility at 3;30 p.m. when he first arrived at the mine and continued in this capacity, with the concurrence of MESA Administrator Barrett until after the second explosion of March 11th.

While rescue efforts were still proceeding, Bill Clemons ordered one of his men, MESA Inspector Herman Lucas, to confiscate records which the mining company was required to maintain under the 1969 Coal Mine Health and Safety Act. Among those were records were those of tests for the methane content of the air at underground locations inside the mine. His belief that methane concentrations inside the mine had not been properly monitored was given by Clemons as his reason for the seizure of the records.

In carrying out Clemon's orders Lucas seized a total of 20 books from the mine office and electrical examination books from nine areas of the mine. The mine office was located about 100 yards from the entrance to the Imboden Seam.

Bruce Jones, a second shift mine foreman, (the author's boss at the time) was present in the office when Lucas entered the office between 5:00 and 6:00 p.m. that afternoon and inquired where the electrical records were kept. He then went to the electrical shop and demanded the records, which were provided for him by David Adams, a maintenance foreman. Lucas understood the instructions for seizure extended to not only fire boss books but extended to the pre-shift books, on shift books, and electrical examination books. Jones stated that "quite a few" people were in the office at that time.

The Scotia Coal Company asked for the records back repeatedly, but did not receive an inventory until several weeks later. Although Clemons denied giving any such order, the books were locked in a government vehicle by Robert Fleming, a coal mine inspector, during the late evening or early morning of March 9 or 10.

A District Court in the early 1980's decided that the records should be suppressed and directed their return to the coal operator. (Blue Diamond Coal Company). Later, the United States Court of Appeals, Sixth Circuit, reversed the district court's judgment and ruled in favor of the Government. 'In so doing, we recognize that the mine industry is a highly regulated one and that a businessman in such an industry, in accepting the burdens as well as the benefits of the trade, is said to consent to restrictions placed upon him. Although the coal mine operator has an interest in the retention of the records, we find that it does not rise to a Fourth Amendment interest which requires their suppression.'

Federal Inspectors West, Sample, and Bowman, along with two other mine rescue teams entered the mine at 4:30 p.m. They were also equipped with self-contained breathing apparatus similar to the other rescue teams, allowing them to join the recovery efforts when they arrived at the fresh air base.

The mine rescue team from the Westmoreland Coal Company discovered the first body of one of the missing miners at 10:18 p.m., at the #22 crosscut in No.2 entry of 2 Left Section, approximately 50 feet inby the 2 Left belt drive. Nearby were the bodies of three other missing miners. They reported heavy and dangerous concentrations of methane gas and carbon monoxide in portions of 2 Southeast Mains as they advanced. The going was slow due to the dangerous explosive mixture of methane and oxygen in the atmosphere and by the fact they were using their self-contained breathing apparatus at this point.

As the rescue team searched the No 4 entry of 2 Left they came up on the bodies of three more miners. Then, just a few yards away they came to the No. 5 entry and discovered six bodies behind the curtained barricade. The left side of the yellow brattice cloth wasn't even fasted into the rib and was hanging loosely when the rescue team members came upon it. It was now 12:30 a.m. March 10, 1976. There were only 2 men that remained on the missing list now.

The National Mines Mine Rescue Team was advancing slowly towards the heading of 2 Southeast Mains. Finally the two locomotives with their load of rails were located near the end of the track at around 1:00 a.m. Both motormen were lying dead just a few feet from their motors. The 15 men were all now accounted for. Some, if not most, of the 15 bodies were burned and mutilated by the powerful force of the explosion they had experienced. The force of the explosion had been greatest in this area (2 Left intersection) as was obvious to the members of the rescue team.

An air reading was taken at the face of 2 Southeast Mains and showed 15-16 percent oxygen and 5 percent methane, but the methane reading was probably even higher according to National Mine Rescue Team Captain John Collins, because the team's methane detector only had a 5 percent scale. A positive carbon monoxide (CO) reading was also noted at the time. The potential rescue of the 15 missing miners was no longer a rescue mission. It had become a recovery mission.

CHAPTER ELEVEN

The Recovery

All that could be done now was to see that the bodies of the deceased miners were treated with respect and returned to their families for a proper burial. The victims had to be carried for a good distance to be transported to the outside of the mine. It was a good 1,800-2,000 feet from the end of the track in 2 Southeast Mains to the No. 4 fresh air base where the locomotives could likely go, but they wouldn't be allowed to go past that point for sure. The distance was much closer from the fresh air base to the 2 Left Section at around 1,000 feet distance.

By 1:30 a.m. all 15 bodies were located and in the process of being removed to the fresh air base where they would be picked up by a crew with three supply cars and a locomotive coupled to each end of the car. (At about 12:30 a.m., I walked over from the bathhouse to the shop and watched as the motor crew prepared the cars with bright yellow brattice cloth in the bottom of the cars.) The motor crew left the shop sometime after 1:30 a. m. and proceeded down the slope and through the portal with their locomotives and supply cars to pick up the bodies. After arriving at the fresh air base sometime after 2:00 a.m., the bodies were loaded into the coal cars for the trip outside. This part of the recovery took awhile, as they were handled carefully and with respect as they were being loaded. Dr. George Nichols, a pathologist from Cincinnati, was possibly also present when the bodies were placed into the supply cars. He was there to make a report on the disaster and examine the bodies. He would be back two days later after the second explosion.

106

Around 3;30 a.m., the locomotives left the fresh air base and slowly eased down the 2 Southeast track-way for 2,000 ft. until they reached the Northeast Mains-2 Southeast Mains switch, then traveled for 5 and 1/2 miles down Southeast Mains, then up the slope and out the portal at 4:46 a.m. As they came very slowly out of the mine and passed up the slope, dozens of coal miners (including this author) were waiting on the steel walkway bridge spanning the slope track. We were standing where our over-head view gave us an excellent vantage point to see the yellow brattice cloth that covered the bodies. As the first locomotive came into view as it came out of the mine portal, all conversation on the bridge went silent and those wearing caps or hats removed them and placed them over their hearts. I'm sure we were all thinking the same thing, "that could have been me." My mind raced back to the day I had asked Rhoda to change me from the Bottom Mine to the B Seam and she did. If she hadn't I might have been one of those poor miners in the supply cars. Rhoda could possibly have saved my life that day.

Some family members who had gathered in the bathhouse were briefed by company officials and others after all the bodies had been located and were told that all 15 men had died in the explosion. Other family members are said to have heard unofficially as word filtered out of the mine that their loved one had died. Either way was devastating to those families. As you can imagine, there was a lot of emotion expressed with those words. There had been so much anxious hope of everyone gathered there that the men had survived somehow.

By 3:00 a.m. some family members started leaving the bathhouse as more hearses started filtering in one by one. Soon there were 15 of them parked around the shop, bathhouse, and mining office waiting to pick up the miners from the supply cars. When the locomotives reached the shop, one of them unhitched and moved into the charging station out of the way, while the other threw the switch and backed the supply cars into the large shop building.

I was standing in the shop door as they were backed inside but was there only to see if any help was needed. I had no want to nor curiosity to view the deceased miners, neither did any others to my knowledge. No help was needed so I quickly left and went back into the bathhouse, where myself and other miners just talked and waited to see if we were needed to help in any way. As it turned out, there was not much we could do. I had now been in the vicinity of the bathhouse for 16 hours while awaiting word on the missing, and now deceased miners.

Medical and coroner personnel were also present inside the main shop when the bodies were backed into the building. I'm almost certain (but not positive) Dr. George Nichols was also there along with the other medical personnel. Several physicians had come to the mine to prepare to treat possible survivors that might be injured. They, like the waiting family members, had endured the cold and chilly weather all evening and night, hoping for a miracle, only to be disappointed by the news of the miners' deaths.

By 9:a.m. the family members at the bathhouse and those others who had bravely withstood the cold weather at the entrance to Scotia's property had all left the scene. The days ahead would be tough ones for survivors of the dead miners but arrangements had to be made for the miners' burials and obligations had to be met. Some of the deceased miners had brothers and other kinfolk who also worked at Scotia, putting them in a unique situation when it came to blaming those whose negligence might have led to conditions which caused the explosion.

With the departure of the waiting family members and after all the bodies had been picked up by the waiting hearses there was no reason for myself and the other miners who had waited through the night (and there were many) to stay around any longer. My brother and I had already gotten ourselves in trouble by neglecting to call home from the mine when we arrived at work and leaving or families to think we might be among the missing men. About 10:00 p.m. on the first night, someone from the mine office came by to tell me to call home on the mine phone, and that my wife had been trying to reach me. I called home from the dispatcher's office and found that Wanda and the children were nearly frantic with worry that they hadn't heard from me. In all that was happening, I had completely forgotten to inform them that the explosion hadn't happened in any New Tygart mining sections. Some people had gotten a nap in during the night by stretching out on the uncomfortable benches, but others, like myself, had gone without any sleep. There was nothing left to do but head out for home, even though the events of the day before and that night felt like a bad dream that would never end.

Some member of the Company personnel passed the word around the bathhouse that Scotia employees would be out of work for at least two days in memorial to the deceased miners. Shortly after 9:a.m. I left the bathhouse and walked across the steel walkway that led to the upper parking lot. When I reached the parking lot I turned around and was looking down the hill at the Scotia main area where the whole complex could be viewed and just stood there, going over in my mine the events of the preceding 20 hours. While I stood there another Scotia miner topped the hill and after we greeted each other we both stood looking at the scene before us. We talked about what had transpired and I mentioned that I would probably have to convince my wife that the upper Scotia mines were much safer than the Imboden Seam Mine, before she would be o.k. with my returning to work again. I'll always remember his reply, "Well, I don't think I'll ever go underground again, I've had it." With those words we parted company and both left the parking lot for our homes. The next day, this same miner that I spoke with that morning was killed in the second explosion.

List of Scotia Miners Killed March 9, 1976

Name	Classification	Age	Mining Experience
Dennis Boggs	Utility Man	27	2yrs.
Everett S. Combs	Ventilation	29	5 Yrs. 3 Mos.
Virgil Coots	Section Foreman	24	4yrs. 2 mos.
Earl Galloway	Shuttle Car Opr.	44	14 yrs. 7 mos.
David Gibbs	Repairman	30	10 yrs. 9 mos.
Robert Griffith	Belt Cleaner	24	2 yrs.
Larry D. McKnight	Motorman	28	3 yrs. 5 mos.
Roy McKnight	Timberman	31	4 yrs. 6 mos.
Lawrence Peavy	Supplyman	25	6 yrs. 8 mos.
Tommy R. Scott	Miner Operator	24	3 yrs. 6 mos.
Ivan G. Sparkman	Bratticeman	34	1 yr. 11 mos.
Jimmy W. Sturgill	Utility Man	20	1 yr. 6 Mos.
Kenneth Turner	Roof Bolter	25	3 yrs. 9 Mos.
Willie D. Turner	Shuttle Car Opr.	25	5 yrs. 8 Mos.
Denver Widner	Ventilation	31	1 yr. 11 Mos.

After the bodies had been removed from the mine, MESA's William Clemons, Assistant District manager, Pikeville, Kentucky office, remained on the scene and continued to be in charge of the surface operations at Scotia. Throughout this entire period, except for a few hours immediately following the first explosion, the Scotia mine was under MESA's effective control. MESA supervised the rescue and recovery operations and was responsible for all relevant decisions and actions.

Even though MESA was in charge of operations, official representatives from the Kentucky Department of Mines and Minerals had been on site from the beginning, including the Department's head man, Commissioner Harrold Fitzpatrick. These State Inspectors and officials also had input in the decision making process, along with Scotia Coal Company representatives and Scotia miners' representatives from the Scotia Employees Union.

Other MESA officials Clemons conferred with when making his decisions on the recovery operations included, Robert Barrett—MSEA Administrator; John Crawford---MESA Assistant Administrator; R. Peluso---MESA Assistant Administrator for Technical Support; Jack Stevenson---MESA Chief of the Ventilation Group; Monroe West---MESA Sub-District Manager; Charles Sample--- MESA Inspection Supervisor; Ben Taylor---MESA Inspection Supervisor; Lawrence Phillips---MESA District Manager and Clemons' immediate supervisor; W.R. Compton--- MESA District Manager; and Herman Lucas--- MESA Coal Mine Inspection Supervisor.

At 5:00 a.m. on March 10, after the bodies had arrived at the surface and the rescue teams had been debriefed and sent home to rest, Clemons met with MESA officials Barrett, Crawford, Peluso, and Compton. At that meeting it was decided to begin the investigation on March 11, once some necessary preparatory work had been accomplished. At this time the damage to the roof at 2 Southeast Mains was yet unknown and the anticipated work was considered to be of a routine nature. According to Clemons; *"It was my conjecture during the conference that the exploration work that remained in 2 Southeast Main entries would be only a matter of routine and could be accomplished easily without any undue hazards once additional ventilation was made available.....the other conferees shared my views...I assumed MESA's position of the responsibility for the work of obtaining the additional ventilation and exploring the remainder of the 2 Southeast entries so that the area could be made ready for the investigating team."*

During the meeting it was decided that MESA rescue teams and Scotia personnel would work during the second shift to attempt to restore ventilation to the mine. It was also agreed to reenter the mine at 7:00 a.m. the next day, March 11, for an inspection tour. After this meeting closed, MESA Washington personnel departed the mine property. MESA Administrator Barrett and Deputy Administrator Jack Crawford returned to Washington, apparently under orders from Interior Undersecretary Kent

Frizzell, who wanted a briefing for himself and for Kentucky's congressional delegation on the explosion.

William Clemons left for home at around 8:00 a.m. and left MESA's Russell Tackett in charge in Clemons' absence. Later that day, just prior to the start of the second shift, Clemons returned to the mine and resumed control of the operations.

About 4:00 p.m. on the evening of March 10, two teams of MESA Inspectors, Company officials, and Scotia Employees Union representatives entered the Imboden Mine from the slope portal located below the bathhouse and began exploring toward the area of the explosion.

At the suggestion of Ben Taylor, MESA Coal Mine Inspection Supervisor, Whitesburg, Kentucky, he and Richard Combs, Scotia General Mine Foreman, began to pre-shift (inspect) part of the mine, but not as far as 2 Southeast Mains. Combs mentioned to Taylor that one of the locomotives involved in the explosion had a compressor as part of its equipment. At that point, Taylor asked Combs if the locomotive compressor could have been a possible ignition source of the explosion. Taylor (allegedly) did not immediately report this conversation to other officials.

Just about 7:45 p.m. the two MESA teams ran into an unexpected problem. MESA supervisor Ben Taylor, of the Whitesburg Field Office, found a place where the drawrock had been jarred loose and was sagging low in the track entry. This could have possibly been caused by the explosion but the exact cause was unknown. The mine roof here was low to begin with, not over 50-55 inches, and the rock that was hanging loose made the roof even lower at this spot. It would be unsafe for motors to travel on the track underneath the rock while carrying supplies to rebuild stoppings and restore ventilation on 2 Left and 2 Southeast Mains. They had no choice, the roof would have to be bolted. That would mean that a roof bolter would have to be brought from another location in the mine and energized from one of the 440 volt power boxes located at the mouth of 2 Southeast Mains and Northeast Main. The loose rock was located in the track entry about 300-500 ft. from the track switch located there.

MESA officials and company officials slowly and carefully worked their way through the mine, making air readings, methane checks, and testing for carbon monoxide in each section. They advanced as far as the area where the last fresh air base had been established by the rescue teams during the recovery of the miners' bodies just hours before. This was at the intersection of 2 Southeast Mains and 2 Left. The last air reading from that area was taken in the track entry at the mouth of 2 Southeast Mains.

No further advancement into the 2 Southeast Mains heading was made, as the interrupted ventilation would have by then likely lowered the oxygen level below what was needed to sustain life, and the methane levels were likely much higher than when the last readings were taken when the bodies were removed. (The oxygen was at 12 percent then and methane readings were 5 percent and possibly higher, as the testing was done with a methane detector that had a detecting scale of only 5 percent.)

The actual area of the explosion wasn't examined. Later, Barrett and other officials would explain that the area could not have been explored further without oxygen apparatus.(The availability or non-availability of such equipment wasn't mentioned at the time.)

At 12:48 a.m. March 11, Mesa Inspectors and Company officials returned to the surface to report on ventilation and roof conditions in the mine. The need for supporting the roof at the mouth of 2 Southeast Mains and Northeast Main was also discussed.

After the crews were withdrawn from the mine, Clemons asked Jack Stevenson, a MESA ventilation expert, to prepare a set of recommendations "as to what was necessary to acquire additional ventilation in 2 Southeast Mains," A few hours after this meeting, Clemons held another meeting to discuss future actions. He later told the House-Senate Investigation Committee, "A meeting was held at 2:05 a.m. March 11 1976, to discuss how to proceed in carrying out Mr. Stevenson's recommendations....This meeting was attended by both MESA and Scotia Coal Company officials." Clemons stated that based upon the meeting a tentative plan was developed, calling for a second work crew to reenter the mine that day. However, "before leaving the mine I informed everyone concerned that the plan was a tentative plan and that no part of it was to be implemented until I discussed it with my superiors." Clemons stated that he called Assistant Administrator John Crawford at about 5:00 a. m. and informed him of the plan. "Mr. Crawford concurred with the plan as I described it to him."

So now we can say that the conditions that would lead to the second explosion of the Scotia Imboden Mine were in place. The Staff Report prepared by the Staff of the House Committee on Education and Labor said this;

With respect to the environmental conditions in the mine between the two explosions, the following is known: Nearly all the physical mine damage resulting from the first explosion was found in the area of the two locomotives located in the upper portions of 2 Southeast Mains; dangerous concentrations of methane gas and carbon monoxide were found in 2 Southeast mains by the rescue teams on March 9-10; work crews and rescue teams on March 9-10 were unable to restore ventilation to the 2 Southeast Mains section; A hazardous roof condition was found at the entrance to 2 Southeast Mains; Perhaps most importantly, the upper portions of 2 Southeast Mains were not inspected or firebossed for hazardous conditions. From the time the rescue teams recovered the bodies of the two locomotive men killed in the first explosion, until now, no one has been in the 2 Southeast Mains section of the Scotia mine. Thus, at the time the 13 man work crew approached the entrance to 2 Southeast mains to repair the damaged roof on March 11, the hazardous environmental conditions in 2 Southeast Mains were unknown.

I arrived at my home in Colson at around 10:00 a.m. on Wednesday, March 10, and finally got a few hours sleep after tossing and turning for a long time before I could go to sleep. I was up after no more than 4 hours of rest, as the events of the night before kept running through my mind.

Wanda wanted me to go over the whole story of what happened, but like everyone else, I knew very little more that what the news reports were reporting. Their reporting turned out to be fairly accurate, as most news broadcasts mentioned that methane gas might have been what set the explosion off.

My mom called me that morning from across the hill in Thornton, Kentucky, and she didn't mince words as she related how worried the family had been when they couldn't reach us nor hadn't heard from us after the news of the explosion hit the air waves. I only learned years later that she had dad drive her to the Scotia entrance and had the guard inquire as to our safety.

He managed to get hold of my brother at the B Seam, where he worked, and Jimmy met them at the guard shack and assured them he was o.k. before going home. I never knew they were there and only remembered that I received a call from my wife at the bathhouse later in the evening. She didn't mince words about my neglecting to call home either.

As I have already related, Scotia declared two days of mourning for the coal miners who had perished in the explosion on March 9th, which meant that those of us who worked on the second shift wouldn't have to report back to work until the evening of March 12th, unless called back for an emergency. I knew that the work was still going on in the Imboden-Seam Mine as they tried to figure out the cause of the explosion, but because I worked on the hill above Scotia at New Tygart, I didn't expect to report back to the mine until the 12th, if then. There was some speculation among the miners at the bathhouse the night of the explosion that maybe Scotia would close down for good now. We just didn't know what to expect, since Scotia had never before suffered a tragedy like what had just happened.

That night, I listened to every news report I could tune in on the radio (our television reception was poor and by antenna only) and heard the same reports over and over. Stations far and wide were talking about Scotia and what had happened there.

Wanda and I discussed the explosion and whether I should continue to work there after this was all over, but in the final analyst we both knew that we had talked about all the what- ifs even before I made the decision to take the job offer one and one half years ago. Every time the families of the men who were killed were mentioned as we were talking, Wanda would start crying and wondering what the little children would do and "how would they make it?" I'm sure she was thinking of our children and how they could easily have been in the same situation.

The next morning, Thursday March 11th, I arose and listened to news reports that Federal officials were working inside the Imboden mine overnight, trying to find the cause of the explosion and to re-establish ventilation. Since I had been home I hadn't talked with anyone at the mine or anyone who worked in the mine to that point, so I didn't have any idea how the investigation was proceeding or even if anyone was working to find the cause. I only knew what little the radio news announcers told us in news reports.

About 10:00 a. m. the phone rang and when I picked up the receiver and said hello I recognized the voice of Scotia's mine office secretary on the other end of the line. "Hello, she said, is this Eddie?" " Yes, I answered, this is he." "Eddie, we're getting a crew together to pick up a bolting machine and take it to 2 Southeast Mains to bolt up some bad top and we need a motorman, would you be interested in coming to work on the second shift this evening?" "Rhoda, I don't know if you know it, but I normally work at New Tygart and I don't know much about the bottom mine. Would you still need me to come out?" "Yes, she replied, there'll be others there who know the mine." "I guess I'll be there then," I said as I glanced up at Wanda who was standing by the phone listing to the conversation.

"No you're not going to work in that mine," Wanda exclaimed. "You've got children here that want you to stay home!"I gave her "the look" as I knew Rhoda heard what she said. Rhoda quickly spoke to me again, "Eddie, I see your wife doesn't want you to work today and that's o.k., I can call someone else. You need to listen to her. This is volunteer work anyway." I then thanked her and hung up the phone. After hanging up I was peeved at Wanda for keeping me from working that evening because, like most people with young families we needed the money. I also wanted to help in any way I could for the humanity side of the equation. I spent the rest of the day chiding her because of her fear that the mine might explode again.

That night at around 12:15 a.m. on March 12, I turned the radio on that was located on a table beside the bed as I listened to a clear-channel A.M. radio broadcast of the news and heard the words, "there has been an explosion at Scotia Coal Company in Ovenfork, Kentucky." I barely heard it while wondering why they were still telling old news of the explosion like it just happened. Then I caught these words, "The Scotia Coal Company mine has exploded AGAIN." I sat up in bed and shouted at Wanda, who was in the kitchen washing dishes. "Wanda, the mine has blown up again!" She said later that I was white as a sheet when she came into the room. What had seemed to be nearly impossible of happening twice in one mine had actually happened. Scotia had suffered an explosion for the second time in two days and the crew of men who were working that night was missing. If my wife hadn't intervened I would have most likely been one of those eleven men then missing after another tragic explosion in Scotia's No.1 Mine.

CHAPTER TWELVE

The Second Explosion

BY 3:00 p.m. on March 11, Clemons had returned to the mine, where the crew that had been assembled were in the process of preparing to enter the mine. It had been decided that a bolting machine that was in Northeast Mains would be brought from that section to 2 Southeast Mains to bolt up the loose rock that had been found there.

Shortly after 4:00 p.m. ten company employees and three Federal Inspectors went underground. Their assignment was to go to Northeast Main and bring a roof bolter from there to 2Southeast Mains – Northeast Main intersection to bolt the loose rock up near the intersection and to attempt to restore ventilation where they could. Two of the ten Scotia Company employees were tasked with operating the two locomotives and two supply cars that they were taking with them.

At 8:00 p.m. Ben Taylor of MESA returned to the mine after resting and told William Clemons about the compressor being a part of the equipment on the locomotive still sitting on the track in 2 Southeast Mains Section. Richard Combs, (Scotia's General Mine Foreman) had told Taylor about it when they firebossed a part of the mine together on Wednesday, March 10th. At 10:p.m., while the crew was moving the bolter from Northeast Mains, Clemons went home and left Taylor in charge.

One member of the work crew that went inside as a union representative was J.B. Holbrook, who was the Secretary of the Scotia Employees Association, the union that represented the hourly workers at Scotia, and who normally worked at the tipple and had never been inside the Scotia mine before.

Another crew member was James "Bird Dog" Williams, who was the second shift section foreman who had been in charge of the 2 Left production crew the night before the explosion.

116

The other members of the crew were: Don Creech, Ernest Collins, Don Polly, Rick Parker, Glen Barker, Monroe Sturgill, James Sturgill, and John Hackworth, all of whom were Scotia employees. Three Federal Coal Mine Inspectors, Grover Tussey, Richard Sammons, and Kenneth Kiser made up the remainder of the 13 man crew. (John Hackworth was attending the Northeast Mains belt drive during the first explosion and had been the first to notify General Mine Foreman Richard Combs that 2 Southeast Mains had suffered an explosion which had destroyed the beltline coming from 2 Left and 2 Southeast Mains. Combs then called all the other active sections and ordered the men to begin walking towards the outside. He then sent mantrip buses to meet them as they walked towards the mine portal.) John had volunteered to go back to the scene to help on the 11th.

By 6:30 the power had been turned on for Northeast Mains, where the crew was to get the roof bolter to take to 2 Southeast Mains. Some repairs had to be made to the roof bolter before it could be moved, which took until around 9:30 p.m. before the repair work was finished and they could begin to tram the bolting machine towards 2 Southeast Mains. They had about 2,500 ft. to go to reach 2 Southeast Mains intersection.

The machine had to be moved on the main line supply haulage all the way to 2 Southeast Mains and the going was slow. An hour after leaving Northeast Main with the bolter they reported that everything was o.k. and they were halfway to their destination, the mouth of 2 Southeast Mains. It was then 10:30 p.m.

Nearly one hour later, at 11:10 p.m. March 11, the crew finally reached the vicinity of the mouth of 2 Southeast with the roof bolter. Their shift was already over and they were on overtime, so the bolting of the loose rock would have to be done by the day shift crew scheduled to come inside in the morning at 7:00 a.m., March 12th. They gathered around the two motors and supply cars in preparation to leave for the outside. One or two men sat in the operators deck of the motors and another man or two climbed in the supply cars to rest from their efforts to bring the bolter from Northeast Main.

The three Federal Inspectors and Scotia employee Don Polly were a little ways from the rest of the crew, probably engaged in making some further checks while waiting on the two electricians to prepare the power cable for supplying power to the bolting machine in the morning.

The Scotia electricians, Ernie Collins and Rick Parker, who were about 30 ft. away from the Federal Inspectors and Don Polly, began tugging and pulling the bolter's trailing cable from the track entry to a 7,200 volt power box located about 150 ft. around the corner in another entry. As the two men began hooking up the 440 volt bolting machine trailing cable to the power source, a tremendous explosion ripped down the 2 Southeast Mains entries, and continued on its path of destruction through the mouth of 2 Southeast Mains where eleven of the thirteen men and the motors and supply cars were located. The force of the blast continued on down the entries and on through some old works before its force was spent. The explosion left the whole area charred and blackened around the mouth of 2 Southeast Mains and extended outward for 100 yards into the track entry leading to the Northeast Mains and South Mains intersection and towards the borehole side of Northeast Mains where the bolter had been brought from. This second explosion had a much greater force than the first one did, finishing the destruction that the first blast started.

Every entry of 2 Southeast Mains was now blackened and charred, with no rock dust remaining to be seen anywhere on the blackened surface. The belt line coming from 2 Southeast Mains and 2 Left Panel was demolished and turned over on its belt rollers. The whole 2 Southeast Mains area was a shambles except for the 7,200 volt power box the two electricians were working at when the explosion happened. The block of coal that the power center was located behind and a gob pile saved the two men's lives when the blast came rushing down the 2 Southeast Mains entries.

The two survivors, Ernie Collins and Rick Parker, later stated they heard the explosion and listened for a few seconds as it thundered down the 2 Southeast entries, which only took a very few seconds to reach the mouth of the section.

One can only imagine the panic and horror the miners who were gathered around the motors and supply cars must have felt for just a few seconds, but there was no time to do anything to save themselves in the short time it took for the concussion from the blast to engulf them.

Collins and Parker were partially protected from the force of the blast due to the gob pile that was at the edge of the break they were behind, but they were engulfed by the heat and temporarily blinded from the dust and debris swirling in the air as the blast swept through the entries.

The concussion from the explosion stunned both men but they were miraculously spared any disabling injuries. The dust and thick smoke surrounded them with a cloud of darkness that was darker than the night. They began walking as fast as they could and reaching for their self rescuers located on their belts, but Collins couldn't get the lid to pop off his rescuer so that he could use it. As they were stumbling away from the explosion and with poisonous carbon monoxide likely in the smoky atmosphere, Parker caught up with Collins and helped him to open his rescuer and put it on, which likely saved his life.

After both got their self rescuers on they managed to feel for and find a telephone line that they knew was normally hung in the main line track and followed that out the main track entry by using the "hand over hand" method. They continued to hold on to each other until they finally reached fresh air that they could breathe without having to wear their rescuers when they reached the junction of Northeast Main and Southeast Main. When they reached the familiar junction the visibility improved enough so they were able to recognize their surroundings. They had escaped the explosion and had walked about 5,000 feet to reach the safety of fresh air.

They used the mine phone positioned nearby on the Northeast Main belt head to call outside to the supply house and report the explosion to the dispatcher. They also asked for transportation to come and get them, but continued to walk out the main line track entry. When they arrived at the mouth of 1-West they heard someone paging them on the mine phone hanging there and Rick Parker answered the call. Parker was told that they were to wait right where they were, as a mantrip was on the way to pick them up. They decided to continue on out the track entry on their own until they met Richard Combs and Federal Inspector Davis whom transported them out of the mine to the surface.

They reached the outside at 12:30 a.m. on March 12, about 60 minutes after the explosion blasted out of 2 Southeast Mains. Eleven more lives had been snuffed out by this second blast that should never have happened but two lives were spared and now safely out of danger.

At 1:00 a.m. William Clemons returned to the mine and resumed control of operations. According to his testimony to investigators he was home when he received word of the second explosion at midnight. He immediately left for the mine.

"*Upon my arrival I was informed that a second explosion had occurred, that two men had escaped from the mine and that eleven were unaccounted for. I talked to the two men who had escaped the explosion and got all the information they could furnish me. From this information, particularly from the extent of the forces, it was obvious to me that it might be necessary to utilize the air shaft in by 2 Southeast Main in the rescue effort. With this in mind and no present means of entering the shaft, I made arrangements for mobil (sic) cranes to be sent to the shaft. There was a constant increase of CO (carbon monoxide)---from 800 ppm to 2,000 ppm---at the fan which indicated a strong possibility of a mine fire and caused much concern for a period of about two hours. I then asked several Scotia Coal Company officials, responsible officials from nearby coal companies who were present, and several MESA officials to meet with me for the purpose of discussing the approach we should take in the rescue efforts....*

Some felt that the effort should be approached from the shaft and some felt that we should approach it from the main slope entries. After listening to all their views, I decided that we would approach it from both directions and that the final approach would be dictated by the conditions encountered."

At 1:00 a.m. MESA's national office in Arlington, Virginia was once again contacted with news of an explosion in the Scotia mine as they were after the first explosion. Also as after the first explosion orders were given to airlift MESA mine rescue teams back to the mine, and to "reactivate MESA's Mine Emergency Operations Plan."

And finally, just like after the first explosion, the sound of ambulances and police cars rushing to the Scotia mine was reverberating through the hills and Valleys of Poor Fork. The same mining companies that had previously sent their rescue teams responded a second time. The teams once again gathered their breathing apparatuses, ropes, pickhammers and other gear they might need in the event another rescue of missing miners might be attempted, and rushed to the Scotia mine.

Shortly after Clemons arrived at the mine, the initial entry into the mine for a rescue attempt was made by two MESA officials on foot at the slope portal followed by two rescue team members. They went all the way to or near the 2 East Main intersection (about 3 miles) before observing any evidence of the explosion. They continued up 2 East, about 9 crosscuts (800 ft.) where they discovered the ventilation was reversed. The men were immediately withdrawn from the mine, using the same route they traveled as they went in the mine. Two rescue teams who were on the scene outside the bathhouse portal were sent to the entrance of 2 East to establish a fresh air base and to make an exploratory investigation to determine the extent of ventilation damage in the area. These rescue teams reported that an overcast had been damaged near the entrance to 2 East and that some 126,000 cubic feet of air per minute was being short-circuited at that point.

After receiving these reports of reversed air and explosion damage to the overcast at 2 East, Clemons made the decision to withdraw the rescue teams from the 2 East area and to concentrate all further rescue efforts via the air shaft.

The air shaft was located in the Frank's Creek area of Eolia, Kentucky about five miles from the main Scotia mining complex. Construction on the shaft had been started in 1975 and was designed to accommodate an automatic elevator to transport the men and some light supplies into the upper reaches of the mine. It would also serve as a fresh air intake to help ventilate the mine more efficiently.

At the time of the explosions the air shaft (or bore hole) was uncompleted. It's 13 and ½ foot diameter shaft was still without the elevator to provide transportation to the bottom of the 386 foot deep shaft. The distance through the mine from the bottom of the shaft to the bathhouse portal at the main office area was about six miles via the track entry.

After the withdrawal of the rescue teams from the mine at the main portal all further efforts were shifted to the Frank's Creek bore hole-air shaft. Sometime before 9:00 a.m. Federal Inspectors West and Merritt, and Scotia Employees Association representative David McKnight were lowered to the bottom of the mine shaft by means of a rope and a bucket to do a pre-examination and inspection of the Northeast Main area where the air shaft was located. Their examination found that the ventilation controls in the area were intact and that the air was flowing in the proper direction and course.

At around 9:45 a.m. (of 12 March) the two inspectors, West and Merritt, and David McKnight, the miner's representative, were withdrawn up the mine shaft and made their report to officials there. Shortly thereafter Clemons, the Nos. 1 and 2 Westmoreland Coal Company rescue teams, and the National Mines rescue team were lowered into the shaft. When they reached the bottom of the shaft Clemons briefed them before proceeding further into the mine. He instructed the Westmoreland teams to travel along the Northeast Main track entry, without using breathing apparatus, in intake air toward 2 Southeast Main. Clemons assigned the National Mines Corporation rescue team to stay at the bottom of the shaft as a back-up team. The Beth-Elkhorn team was standing by on the surface of the air shaft.

The Westmoreland teams advanced along the track entry cautiously and carefully towards the mouth of 2 Southeast Mains where the missing miners were last seen and heard from, occasionally testing for oxygen, carbon monoxide, and methane as they advanced. It was approximately one mile from the bottom of the air shaft to the mouth of 2 Southeast Mains.

Around 12:00 noon the teams reached the intersection where they found the eleven missing men dead. After determining that there were no signs of life, the teams were ordered to return to the surface without recovering the bodies because of the danger of another explosion occurring. All the people who went underground were back outside the air shaft by 1:02 p.m. According to Clemons;

" *Following my instructions closely, the teams advanced bare-faced to the entrance of 2 Southeast Mains where they found the eleven men (approximately 12:00 noon)... Since all eleven were dead, and I had drastic fears of another explosion, I told the rescue teams to return to the shaft bottom as quickly as possible (from which they were withdrawn from the mine without recovering the eleven bodies.")*

MESA Administrator Barrett had arrived back at the mine at 5:30 a.m. on March 12, and after Clemons made the decision for the rescue teams to not recover the bodies, Barrett held a series of meetings among representatives of mine management, the Scotia Employees Association, The Kentucky Department of Mines and Minerals, MESA, and joined by representatives from the Secretary's office of the Department of the Interior. The consensus decision resulting from these meetings was to seal the Scotia Mine. All parties had concurred that the chance of another explosion was too great to permit anyone to reenter the mine.

After the decision was made by all parties (except the families, who had no input into the decision) preparations began immediately to gather the materials to build the seals in all openings of the Scotia No. 1 Mine. The mine portals were sealed with two rows of concrete blocks with a "fill" material between the two rolls of blocks that was of a porous nature. After some leaks were detected, the seals were reinforced.

All the openings had been sealed by 2:10 p.m. on March 19, 1976. Just four days before, on March 15, MESA mining engineer Rick Keene issued a 104 (a) Order which covered the entire mine. This order is worth repeating as to what it meant:

Imminent Danger---Section 104 9a) provides that if an authorized representative of the Secretary of the Interior (MESA) finds that an imminent danger exists in a coal mine he shall forthwith issue an order requiring all persons to be withdrawn immediately from the mine, or affected mine area, until such time that the representative determines that the imminent danger no longer exists.

So whether it was now closed by order of the Department of the Interior or by the concrete blocks which had been installed in all entries to the mine, Scotia's No. 1 Imboden Seam Mine was closed until a plan could be put in place to rebuild the many shattered stoppings, pump the water out, and ventilate the mine in order to recover the eleven bodies still lying at the mouth of 2 Southeast. It would be a long wait.

List of Scotia Miners Killed March 11, 1976

Name	Classification	Age	Mining Experience
Glenn Barker	Motorman	29	5 yrs.
Don Creech	Utility Man	30	8 yrs. 4 mos.
John Hackworth	Timberrman	29	2 yrs. 6 mos.
J.B. Holbrook	Tipple Operator	43	13 yrs.
Kenneth Kiser	Federal Mine Insp.	45	27 yrs.
Carl Polly	Roof Bolter	47	7 yrs. 2 mos.
Richard M. Sammons	Fed. Mine Ins.	55	26 yrs.
James Sturgill	Belt Cleaner	46	11 yrs. 11 mos.
Monroe Sturgill	Roof Bolter	40	13 yrs 10 mos.
Grover Tussey	Federal Mine Ins.	45	26 yrs.
James Williams	Section Foreman	23	4 yrs.

The second Scotia Explosion, March 11, 1976

Map courtesy of *The Mountain Eagle* Whitesburg, Ky.

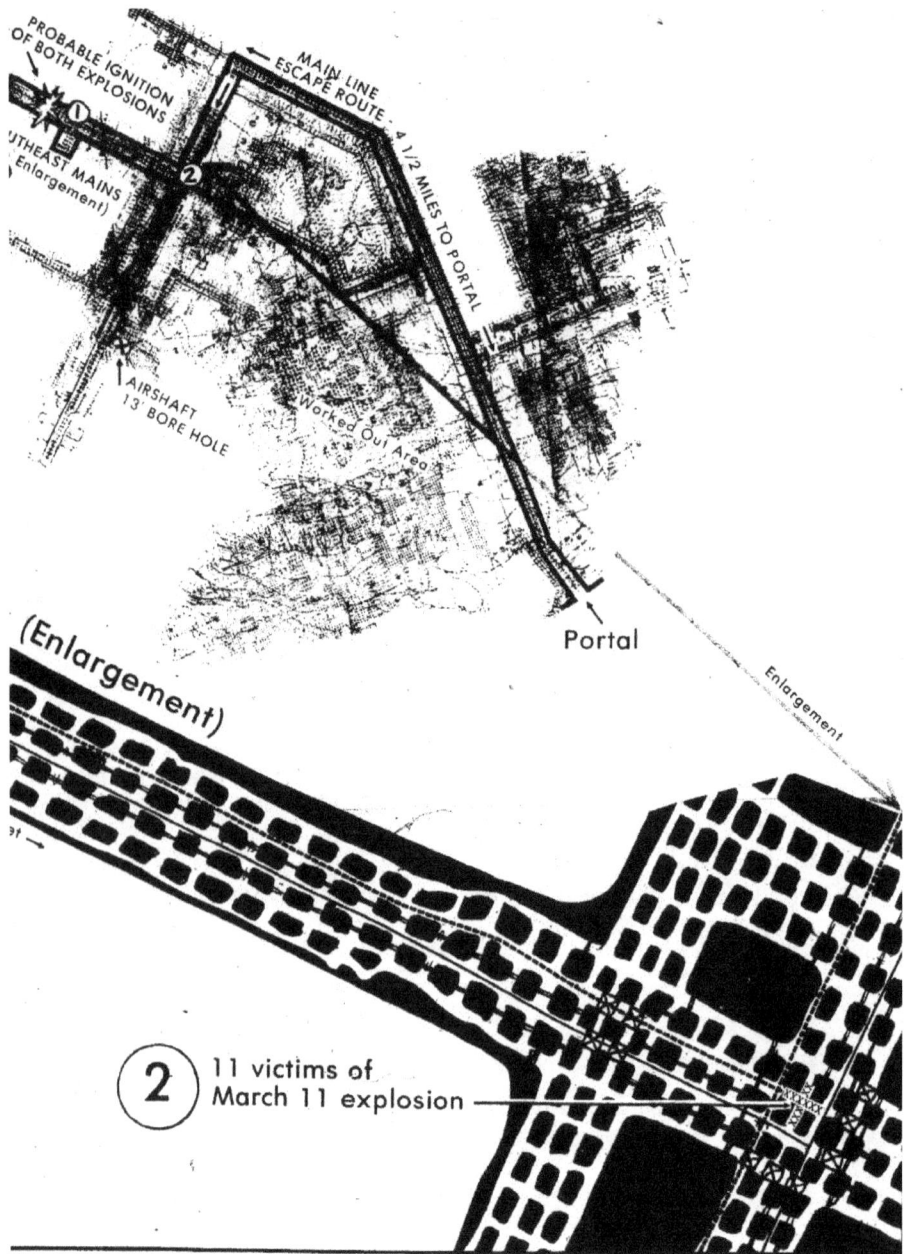

CHAPTER THIRTEEN

Aftermath

After the mine openings had all been sealed and the leaks stopped, a number of Scotia related events took place in the form of several public hearings to try to get to the bottom of how the tragedies could have happened and they might have been prevented.

There was one day of public hearings in Washington, conducted by the Subcommittee on Labor on March, 24, 1976;

The convening of a MESA investigation panel which held nine days of public hearings on April 5, 6, 7, 8, 9, 27, 28, 29, and 30, 1976, in Whitesburg, Kentucky;

Three days of public hearings conducted by a joint Committee of the House Education and Labor Committee and the Senate Labor and Public Welfare Committee on May 7, 1976, in Whitesburg, Kentucky, and on May 13 and June 16, 1975 in Washington, D.C.

With respect to the composition of the MESA investigation panel, the following individuals served as members:

Robert Barrett, MESA Administrator, panel chairman;

Thomas Mascolino, Assistant Solicitor, U.S. Department of Interior

Fred Karem, Deputy Undersecretary of the U.S. Department of Interior;

Harold Kirkpatrick, Commissioner of the Kentucky Department of Mines and Minerals;

George Eadie, Professor of General Engineering, University of Illinois;

George McPhail, Senior Mine Rescue Officer, Province of Ontario, Canada.

Of this group the first factor to be noted is that two of the members, Barrett and Kirkpatrick--- were directly involved in the events which occurred at the Scotia mine following the first explosion. It is not our intention to question the integrity of either man---both are outstanding professionals in their field---however, the very fact that they were inves-

tigators of events to which they were parties should be noted for the record. While there is nothing in the record to suggest that either man conducted himself in a manner detrimental to the investigation, the fact remains that both, in varying degrees, participated in the decisions that were made following the first explosion.

The second point to be noted is the glaring absence from the MESA panel of any miner representatives. Even though the Scotia mine was, in effect, a non-union mine, the miners who work at the Scotia mine have a direct and continuing interest in the twin disasters. It seems to us that a miner representative, at the very least, would have added to the panel's credibility.

The MESA hearings themselves have been subject to some criticism by the news media, Scotia miners, and company officials because of the manner in which they conducted. The only witnesses to be called were those selected by MESA and there was little effective cross- examination by anyone other than the MESA panel.....

Following the decision to reopen the mine, MESA Administrator Barrett assured the families of the victims that the recovery would proceed through the ventilation shaft which enters the mine some 3,000 (or more) feet from where the bodies are located. It was estimated that such a route would enable the bodies to be recovered in about a week.

However, Barrett has reversed himself on the recovery route and has approved a Scotia Company plan that approaches the recovery of the bodies through the main shaft. Under this plan, it has been estimated that the recovery would take a minimum of 60 days. At the present time reports from the mine indicate that the recovery operation is confronted with difficulties due to mine flooding.

The point is to be made that by following the company's plan the mine will be placed back into production much sooner than if the recovery took place through the ventilation shaft. Thus, it appears to the committee staff that MESA--- which still effectively controls the mine--- acquiesced to the Company's production oriented wishes, rather than insisting on the more humane approach of affording the families of the eleven men the opportunity of providing their loved ones with a decent and respectful burial.*

According to the staff study prepared by the Senate Subcommittee on Labor, of the 420 safety and health violations that Scotia was cited for be-

---

* A Staff Report; House Committee on Education and Labor, Washington: 1976

tween January, 1974 and February 1976, at least 63 of the violations were directly related to ventilation and methane conditions.

Another critical aspect of Scotia's safety record was the complete lack of an adequate safety education and training program. (During the period January 1974, through February 1976.) Testimony presented by Scotia miners, Company officials and MESA professionals clearly indicated that Scotia's training and education program was a "sham." According to the testimony, training in the use of self-rescuers was sporadic, and fire and mine evacuation drills were nearly non-existent.[+]

In terms of the March 9 and march 11 explosions, the issues most directly related to Scotia's safety record include (1) the history of ventilation and methane problems, and (2) the lack of education and training programs.... In the opinion of all those associated with the Scotia mine disaster, these three conditions apparently led to the explosions on March 9 and March 11, (1976.)

Most people knew, and it was an accepted fact, that Scotia was the most gassy mine in Eastern Kentucky. If compared with mines in other states, including the neighboring state of Virginia, the Scotia mine was not considered as heavily gassy. MESA had calculated that Scotia liberated an average of 250,000 to 500,000 cubic feet of methane in a 24 hour period. The aggregate amount of methane liberated is relatively unimportant if proper and adequate ventilation exists to keep the methane concentrations below the ignition level.

MESA regulations require tests for methane at the start of each shift and at each working place by qualified individuals. If 1.0 percent or more of methane is detected, electrical equipment must not be taken into, started, or operated at the working place. Examinations and monitoring for methane are also required at 20 minute intervals during the operation of electrical equipment. In addition, the regulations require a pre-shift examination for accumulations of methane within three hours preceding the beginning of any shift, and before any miner in such a shift enters the active workings of a coal mine. If 1.5 percent methane is detected at any time, all miners must be withdrawn from the endangered area.

With respect to the Scotia mine the following facts are known:

High concentrations of methane gas had previously been detected by the MESA inspectors and Scotia company officials;

_____

[+] After the explosions the safety programs were excellent.

Pre-shift examinations were not always conducted in accordance with the law;

Methane monitoring at the required 20 minute intervals was not always complied with; and

Federal ventilation requirements were frequently violated.

On at least seven separate occasions between January 1974 and February 1976, MESA issued violation notices of high methane concentrations. On at least two separate occasions---November 18, 1974 and January 7, 1975---the Scotia mine was ordered closed because high concentrations of methane were found by the MESA inspector. The January 7, 1975 closure order indicated that an imminent danger condition existed due to a combination of 1.2 percent methane and inadequate ventilation.

In addition to the methane violations found by MESA, Charles Fields---third shift fire boss at the Scotia mine---testified before a MESA investigation panel that on a number of occasions he detected excessive concentrations of methane gas throughout the mine. During the MESA hearings Fields was asked:

How often did you find more than say two percent of methane in work areas or idle areas?
Fields. Well sometimes it will be a long time. And maybe you will find not over two-tenths. And then sometimes you will get it where it will be *nine percent* or *three percent*. (Emphasis added.)

At the same hearing, Fields also testified that he had been aware of a methane gas feeder located in the same section of the mine where the two explosions occurred. (2 Southeast Mains.) Fields said he measured at least a five percent methane concentration at the floor of the mine where the feeder was located. According to Fields, the concentration could have been higher but his methane monitor measured only up to a 5 percent level. Fields further testified that when he took the same reading at a level somewhat above the mine floor, "it showed nothing."

Other miners also testified to the existence of a methane gas feeder in the 2 Southeast Mains section of the mine. Pat Pate, a shuttle car operator, told the MESA panel that whenever the mine floor was wet in the 2 Southeast Mains section, methane gas could be seen bubbling up through the water. According to Pate, "it boiled just like boiling water on a hot plate." Others who testified that they knew about the gas feeder included

Arvil Cornett---Scotia mine foreman, James Maggard---second shift maintenance foreman, Fred Maggard---general superintendent of the Scotia mine, Harvey Creech, Scotia staff foreman, and Earnest Collins, a Scotia miner. (The same Ernest Collins who had survived the second explosion.)

Fields also told the investigating committees that he sometimes fire-bossed the entire mine and sometimes had help from Arvil Cornett, third shift mine foreman. Company records---seized by MESA after the (first) explosion---showed that Fields signed the inspection records. Under questioning, he said he had not fire bossed 2 Southeast Mains on March 8, even though the records show him as having done so; he said Cornett had actually made the inspection of the area. Cornett however, testified that he had checked only the active 2 Left section and not the area of 2 Southeast Mains where the explosion later occurred.

Their testimony suggests that on the morning of March 9, when two miners entered the heading of 2 Southeast Mains with spark producing locomotives pushing a load of steel rails, they were entering an area which was producing methane and which had not been fire bossed for at least a week.

The Fields---Cornett testimony demonstrated that there was no set pattern for dividing up the fire bossing responsibilities between them. This led to apparent confusion and a failure on occasion to cover the whole mine.

With respect to the pre-shift mine examinations (fire bossing) required by the law, the MESA hearings clearly established that the examinations were not regularly made in all working sections of the mine. According to the transcript of the MESA hearings:

Question. This (the fire boss book) begins on March 5, and those are the records of the pre-shift examinations that were signed for by Mr. Fields prior to the explosion Those are your signatures at the bottom of this particular page? You agree they are copies of the fire boss book?
Fields. Yes sir.
Question. And you signed for the exams?
Fields. Yes.
Question. But you did not make them (the examinations?)
Fields. No.

Robert Barrett, MESA Administrator, also questioned Fields at the hearing. According to the transcript:

Barrett. Were you in 2 Southeast Mains after the (continuous) miner pulled out of that section of the mine where the explosions occurred?
Fields. Yes.
Barrett. How often did you get up there?
Fields. Well, not very often.
Barrett. There were approximately six weeks between.... the time the equipment was pulled out of the Mains and moved into 2 Left... How many times would you say during that five or six week period were you up the Mains?
Fields. Really I was up in there I would say twice.

Not only did the testimony affirm that the 2 Southeast Mains Section was not fire bossed immediately prior to the shift in which the March 9 explosion took place, but also that the 2 Southeast Mains Section was excluded from fire bossing when the March 11 explosion occurred.

William Clemons stated; "Prior to the first work crew going into the mine on the afternoon of March 10, a fire boss examination was made in the areas that required such an examination." In addition, a second fire boss examination was conducted on the morning of March 11, at 8:14 a.m. prior to the thirteen man work crew entering the mine at 4:15 p.m. later that same day. According to MESA Administrator Robert Barrett:

The MESA and Scotia Coal Company men who began to enter the mine at 8:14 a.m. on March 11, were to examine ventilation controls and to make examinations for hazardous conditions. This is a standard procedure to determine whether it is safe for men to enter the mine. This in effect was a pre-shift examination. These examinations were completed. *The examiners determined that the mine was safe,* and a work crew began entering the mine at 4;15 p.m. (emphasis added,)

While it is clear that these two pre-shift examinations did in fact take place, it is also clear that they were both limited to that portion of the mine where the two crews were intended to work, which excluded 2 SEM. Ben Taylor told the joint House-Senate Committee, " Two Southeast Mains themselves were not fire bossed." Clemons testified that " I personally instructed no one to go into 2 Southeast Mains.

According to Barrett:

....*an examination of the entire mine had been made using company fire bosses accompanied by MESA inspectors. Except for Two Southeast sections. Now, that section we had given orders that no one was to go in there.--- I shouldn't say no one---they were given instructions that no one was to touch anything because of the possibility of destruction of evidence. The only people who were in that section after I left was our MESA mine rescue team on the night before (the early morning hours of March 10.)*

Thus at the time the thirteen men entered the mine on March 11, the environmental status of the 2 SEM was unknown. However, what was known was that the last reports from the rescue teams on March 9 indicated dangerous concentrations of methane gas in an area where ventilation had not been restored.

The evidence that the 20 minute methane monitoring rule was repeatedly violated was brought out in the hearings also. On at least one occasion (July 8 1975,) Scotia was cited by a MESA inspector for failure to test for methane at the required 20 minute intervals. Furthermore, testimony taken from Scotia miners indicated that the 20 minute rule was seldom followed. According to Carlos Smith, a Scotia continuous miner operator, this requirement was repeatedly violated. According to the MESA hearing transcript:

Question. Are you aware of a requirement that gas has to be checked periodically?
Smith. Yes, Sir.
Question. Do you know how often that is?
Smith. Every 20 minutes, I believe.
Question. Would you say that gas was being tested for every twenty minutes?
Smith. No, Sir.

Smith also testified that while he was not qualified to test for methane gas, he nonetheless regularly made such tests at the miner which he operated. Additionally he stated that while the section foreman was supposed to test for methane at the miner, he, Smith, was "not sure" how often the tests were made. Smith did state that the tests were very seldom taken while he was operating his equipment.

Methane Feeder

Smith and other witnesses indicated that at least two weeks before the disasters, crews in 2 Left noticed methane coming into the section in their intake air which passed through 2 Southeast Mains en route. Ordinarily, they said, intake air would be methane free.

"Two weeks previous to this (first) explosion, our gas had been real bad," Smith testified. "It sort of throwed (sic) me, me too, because it was coming on the intake, and all the experience I'd had with gas, the further off the air, the more gas you have. And I had mentioned it to the section foreman." Later, when the curtain was down across the track entry, " we got less gas," Smith said. Other witnesses agreed that the presence of methane in the intake air was a tip- off that gas was building in 2 Southeast Mains. Nevertheless, no special effort was made to locate the source or increase ventilation to compensate for the build-up.

Federal investigators came to believe that there was probably more than one methane feeder located in the track entry of 2 SEM, as several witnesses testified that they knew of at least one feeder which had ignited when a welder's torch had came into contact with the methane gas rising from the "feeder." "A piece of hot metal fell down in a hole," one miner remembered, and the fire just boiled out We poured a bag of rock dust down on it to put it out." The witnesses also testified that company officials knew of the ignition. Shuttle car operator Pat Pate told the investigating committee that miners had hung a warning sign ---- "check for gas"----at the site of the ignition.

Scotia General Mine Foreman Richard Combs contradicted this testimony, claiming that he had not been able to locate the source of the ignition and was not aware of any methane feeders in 2 SEM. Had the company known of the ignition, it would have been in violation of federal regulations for failure to report it to MESA, and would be subject to prosecution. Company fire boss Charles Fields testified however, that he had heard about the ignition, and second – shift maintenance foreman James Hargus Maggard said he had been told of the ignition but had not thought it sufficiently important to report it to superiors.

Ventilation History

In the two year period preceding the two explosions, the Scotia mine had been cited 63 separate times by MESA for ventilation violations. Of this total, 26 violations were attributed to not enough air reaching the working face of the mine, and 18 violations were for failure to follow the MESA approved ventilation plan. Other ventilation violations included line brattices being out of position, inoperative methane monitors, high methane concentrations, permanent brattices unconstructed, lost (spilled) coal and coal dust, and fans and other equipment not properly equipped or operating.

At the Joint House and Senate committee hearings, former Scotia coal miner Ronald Ledford testified that he personally witnessed air being diverted from one section of the mine to another in anticipation of a MESA inspection. Under questioning by Chairman Carl Perkins, Ledford said that he had accompanied James Bentley, assistant mine foreman for ventilation at Scotia, on three occasions when air was diverted. According to Ledford,

We would go to the (air) regulators, and whatever section he (the MESA inspector) was coming on, he (Bentley) would kind of slide the doors closed over another section, and they could put more air into another section---the section that the inspector would come in---for more air, and then) they would shut it down.

According to the hearing transcript:
Perkins. You mean they would switch the air around?
Ledford. Right.
Perkins. How often would they do this?
Ledford. I went with him (Bentley) three times when he done it.
Perkins. Over what period of time did this take place?
Ledford. Back in about seven or eight months.

A number of other Scotia miners gave testimony which essentially substantiated Ledford's assertions. Furthermore they also testified that they personally were involved in instances where MESA inspectors were intentionally misled as to ventilation and other safety conditions in the mine. Taken as a whole, the testimony of Gary Smith---a utility man, Carlos Smith---a continuous miner operator, Merle Rhodes----second-shift foreman, Glen Sturgill---former Scotia miner, Everett Boggs---former Scotia miner, and Pat Pate---shuttle car operator, presented a ringing indictment in the manner of which the air in the mine was diverted, and inspectors misled.

Education and Training

Robert Barrett, MESA Administrator, testified before the joint House and Senate Committee that MESA's investigation " clearly revealed that the Company's training program at Scotia was a sham." The staff report of the House Committee on Education and Labor stated that "Nothing more tragically demonstrates Scotia's sham program than the fact that six of the miners who died on March 9th probably could have saved themselves had they received proper training in fire drill techniques and evacuation procedures. These six men did not die as a result of the initial explosion, but suffocated to death when their self-rescuers became inoperative. ± Following the initial explosion, the six apparently barricaded themselves in the 2 Left Panel, off 2 Southeast Mains and sat there until they died."

MESA and Kentucky State officials reportedly said that the six miners who suffocated might have survived had they simply tried to walk out of the mine following the explosion. According to Harrold Kirkpatrick, Commissioner of the Kentucky Mines and Minerals, "We feel that the self-rescuers, with what we know now, they (the six miners) could have walked out 3½ miles in an hour." In testimony before the Joint House-Senate Committee, Monroe West, Sub-district manager of MESA's Norton, Virginia office, said, "Sir, if they (the six miners) attempted to come out of there (the mine) there is a good possibility that they could have made it." MESA Administrator Robert Barrett, at a congressional briefing on March 15, 1976, also expressed the opinion that the six men probably could have saved themselves by walking out of the mine.

Author's Note: While it is true that these six men could have walked the return entry for 2,600 feet and came out into fresh air at the mouth of 2 Southeast Mains, it is impossible to second guess their decision to go back on the 2 Left Section, barricade, and wait for rescuers to come to their aid. All of the men had the option to act as an individual and leave the group and try to reach safety on their own, and yet all chose to stay together and barricade. This tells me that they agreed that to barricade would be their best bet under the circumstances.

I had the opportunity, as a member of the "fresh air crew" that helped to ventilate the mine and build new stoppings that had been destroyed by the explosions, to observe 2 Left in the state it was in after the explosions. I followed the steps of the six men down the return of 2 Left and saw the very spot where each man had put on his self-rescuer as he went down the return. Imagine if you can, going down that darkened entry with heavy smoke obscuring your vision and with each breath of air you struggle to inhale saturated with smothering smoke and dust that sears your lungs. Then you come to the mouth of 2 Left Section where you enter the 2 SEM

± Self-rescuers only provided protection for one hour, at most.

return entry and discover that the smoke and dust is even heavier and no ventilation is moving through that entry. Your first thought is that maybe the whole mine is blown up. There's no air to breathe except what is remaining after the explosion blasted through and the oxygen level will probably get lower by the minute. Should you continue on down the entry and maybe not even be able to tell where you are or even where you should go? Is the whole mine blown up? What should I do? Or should I do what I am told to do if there is a *serious mine fire or explosion and escape to the surface is cut off?*

They made the decision to barricade because it seemed like the best thing to do under the circumstances, as they had some fresh air left on the section (they went several hundred feet before putting on their self-rescuers) and they knew that if escape through the return was cut off, (they thought) their only option was to barricade. They went back on section and did so.

They were experienced coal miners. All but one had at least one year in the mines, and he was only one month short of having his first year in. Every new miner had to wear a yellow mining hat at Scotia until they had worked there for a year. When the miner achieved that symbolic goal of becoming an experienced coal miner, he was allowed to wear the color of mining hat he wanted. I'm sure they had discussed what to do in case of a tragedy because I know that every crew I worked with before and after the explosions would sit around the dinner hole and discuss what we would do as an individual if escape from a disaster was impossible or improbable. Every man always agreed that if he could he would walk out with his self-rescuer he would do so, but if that was an unlikely possibility, then he wouldn't hesitate to barricade on section so he could be easily found. For these reasons, the six miners should not be faulted for the decision they made on the spot to barricade.

Nearly every coal miner is given a sticker to attach to the inside of his hat to have handy in case of such a tragedy as happened at Scotia:
When escape is cut off;
1. Barricade
2. Listen for 3 shots then;
3. Signal by pounding hard 10 times. Rest 15 minutes then repeat signal until:
4. You hear 5 shots, which means you are located and help is on the way.

Below is the long version:

In case of a serious mine fire or explosion and escape to the surface is cut off:

<u>Barricade</u>

1. Do not panic.

2. Select large area with good air quality.

3. Gather useful items. (Food, water, tools, safety lamps, barricade material, etc.

4. Short circuit ventilation outby barricade sites.

5. Promptly erect airtight barricades.

6. Post signs outside barricades with date, time, and number confined.

7. Extinguish flame safety lamps.

8. Rotate cap lamp use to conserve batteries.

9. Ration food and water.

10.Keep quiet to conserve energy and oxygen.

11. Do not congregate in one place.

12. One person walk around periodically to mix air.

13. Employ signaling methods:

(A) When you hear 3 shots, pound hard 10 times.

(B) Rest 15 minutes-repeat cycle.

(C) When you hear 5 shots, you have been located.

However tragic this example of six dead men might appear, (says the staff report) their failure to act should not be surprising in light of Scotia's record on safety education, particularly with respect to fire and evacuation drills. Testimony taken from Scotia miners and officials clearly established (during the hearings) the lack of an overall, adequate safety education program at the mine.

With respect to fire drills, (continues the report) escapeway procedures, and disaster-type situations, the hearing record is replete with evidence that most of the miners never had received proper training and instruction. Freddie Maggard, the General Manager of the Scotia mine, told the investigation panel that he did not know when the last fire drill had been conducted. His testimony indicated that he knew very little with respect to anything related to training and education. Maggard said that all safety training and education activities were the responsibility of the Company's safety personnel.

Charles Kirk---the only safety man employed by the Scotia Coal Company ---testified that to the best of his knowledge not one fire drill had been conducted at the mine during his tenure as the Company's safety inspector, approximately 3½ years. He further testified that he was the only Company safety inspector and was responsible for all three of Scotia's mines including Scotia No. 1 where the disaster occurred. Kirk stated that he had not been in the Scotia No. 1 mine during the 3-month period prior to the disaster.

Richard Combs, Scotia General Mine Foreman, told the MESA panel that while he was aware that evacuation drills were required, he was not familiar with the federal regulations as such.

David McKnight, President of the Scotia Employees Association, in response to questioning from Chairman Carl Perkins, told the Joint House-Senate investigation committee that "I have never known of a fire drill" and "as far as escapeways, sir, nothing about escapeways. I could go into those mines and never get out myself." Others who testified concerning the lack of safety training and fire and evacuation drills included Roger McKnight, Jasper Cornett, Carlos Smith, Glen Sturgill, and Everett Boggs.

CHAPTER FOURTEEN

Scotia Safety Practices

With 420 citations for safety and health violations between January 1974, and February 1976, combined with its complete lack of an adequate safety education and training program, it was no wonder MESA called it a "sham." Testimony that came out in the many hearings held after the two disasters confirmed that the health and safety training was sporadic at best.

The miners testified that they were paid for attending the required classes offered by Scotia outside normal working hours, but they seldom went. Several say they didn't go because the classes are only simplistic explanations, not comprehensive training.

Others said they didn't go because they wanted to go home after work, they didn't want to bother with classes in their free time. A continuous miner operator, who has worked at Scotia for five years and in the mines since 1948, said of these classes, "I don't go because it's the same thing over and over. If we got something that was going to teach us anything on a more in-depth level, I'd be the first man there.

Rick Parker, one of the two men who survived the second explosion, said, "The safety program in my opinion , isn't what it should be, and I know the majority of the miners feel that way." Parker said he would continue to work for Scotia if offered "the right job with the right pay," but not in the No. 1 mine. "Scotia is safe with the exception of ventilation," said Parker. That's why I won't go back into that gassy (No 1) mine."

Another miner however, said that not only was the ventilation poor in the Scotia Mine, but that the company allowed widespread disregard of federal and state regulations. He said it is common to see miners using nails to connect equipment to electric cables, rather than the required proper connectors.

He also said that many of the shuttle cars (buses) that take miners in to their sections do not have brakes and sometimes "jump the rails." Required methane readings are often not taken before a welding job is begun said the miner, who summarized the company's safety program as being "one film on safety, but I've never seen it."

"There's an understanding among miners around here, he said, "that if you can find work in another mine, it's better, you're more likely to survive." "But, he said, Scotia pays well ($62 a day is the top pay) and it is an expanding mine that hires young or inexperienced people."

Of about 15 miners interviewed about Scotia's safety program, the one who gave it the most credit said it included an annual "course in first aid, a safety course, and class in roof and rib control."[*]

One man who has been operating a shuttle car at the Upper Taggart Mine for almost two years said he was instructed in the use of a self-rescuer "for the first time ever" a week ago. Since the explosions, they've been cracking down on safety. But if hadn't happened, you can bet we wouldn't have been taught that self-rescuer."

And accounts of similar scanty training stories go on and on:

" They just told me not to smoke, gave me a self-rescuer and sent me down."

"They never showed me how to use a self-rescuer. When I hired in, I was given a self-rescuer. (Charles) Kirk, (Scotia Safety Director) said he would tell me how to use it that evening. That evening he was busy, he said he'd do it tomorrow. That went on for a week, and another week, and it never happened."

"A week before the explosion, the section I was on drilled into a pocket of methane. But nobody knew what to do, what we should do to be safe."

"All the time, you'd see someone or the other welding without using methane readings. We just weren't afraid of gas, we didn't think it would explode."

"You're supposed to take all the safety classes they have to offer, but mostly you don't go. They don't make you and it's after work on your own

---

[*] *The Mountain Eagle* , Whitesburg, Ky. Thurs. March 18, 1976.

139

time, you've got other things to do. If it were during the shift, you wouldn't see anyone working instead of taking a class."

At the B Seam in 1975, Scotia reported that 20 non-supervisors were trained in 14 courses ranging from roof and rib control to use of a flame safety lamp to test for gas. Seven men took the roof and rib class; the other courses had one man each.

During the same year at Upper Taggart, 10 supervisors took a course in roof and rib control and 10 in first aid. Training in these two areas is particularly encouraged by MESA officials since most mine fatalities result from roof falls. First aid can mean immediate treatment for a person injured within the mine.

Also at Upper Taggart in 1975, hourly workers completed 150 training courses. Ninety six took roof and rib, 12 took first aid and a group of three took 14 other courses. Some of those who took first aid also took the roof and rib course.

In 1974 at Upper Taggart, 352 courses were completed by hourly workers. Many of these miners took several different courses, bringing the actual number of individuals trained well below the number of course completions. The course with the largest attendance----43----involved the flame safety lamp, followed in size by three courses in the use of methane monitors.

That same year (1974) at the B Seam mine, non-supervisory miners completed 56 safety training courses. In 1973 Scotia employees completed 22 roof and rib or first aid courses at Upper Taggart, while two employees completed five safety courses at the B Seam.

The figures listed above are proof that at least in Scotia's Upper Taggart mine and the B Seam mine, a good effort was made to see that the miners who worked those mines received adequate safety and health training even before the two explosions occurred. This writer was one of those miners who was employed at Upper Taggart (or Tygart) beginning in 1974 and attended many classes in first aid, roof and rib, and ventilation classes during that time and afterwards. I also took some classes on the flame safety lamp before it began to be phased out in the late 1970's.

During the House-Senate hearings, Senator Harrison Williams (D. N.J.) told Blue Diamond officials that he found their safety record, and the record of the national mining industry, disturbing. He added that fines for violations, usually in the hundreds of dollars, have been too small to force Blue Diamond (the parent Company of Scotia Coal Company) or other mining companies to adhere to mine safety laws. Williams, Sen. Richard Schweiker, (R-Pa.) and Kentucky Senators Wendell Ford and Walter Huddleston criticized safety training procedures at the Scotia mine.

Williams told Blue Diamond officials, "We've been advised that if men killed in the first explosion had been trained properly, they wouldn't have built a barricade, but would have gone to an open area to escape."

Jasper P. Cornett, vice-president for operations at Scotia, replied that lack of training might not have been the reason the men built the canvas barricade. Cornett told Williams, "I wonder what you or I would do if such a thing happened," arguing that a mine explosion might cause anyone to panic.

R.C. Cornwell, general manager of the Scotia mine testified, "We have a mandatory safety program for our foremen. We have a voluntary program for all miners." Most of this training is done on the miners' own time, he said.

Committee investigator Roy Wade testified that Scotia told him foremen held five minute weekly training sessions with miners. He said the Scotia miners were apparently not given safety manuals.

Blue Diamond officials admitted that miners were offered no training sessions in use of self-rescuer breathing devices, which provide an hour's worth of oxygen. (Author's note: the self rescuer does not provide ANY oxygen. It merely filters out carbon monoxide). Only printed instructions for use of the device were given miners. When Sen. Ford said all miners should be trained in the use of the self-rescuer, Cornwell replied, "That suggestion doesn't have merit."

Sen. Williams surprised Blue Diamond officials by stating that the present Coal Mine Health and safety Act requires mine operators to equip each miner with a self-rescuer and to train miners in the use of the device. Later, MESA Administrator Barrett admitted that his agency had failed to enforce this provision, at least at the Scotia mine.[+]

MESA Hearings

During the MESA hearings, Richard Combs, Scotia General Mine Foreman, claimed that he had no decision making functions when he

---

[+] The Mountain Eagle, Whitesburg, Kentucky, April 8, 1976

went underground with MESA's Whitesburg inspection supervisor, Ben Taylor, to fire boss the mine after the first explosion. "From the outset, he said, company officials did whatever they (MESA) told us to do." When bad roof conditions were encountered, Combs said, Taylor ordered him to set timbers. "I didn't ask questions, I did what he said," Combs said.

Describing a meeting held between MESA and Scotia officials to determine a course of action after the mine roof needed additional support, Combs said he raised no objections to the plan as adopted---the plan which ultimately left 11 men working directly in the path of the second explosion. " I was taking orders," he said, adding that all I was there to do was what I was told to do."

In response to practically every question from the panel, Combs stressed this same point in different ways:

"I wasn't aware of anything. All I was doing was working."

"I considered myself to be a chauffeur for (MESA's Whitesburg, Kentucky Field Office Inspection Supervisor) Ben Taylor.

"We didn't discuss any conditions...we didn't observe anything."

In testimony on April 9, 1976, Taylor had acknowledged learning of the compressor from Combs in the course of discussing the braking equipment on the two locomotives in 2 Southeast Mains. Combs recalled the incident differently, remembering Taylor as having said: "I understand there's a motor up there with a compressor." Combs said he acknowledged that there was, and later told a MESA team about the compressor as they prepared to explore the area adjacent to the origin of the explosion.

" I warned the---well, talked with the MESA mine rescue team," he testified. " They didn't seem to be concerned," he added. When panel member Fred Karem, Deputy Undersecretary of the Interior, attempted to pursue the point---asking Combs directly whether he considered the compressor a danger---Blue Diamond attorney Maxwell Barrett interrupted: " You're asking him to speculate, and I don't see any point in him doing it." Karem's line of questioning was dropped.

General Mine Superintendent Freddie Maggard told the panel that he, too, was simply following MESA instructions during mine recovery work after the first explosion. "I was not asked for approval or disapproval" of recovery plans, he claimed.

Maggard--- after first telling the panel that he could not recall when he first learned of the compressor---acknowledged being told about it by

Combs after the first explosion. Kerem asked him if he felt it posed "any special danger." Attorney (Bert) Combs would not let Maggard answer.

(Blue Diamond had hired the former Kentucky Governor as their legal counsel after the mine explosions. Comb's law firm had recently completed their successful defense of Finley Coal Company, the operator of the mine in Leslie County, Kentucky which had blown up with the loss of 38 coal miners in 1970.)

Repeatedly, Combs chided the panel:

" You're trying to do something not within the scope of this hearing... I object to your going over and over the same thing."

In the face of Comb's objections, Karem occasionally attempted to persist with his questions: other panel members, including Barrett, generally backed off. Key areas of conflicting testimony were left unresolved, at least temporarily, as a result.

Combs also cut off questioning of mine Superintendent Freddie Maggard concerning fire boss runs made in the explosion area. At one point, Maggard had apparently begun to contradict testimony by company officials delivered in early April that the explosion area was fire bossed infrequently since it was "temporarily idle." Maggard said that daily fire bossing of the area was "routine," but on Combs' advice refused to clarify the statement.

On several occasions miners' testimony contradicted that of the company officials, particularly when it concerned ventilation of the mine.

One MESA official, who wished to remain anonymous, said when the hearings were originally scheduled that he didn't think the sessions would be significantly conclusive since company officials could not be forced legally to reveal crucial information.

Gordon Bonnyman, President and Chairman of the Board of Blue Diamond Coal Company, refused for example, to reveal his corporation's profit figures. He testified he didn't know what percentage of these profits went toward mine safety programs nor what part went to paying penalties for violations of federal health and safety regulations--- information that would have shed light on the corporation's commitment to safety and the effectiveness of MESA's penalty program.

Both the coal company and MESA promised during the last days of the hearing to make changes that might avert similar disasters in the future. Bonnyman said that changes he was considering implementing included:

----Placing only permissible equipment in mines like Scotia which liberate highly combustible methane. Permissible equipment does not produce open sparks or flames.

----Placing more emphasis on the training of mine supervisory personnel and on the training of new miners before they are sent underground. David McKnight, President of the Scotia Employees Association, entered into the hearing record a list of 85 miners who had not been instructed in the use of a self-rescuer before going underground at Scotia. Reports on the company's training records indicated that the training of supervisors at the Scotia mine did not meet MESA requirements.

----Devising a "better method of control and processing to the violations and citations" issued at the company's mines.. Bonnyman said there is no regular analysis of safety violations.

----Implementing the training of mine rescue teams.

 MESA Administrator Barrett promised to:

----revamp the MESA penalty program in order to increase fines for violations. During an 18 month period in 1974 and 1975, the Scotia Company paid an average of $139.45 for each ventilation violation found at its Scotia mine.

Garland Lewis, until recently (in 1976) chairman of the SEA's mine committee, called MESA's fines "pitiful" and said they didn't amount to "a bucket of coal for the company." Lewis also described the safety program at Scotia as "lacking" and "far behind."

----have MESA inspectors make closer checks on fire bosses. Testimony in early April (1976) revealed that the explosion area had not been fire bossed the day before the disaster, although company records showed it had been.

----to make more frequent "blitz" inspections, which would entail groups of inspectors being sent into mines to check ventilation in all working sections at once. This would prevent operators from shifting air from one section to another in order to fool a lone inspector about ventilation adequacy. Several miners have claimed that shunting air was a common practice at the Scotia mine.

Hershal Potter, chief of MESA's safety division, said he was working on plans to:

----organize a "mine profile" system that would alert MESA to mines with high violations frequency rates, such as Scotia.

----train inspectors in mine rescue techniques and in the examinations of gassy mines.

----identify which violations most frequently result in serious accidents or deaths.

The hearings left unresolved the question of how much the company was involved in the mine recovery operations that led up to the second explosion.

Testimony at the hearings also indicated that the Blue Diamond officials responsible for drawing up ventilation and safety plans at the Scotia mine did not routinely check to see if those plans were accurately implemented.

Bill Foutch, Blue Diamond safety engineer for the Leatherwood and Scotia mines, testified his responsibilities at the Scotia mine were "to gather information and formulate plans." He said he didn't check to see if the plans were met or if the information given to him by company officials was always accurate.

Although he is responsible for notifying MESA of the development of new sections in the Scotia mine. Foutch said he didn't report the development of the 2 Left Section and the concurrent removal of a crucial stopping wall used to channel air because the mine management didn't give him the information.

In other testimony, District manager Phillips said that in investigating a three-hour shutdown of a fan at Scotia's Upper Taggart Mine, MESA inspectors found that the fan charts were missing a two-week period surrounding the day the alleged incident occurred. This incident caused one miner to decide to quit his job at Scotia.

"The ventilation a lot of times would be really poor," said Daniel Sturgill (at the hearings). "I'd tell the old lady when I'd go to work---maybe I'll come back, maybe I won't." His comments collaborated other statements made in interviews by several other miners that they expected a methane explosion in the Scotia mine.

"No sir it wasn't" was the response of continuous miner operator Carlos Smith when asked by Barrett if the ventilation on his section was adequate. Smith who testified during the first five days of the hearing held in Whitesburg held in April, 1976, worked the 2 Left Section off 2 Southeast Mains. (The same 2 Left that was involved in the explosions.)

In the same hearings miner James Miles, an electrician, testified that a spark from his welding torch ignited methane coming from a crack in the mine floor near the explosion site about a month before the disaster. Miles said he stamped out the small blaze, filled the crack with rock dust and then put up a sign reading, "Danger Methane."

Miles said he reported the incident to Assistant Mine Foreman Bruce Jones. Foreman Jones testified in early April that he didn't notify his superiors or MESA of the ignition because he didn't think it was serious. However, Rick Keene, a MESA ventilation expert who oversees the ventilation plan at the Scotia mine, testified that he would have considered requiring more air in the straights upon report of the ignition.

MESA officials who supervised the Scotia operations maintained that the design of the ventilation system for the Scotia Mine was adequate. Dow Phillips, MESA District Manager, for the Pikeville District, acknowledged that he has some reservations about its functioning. When an airshaft---recommended by MESA to increase ventilation---was completed last year, Phillips testified he could "not tell from air measurements where the shaft cut through."

Phillips theorized at last week's hearing (early April, 1976) that the airflow was not increased by the new shaft because a belt on the mine's main fan was slipping, but emphasized this was his "opinion, not proven fact."

The district manager also said he wasn't certain that the ventilation through a worked-out section near 2 Southeast Mains was adequate to prevent a possible methane build-up. "I do not consider it (the ventilation system of leftover gob in the worked-out section) a good one: it may be adequate," he said. "You cannot be assured where that air is going through that gob. It may be seeping one path down there."

Testimony also brought out two instances of disruption of the ventilation system on 2 Southeast Mains:

The night before the first explosion, curtains were hung across entries carrying fresh air up the straights, miner Gary Smith testified. Smith said he was ordered to hang the curtains by his section foreman in order to shunt extra air into the 2 Left Section.

The curtains were pulled down at the end of the shift, miners said, but while they were up they prevented air from clearing constantly accumulating methane from the straights.

A MESA inspector and several miners testified that a ventilation curtain on the track entry leading into 2 Left was not kept in place. Without this curtain, air again would be short-circuited into 2 Left from the straights where the blasts occurred.

Miner James Miles told the panel last week that he had been into 2 Left three times during the week before the disaster and had never seen the curtain up. James Powell, another miner, stated he had been on the section the night before the first explosion and "never went under a curtain on the track itself."

Despite the testimony by several Scotia miners, company officials generally held in their testimony that the crucial curtain was in place.

According to one miner who was interviewed by a local newspaper and who worked on the 2 Left Section, a stopping critical to the ventilation of 2 Southeast Mains was removed in early February, 1976,(about the same time the 2 left section was started.) However, the remover stopping was shown as still being in place in Scotia's ventilation map.

The miner, who wished to remain anonymous, said when crews were laying track into 2 Left about a month before the (first) explosion, "they had to knock out that stopping, but no curtains were put up in place of it."

With the stopping out and when no curtain was up, some of the fresh air that should have gone into 2 Southeast Mains to clear the liberated methane out was either going straight down the return or seeping into the 2 Left Section.

MESA Chief Engineer Keene commented that the March 1,1976 mine map submitted to MESA showed the stopping to be still in place where a track line extended into the 2 Left Section. Keene also noted that he was meeting with Jack Collins, the Whitesburg MESA field office ventilation expert, and Larry Ison, a Scotia official, to "talk over discrepancies in the ventilation plan on the morning of March 9, the day of the first explosion.

Keene also said that the track line into 2 Left wasn't shown on Scotia's mine map, even though MESA's safety regulations "require track lines, stoppings, all curtains and anything else pertaining to ventilation to be shown on the mine map. Therefore, when the mine map was submitted by Scotia for approval Keene said he would have had no idea that the track had been extended into 2 Left or that the required stopping had been removed.

In the investigation to determine the cause of the explosions of March 9, and 11, 1976, public hearings were held before a panel appointed by the United States Secretary of the Interior in the Fiscal Courtroom, Letcher County Courthouse, Main Street, Whitesburg, Kentucky, at 9:00a.m., on April 5-30, 1976, before Robert E. Barrett, Chairman.
Appearances on behalf of the Mining Enforcement and Safety Administration (MESA): I. Avrum Fingeret, Esq. Assistant Solicitor, Court Litigation, U.S.Dept. of the Interior; on behalf of the Scotia Coal Company:

Bert T. Combs Esq. and Robert Cusick, Jr., Esq., Tarrant, Combs & Bullitt, Maxwell Barret, Esq. and Richard Ward, Esq., Craft, Barret, Haynes,and Ward.

Below is a list of the witnesses who appeared before the panel and the days on which they appeared:

April 5, 1976
1. Arvil Cornett; third shift mine foreman
2. J.P. Feltner; construction foreman
3. Cecil Davis; federal inspector
4. Harold Sexton; repairman
5. Gary W. Smith; Scotia miner
6. Carlos Smith; continuous miner operator
7. Merle Rhodes; second shift assistant mine foreman
8. James H. Maggard; maintenance foreman
9. Bruce Jones; assistant mine foreman
    April 6, 1976- Bruce Jones; continued testimony
10. James Bentley assistant mine foreman-ventilation
11. Rick Keene; MESA engineer
12. Pat Pate; shuttle car operator
13. Roger McKnight; Scotia miner
14. Robert Holcomb;
15. Richard Combs; general mine foreman
    April 7, 1976- Richard Combs; continued testimony
16. Jack Brown; belt man
17. Freddie Maggard; Scotia Superintendent
18. Charles Kirk; Scotia safety inspector
19. Hubert Payne; Captain, U.S. Steel Mine Rescue Team
20. James Vicini; map man, U.S. Steel M.R.T.
21. Albert Wagers; MESA chief mine inspector
22. John F. Collins; Captain and safety dir. National Mines Rescue Team
23. J.C. Spencer; map man and asst. safety dir.   "   "   "   "
24. Burley Wright; Team Captain National Mines-Wayland
25. Jack Quillen;   map man   "   "   "
26. Warnie Flint; National Mines rescue team
27. Jerry Fritz; team Captain, Westmoreland Mine Rescue team

28. Lewis Henager; team trainer, Westmoreland Coal Co. M.R.T.
29. Bill Person; team Captain, Westmoreland Mine Res. Team.
    April 8, 1976
30. Jasper K. Cornet; Scotia vice-president for operations
31. Harvey Creech; staff foreman
32. David McKnight; president, Scotia Employees Association
33. Monroe West; MESA Sub-district Manger, District 5
34. William Clemons; MESA Sub-district manager, District 6
    April 9, 1976
35. Cecil Lester;
36. Ben Taylor; MESA coal mine inspector supervisor
37. Rick Parker; repairman (survivor of second explosion)
38. Ernest L. Collins; repairman (survivor of second explosion)
39. L. Thomas Galloway;
40. Robert E. Barrett; MESA Administrator
41. Harreld Kirkpatrick; Commissioner, Kentucky Department of Mines and Minerals
    April 27, 1976
42. Richard Combs; general mine foreman
43. Freddie Maggard; Scotia Superintendent
44. Gerald (Jerry) Davis;
45. Herchel Lough; MESA mine inspector
46. William Dupree;
47. Stephen Miles; Scotia miner
48. Sam Johnson; Asst. Commissioner, Kentucky Department of Mines and Minerals
49. Everett Bartlett; Kentucky State mine inspector
    April 28, 1976
50. Dow Phillips; MESA manager District 6
51. William Clemmons; MESA manager District 5
52. Henry R. Simpson; chief repairman
53. James Arnold; MESA electrical inspector
54. James Miles; repairman
55. James Powell; committeeman, Scotia Employees Association
56. Herbert G. Lewis;
    April 29, 1976
57. David McKnight; President, Scotia Employees Association
58. Gordon Bonnyman; chairman of the board, Blue Diamond Coal Company, Knoxville, Tennessee

59. Daniel Sturgill;
60. William Foutch;
61. Arnold Miller; U.M.W.A. president
62. Dow Phillips; MESA manager District 6
     April 30, 1976
63. Ben Taylor; MESA coal mine inspector supervisor
64. Herman Lucas; MESA coal mine inspector
65. Reed Kiser; MESA coal mine inspector
66. Jean Gilbert;
67. Geraldine McKnight;
68. Jennifer Boggs;
69. Hershell Potter; MESA coal mine inspector
     April 6, 1976
70. Kester Halcomb; section foreman

During these hearings held in Whitesburg, MESA manager William Clemons defended the decision he had made to a sent work crew underground to the area of the first explosion despite the fact that it had not been fire bossed or explored. He also stated for the first time that MESA Assistant Administrator Jack Crawford had, during a telephone conversation, concurred with the basics of the plan to send in work/repair crews.

Clemons only had a few hours sleep during the two-day period that he directed recovery operations at Scotia, but he stated that he was "mentally alert and physically capable. I was tired, but not too tired to think clearly,"

MESA inspector Jim Hackworth (whose brother John had been killed in the second explosion on March 11) told the panel that he had experienced problems enforcing the (1969 Mine health and Safety) Act because there were no means to severely penalize an operator for health and safety violations. Referring to the relatively small fines exacted for violations, Hackworth said that operators "just pass this penalty on to the consumer of this product."

Kentucky Representative Carl D. Perkins directed criticism towards Hackworth and several other MESA employees that the Scotia Mine should have been shut down because of its history of violations. "They ought to have had that mine closed long ago," he said.

Hackworth vehemently replied, "You can't make this mine stay down. If a violation is corrected an operator cannot be kept under a closure order."

Pointing out that many closure orders issued because of imminent danger are not upheld when appealed by the mine operator, Hackworth replied, "I think this is why inspectors are reluctant to issue closure orders." Perkins then said, "That's what brought on these explosions...these fast fixes." "You know the act, Mr. Perkins, replied Hackworth. Why are we sitting here arguing about this? Let's quit playing politics and do something for health and safety in the coal mine."

Some relatives of the victims of the explosions who were in the audience applauded when this exchange took place. Perkins glanced at his watch, gathered his papers and said he had to leave. It was then 4:00 p.m. and three other panel members had already left. Perkins had declared in his opening statement that "I would be willing to stay here until midnight and later if that were necessary or helpful."

Mrs. Geraldine McKnight, widow of miner Roy McKnight, read from a prepared statement on the other miner widows' behalf, "The buck has been passed around. Gentlemen, who is going to step up and say, the buck stops here? Everybody has been busy with the making of laws. Who has cared enough to enforce them?"After pointing out to Rep. Tim Lee Carter (member of the investigating panel) on a map of the Scotia mine the locations of bodies following the first explosion, "I don't think this panel is as knowledgeable in the coal mines as they could be."

She also defended Clemons and Barrett, whom she praised for being "a coal miner." She continued, "We hope this committee will be careful so that in all the department 'shuffling around' the coal miner himself will not be lost."

Iva Stidham, sister of miner Dennis Boggs, who was killed in the first explosion, concluded that, "Mr. Perkins and most of the others (members of the panel) are just up there politicking."

As Perkins was leaving the Whitesburg courtroom, he told reporters that MESA Administrator Barrett was not to blame for the disaster since he has only held the administrator's position since last winter. "But, he concluded, this (hearing) closes beyond any doubt the fact that local inspections have not been good. We're placing a lot of the blame on MESA."

As the door closed behind Rep. Perkins, MESA Inspector Hackworth replied, "They (the congressmen) just didn't want to listen."

CHAPTER FIFTEEN

Grieving for the Miners

When the 15 deceased miners were brought out of the Scotia #1 Mine, the hearses were ready to pick up the miners' bodies and transport them to the various area funeral homes. The bodies were transported to the following funeral homes:

David Gibbs, Virgil Coots, Gail Sparkman, Kenny Turner, Denver Widner, Tri-City Funeral Home, Cumberland, Kentucky.

Roy McKnight, Larry McKnight, Everett Scottie Combs, Willie Turner, Parker Funeral Home, Cumberland, Kentucky.

Jimmy Sturgill, Colonial Chapel, Harlan, Kentucky.

Tom Scott, Earl Galloway, Blair Funeral Home, Whitesburg, Kentucky.

Lawrence Peavy, Johnson, Benham, Kentucky.

Robert Griffith, Banks Funeral Home, Neon, Kentucky.

Dennis Boggs, Baker Funeral Home, Pound, Virginia.

On Friday, March 14, 1976, the last of the 15 victims of the March 9 Scotia Mine explosion were laid to rest. Eleven victims of the March 11 explosion were now sealed inside the Scotia #1 Mine and their recovery would have to wait until the mine was deemed safe enough to enter again.

The "blue ribbon" panel that the U.S. Department of the Interior set up to investigate the disaster included no rank-and file Scotia coal miners and no ventilation experts. The mission of the panel was to investigate all the circumstances related to the mining disasters of March 9 and 11, 1976, at Scotia.

The panel is listed in a previous chapter but is worth repeating here:
Robert Barrett, MESA Administrator, panel chairman;
Thomas Mascolino, Assistant Solicitor, U.S. Department of Interior;
Fred Karem, Deputy Undersecretary of the U.S. Department of Interior;
Harrold Kirkpatrick, Commissioner of the Kentucky Department of Mines and Minerals;
George Eadie, professor of General Engineering, University of Illinois;
George McPhail, Senior Mine Rescue Officer, Province of Ontario, Canada.

One point of contention was raised about the panel because Barrett and Kirkpatrick were directly involved in the events which occurred at the Scotia Mine following the first explosion. The staff report of the Committee on Education and Labor had this to say: "while there is nothing in the record to suggest that either man conducted himself in a manner detrimental to the investigation, the fact remains that both, in varying degrees, participated in the decisions that were made following the first explosion."

The second point, as pointed out by the staff report, was the absence from the MESA panel of any miner representatives. Even though, according to the report, the Scotia mine was, in effect, a non-union mine, the miners who work at the Scotia mine have a direct and continuing interest in the twin disasters. It seems to us (the staff) that a miner representative, at the very least, would have added to the panel's credibility.

Author's note; in one respect the staff report was mistaken in calling Scotia a non-union mine. It's true that the Scotia Employees Association was a non-United Mine Workers of America (UMWA) union, but even as an independent union, they enjoyed all the rights and privileges that any union organization had under the U.S. Department of Labor. In the several personnel issues, labor disputes, and other minor and major work disputes that occurred over the years, I personally felt that the company always negotiated in good faith. In saying this, I realize that others who were employed with Scotia might have a different opinion though.

The method of recovery of the miners' bodies, which still remained in the mine after the explosion of March 11, became a major issue between MESA, the blue ribbon investigating panel, the Scotia Company Officials, the victims' families, and the Scotia Employees Union.

MESA Administrator Barrett assured the families of the victims that the recovery would proceed as quickly as possible after the re-opening of the mine. Barrett was reported to have at first stated that the recovery would proceed through the ventilation shaft which enters the mine about 4,000 or so feet from where the bodies were located. It was estimated that such a route would enable the bodies to be recovered in about a week.

However, Barrett reversed himself concerning the recovery route and approved a Scotia Company plan that would approach the recovery of the bodies through the main shaft. Under this plan the recovery was projected to take a minimum of 60 days. Mine flooding and other complications would later extend the time needed for recovery to months instead of days, as we shall see.

David McKnight, the Scotia Employees Association President, disagreed with the plan to re-open Scotia through the drift mouth and threatened to use his veto power as the representative of the Scotia miners to block the proposed plan. The plan was considered as too slow and as taking too long when compared to the alternative method of using the air shaft at Frank's Creek to enter the mine. The air shaft was three miles or more nearer to the area where the bodies were located than was the route using the bathhouse portal at the main Scotia complex. In the end, all parties acquiesced in using the longer route as proposed by the Company, as that route was considered the safer route with all things considered.

At 2:10 p.m. March 19, 1976, the Scotia #1 mine was officially sealed with no tentative plans of when the mine would be opened to attempt to recover the eleven miners who were killed in the second explosion. That decision would have to wait until after the hearings into the explosions had been completed and until conditions in the mine were such as to make if reasonably safe to re-open the mine. That safe point would not be reached until the mine's methane content had reached peak volatility. That is, when the mine atmosphere reached the point where there was too much methane and too little oxygen to explode.

In the interim, Scotia would begin the training of its own Mine Rescue Teams. A few weeks after the sealing of the mine, the call went out for volunteers from the Scotia miners' ranks to fill the positions of the three mine rescue teams which had been authorized by Company officials. At the same time, two mine rescue teams were being organized at Blue Diamond's Leatherwood Mine near Hazard, Kentucky.

During the hearings and investigations held after the explosions Blue Diamond and Scotia Officials came under heavy criticism for not having adequate safety training and mine rescue teams. The events of march, 1976, convinced those officials that the time for procrastination was over and that they must not be caught off guard should another tragedy happen at their mines.

It became a common occurrence while the mine was still closed to encounter a group of miners walking the roads of Scotia property while under oxygen with their breathing apparatuses (Dragers) strapped on their backs. They were obviously practicing to be ready for when the officials gave the go-ahead to re-open the Scotia mine to recover the bodies. They took their training seriously because they knew that they would more than likely be called on to be "the point of the spear" when the time came to re-enter the mine.

MESA objected to one point in the forming of the Scotia rescue teams because one team had as their Captain Charles Kirk. Kirk was the Scotia Safety Director who the April, 1976 hearings had revealed had never worked inside an underground coal mine. His seven years at Scotia had all been spent as safety director.

Kirk had admitted his limited knowledge of both the lay-out of the mine and the ventilation plan in use. He was also criticized for the safety program's failure to train Scotia miners in even the most fundamental safety measures.

MESA attempted to have Kirk removed from the list of men participating in the recovery operations, but they were unable to veto his participation. MESA's veto attempt was because of his absence of inside mining experience and mining knowledge as revealed in his testimony given in the Department of Interior hearings into the Scotia disasters.

On Monday, March 17, 1976, two memorial services for the 26 miners was held at Cumberland, Kentucky. Cumberland businesses closed for four hours during the memorial and miners at Lynch remained off their jobs for a full day as a memorial to the 26 men.

Five days later, on March 21, another memorial service was held at the Whitesburg, Kentucky First Baptist church, with the pastor of the Lynch Church of God and Rev. Bill Mackey, of the Whitesburg First Baptist Church delivering sermons to the friends and relatives and in tribute to the 26 deceased miners. [*]

---

[*] *The Mountain Eagle*, Whitesburg, Ky. March 25, 1976.

One sad incident that was related to the two explosions was the death of a Scotia miner by suicide on March 16, 1976. The miner shot himself after having difficulty coming to terms with losing so many co-workers in the short space of two days. His widow said that he had not been able to get "straightened out" since the first explosion. She said her husband had worked with the 15 who died in the explosion and was a friend of theirs. The miner had been scheduled to go on shift at midnight March 11, half an hour after the second explosion, and had been "upset and depressed" since then, his wife said. He had also been hearing the voices of the dead miners.[+]

On the same day of the second explosion at Scotia, March 11 1976, a fatal auto accident claimed the life of Hassel Foutch, a 54 year old Harlan County man, who was rushing to the Scotia mine where his son-in- law, Glenn Barker, was one of the men involved in the explosion. Barker's wife and other family members were in the car and sustained minor injuries in the accident.[±]

March 14, 1976

(Whitesburg, Ky.) "I don't believe I'd like to work anywhere BUT in a mine," Eddie Nickels said. "It's different from working on the outside in a way that you can't explain." Nickels, 28, voiced an idea that has been repeated frequently by Letcher County coal miners during this week, even while they waited for word from crews working to reach the bodies of 26 men killed in the Scotia mine at Oven Fork. (sic) But his mother, Mrs. Nell Nickels, said she won't feel comfortable until Nickels and his brother Jimmy Don, and her two sons-in-law leave the mines for good. And she spoke for the Oven Fork (sic) widows, and her daughters and her sons' wives, and for many others in this county where no one is unaffected by a mine disaster. As Nickels spoke at his sister Kathy's drive-in restaurant here at Whitesburg one of his brothers-in-law was in the Scotia mine helping with rescue efforts for 11 men trapped Thursday night by a second explosion there. At Neon, across Tunnel Hill from the restaurant, American Legionnaires were preparing for the military burial of Robert Griffith, one of 15 men killed in a blast at the mine Tuesday. Nickels himself had arrived for work at Oven Fork shortly after the first blast. His mother and sisters were tense and worried, and even the res-

---

[+] ibid
[±] *Letcher County Community Press* March 18,1976

taurant's customers spoke in hushed tones and showed the effects of the tragedy on this and nearby Harlan County. Nickels sympathized and was sorry and concerned that the two explosions had occurred. But he said when he thought about it, it just didn't affect his willingness to go back to his job at the mine whenever it reopened. "To me, it's just like any other job. You can get killed doing anything," he said. But he said mining coal is "not like any other job" in other respects in a way you can't explain. I was in the service, he said. It's kind of like in the service. You've got comradeship there." His mother, reflecting a nagging fear of the mines that seems common among many who don't go in them, said she wishes her two miner sons would get "safe" jobs such as that held by a third son, Philip. Philip, 25, is a state trooper. "I suppose his job is dangerous too, but I just don't worry about him as much as I do them," she said. Information provided yesterday by a life insurance agent indicated one insurance company thinks her deepest worry may be misdirected, and a second thinks it is out of proportion. The insurance companies figure the odds on death accidental and otherwise as a means of deciding what they should charge the insured. The Insurance Co. of North America schedule shows that a police officer such as Philip Nickels must pay that company twice as much as most persons, while an underground coal miner pays only 1.5 times as much. The Kansas City Insurance Co. figures the danger about even. It charges twice the price charged most persons for both miners and policemen. And Metropolitan Life considers the most dangerous policeman's job as somewhat less dangerous than the safest underground miner's job twice normal, as compared to 2.5 times normal. Metropolitan Life, in fact, considers the most dangerous job in mining that of an explosives handler as equal to the most dangerous jobs whose holders can get Metropolitan life insurance. It ranks with explosive handlers in tunnel and shaft construction, with power line workers and with loggers. The company charges all of those occupations four times the normal rate for the accidental death benefit. But the people here don't base their fear of the mines on statistics. They base it on such sights as the two funeral processions that passed in opposite directions within three minutes on Main Street in Cumberland yesterday, and on such sounds as the sobs of Robert Griffith's wife as friends urged her away from his grave site. Mrs. Nickels said her father died in a mine accident. Her husband, Ed, worked in the mines for 22 years, and her brothers also worked there. In short, she, like many of the women here, has not been free of that nagging fear since she was old enough to know *what death is." "And unless you've had somebody in there, she said, you just don't know what it's like."*[*]

About a week after the second explosion, Scotia officials and the Scotia Employees Association called a special meeting with the miners employed in all the Scotia mines. Since Scotia Mine#1 was now sealed until conditions were right to ventilate the mine and recover the bodies of the entombed miners, the miners would either have to be assigned to one of the other two mines on the property or suffer a layoff, or both. I assumed they were calling us together for a lay-off and I was partially right.

All 450 or so of the miners met at the upper Scotia parking lot on a cold day that required a warm coat instead of a jacket. A Scotia Company Official and one or two union officials stood in the back of a pickup truck and explained that the Company had no choice but to move some miners around and others would have to be lain off for an unspecified time. It all depended on when the Bottom Mine could be re-opened and recovered.

Some complaining and groaning was expressed with those words, but I'm sure the other miners were like me and had expected that a lay-off would have to be in order, at least for a period of time. Hardly any miner there wanted to have to change jobs or go to a different mine to keep his job, but most accepted the decision with grace and understanding, although there was, as always, some complaining and yawing back and forth.

When the explosions happened, I was still working at New Tygart, New Taggart, or Upper Taggart, as I and others called the newest mine. Either name was correct and was familiar to Scotia miners, but the correct name was Upper Taggart. The other working mines at Scotia was the "B" Seam mine, and the Old Taggart, Old Tygart, or Middle Taggart, the last mentioned of which was the correct name for the C Seam mine.

The miners that were to be laid off were determined under Article 11 and Section 3 of the contract signed between Scotia and The Scotia Employees Association members on July 14, 1973, and extending through July 14, 1976. Section 3 read thus:

In all cases where the working force is to be reduced, employees in each job classification at the mines with the least total service at the mines shall be laid off first; however, in the event any employee who has more

---

[*] *Louisville Courier Journal* interview with author, March, 14, 1976

seniority is to be cut off and put on panel, mine management shall offer such employee a job in another classification for which he is qualified, and shall, if accepted by such employee, cut off the man having the least seniority in this classification.

By contract, miners would be laid off by seniority in classification; meaning the youngest person in a job would be laid off first. I was a classified motorman at Upper Taggart, along with Wayne Morgan, who was also a second shift motorman like me. Even though I was younger than some of the men in seniority with the company, I was older than some in my motorman classification, so I was able to keep my job as it was before the explosion. Morgan and I continued in our job at Upper Taggart on the second shift.

Our mine foreman remained as before the explosions, Bruce Jones, who I always liked and respected as a boss.

The Company resumed the production of coal on March 22 1976, at the Middle and Upper Taggart mines with a lot of changes in personnel. Some of the miners were men who had worked in Scotia's Imboden Seam with its 6 ft. or better height came to a mine with the height of the coal averaging around 50 inches. It would take some time for them to adjust to working in lower coal. Most of the transferred Scotia Imboden Seam miners that I talked to expressed to me that they couldn't wait until the bottom mine was re-opened so they could get back to "God's Country," as they put it. Even with all that had transpired before and after the explosions, they still preferred to work where they could stand up without bending over.

Our work at the Upper (New)Taggart Mine soon got back in order after the long idle period between March 9 and March 22nd. A lot of rock dusting and supply hauling kept Morgan and myself busy every shift, and we worked in a rush all the time. After pulling the mantrips each evening, we loaded and hauled supplies to the sections, then went back outside with our 6 and 5 ton motors to hook up to the track rock duster. Each of the large steel "bubbles" on the duster held around one ton each. After loading the dust by hand, one 40lb bag at a time, we hitched a motor to each end of the duster and off we went. We then stopped our motors on the track somewhere in the mine and stretched the 3 in. diameter hose to one of the beltlines and sprayed until it was white with coal-dust suppressing, beautiful rock dust.

It may have been a beautiful sight when it was spread over all the coal dust but handling it and breathing it was not a lot of fun. Even though we usually (I always did) wore dust masks while spreading the dust, the masks were nearly impossible to get to a point in tightening where they would be airtight. Breathing with one worn on the face was a trial, as one had to struggle to get a breath of air through the filter, and the feeling of smothering while wearing one was difficult to suppress for the wearer. One might imagine the difficulty of breathing through the filter after rock dust had completely covered the filter and has seeped through every minor loose point of the mask. The struggle to drag 100ft of more of 3 in hose full of rock dust while struggling for breath makes for a trying time for the hose-dragger. There's a reason every coal miner has to take a physical before his employment. The weak hearts and backs wouldn't or couldn't last long in a coal mine.

Having a boss like Bruce Jones made life just a little easier for Morgan and myself at times. He didn't mind "getting dirty" and joining us when the rock duster had to be loaded. He would take his turn just like the union miners of tearing open the bags of rock dust and pouring the dust into the bubbles of the track duster. That was the dirty job avoided by most when they could. After filling one of the bubbles up, your arms were aching and you were completely covered in white dust, eyes, mouth, hair and all. The man doing that job never failed to be laughed at and mocked about his appearance after his turn at loading the bubble.

Even after all that had occurred with the two recent explosions at Scotia, the miners of New Taggart were still capable of having a little fun at the expense of one of their co-workers. Once, when the men reached the outside of the mine after the end of their second shift, one of them came into the office where I was talking to my motorman buddy Morgan, and said his transmission had gone out of his truck and he needed to call a ride. Some of the men who had just come outside offered to take a look at his truck with him to see if they could help in any way.

About half a dozen of them, myself, and my motorman buddy, walked across the walkway spanning the beltline and watched as the truck owner started his truck and put it in gear, only to have it again refuse to move no matter how much gas he gave it. He had his engine roaring, trying his best to get it to move, with the exhaust blowing out puffs of black smoke. What was curious about the situation was that his rear tires were spinning furiously while he was giving it gas. I wondered how that could be, while I was watching it. One of the men shouted for him to "let off the gas before you blow your engine!" The miner climbed out of the truck cab, cursing every breath about how sorry a truck he had. One of the miners stooped down and shined his caplight under the rear of the truck and burst out laughing. Someone (several men) had picked his truck up at the rear and had placed a concrete block under his differential so that it raised the rear tires just far enough off the ground that you couldn't tell it without looking under the truck.

After five minutes or so of cursing and threatening to kick the rear ends of those who had done him that way, he finally settled down and drove down the hill towards the bathhouse. It gave all of us a little relief from the tension we had been under since the explosions. The miner who had been tricked (and who shall go unnamed) took a lot of kidding from his co-workers after that incident. No doubt, he made it a habit to check under his truck before trying to leave the parking lot after that embarrassing incident.

With the Scotia #1 Mine now being shutdown, the federal and state inspectors had nowhere else to go at Scotia but to the remaining 3 Scotia coal producing sections, B Seam, Middle and Upper Taggart. They made good use of their time, and understandably so, because past health and safety practices had put Scotia and their workers in somewhat of a bad light.

In the first two weeks after returning to work in the 3 upper coal producing seams federal inspectors alone cited Scotia for 67 violations. Six of the violations resulted in closure orders when the violations failed to be corrected on certain pieces of machinery or entire mine sections.

Of the six closure orders, two concerned improper grounding of electrical equipment, three were placed on pieces of equipment, and the final order closed a mine section because of failure to follow the roof control plan.

During this time period, federal inspectors often found the sections they were going to inspect were shut down and not producing coal. On two of the days he inspected the Scotia mines, Reed Kiser reported that "coal was not produced while I was on section."

The inspectors did report that Scotia now seems to be emphasizing safety. Safety Director Charles Kirk had once even called the crew of one working section and held a safety meeting and informed the crew that if they could not mine coal safe, to "pack their buckets and go to the office."

The last week in March 1976, Scotia sent $5,000 checks to the 26 families of the men killed in the explosions, as a death benefit. This was in keeping with an agreement reached between the Company and the Scotia Employees Association.

"Young miner quits Scotia company for safety," read the headline of a story in the Whitesburg, Kentucky, _Mountain Eagle_ on March 18, 1976. There was probably more than one miner who decided to call it quits after the explosions, but this is one miner's story:

"I went to work there for the money. That's all. They paid real good, and they had that bonus for perfect attendance." For Danny Mullins, perfect attendance at the Scotia mine ended abruptly on March 9. Within minutes after the news of the explosion at the mine, he was on the phone, looking for another job.

Almost any job, at almost any pay. "They say money isn't everything, and buddy, that's the truth," Danny Mullins says. "I'm going back there just one more time, to pick up my clothes at the bathhouse."

Danny Mullins isn't his real name. He doesn't want his real name used. "I'd like to get a job at Jenkins," he says. "They won't hire me if they read about me bad-mouthing Scotia. It's the blacklist. My uncle couldn't get a job for years after they got him on the blacklist trying to organize Scotia some years back. It's not changed. They know who you are."

He is 19, rides a motorcycle, lives in a small pin-neat frame house set back from a side street in Whitesburg, and would like to go to college. His wife attends Hazard Community College now, hopes to go on to Union College and then to find a job to pay for Danny's education.

He went to work for Scotia 18 months ago."There's things about the mine I never liked. The air---it gets so hot I'm in a sweat after one cable splice. Some of the equipment's twice as old as me. But I never worked any other mine, can't really make any comparisons."

He admits he didn't worry much about safety protection until the disaster. Now he realizes he wore his self-rescuer into the mine more than 360 times without ever knowing how to use it if he had to. Sometimes, he says, his section worked a whole shift without supervision. "I don't know where the foreman was , or even if he was in the mines," he says. "Nobody seemed to care as long as we got paid.

Even though Danny Mullins slotted in a low- pay classification at Scotia, his gross earnings for a two-week period would average nearly $600; he would take home about $445. He figured he would be running a continuous miner in a few months, with his pay at $62 a day, nearly $5 a day more than the $57.20 top rate for a UMWA continuous miner operator at Lynch, the U.S. Steel mine where he wants to work.

Then why make the switch? I want the protection," he says. On the coffee table in front of him are copies of a United Mine Workers contract and a Scotia Employees Association contract. He has marked the comparison that interest him.

In the UMWA contract, which covers 150,000 soft-coal miners in 20 states, safety provisions are spelled out in the largest single section of the contract, covering nearly 15 pages. He points out that a UMWA Safety Committee can close a section or a whole mine on its own authority in situations of immediate danger, and the individual miner's right to refuse unsafe work is spelled out in detail. Elsewhere, the contract requires manning by two men on continuous miners and roof-bolters, a provision negotiated in 1974 to help down on the most frequent cause of fatal accidents.

In UMWA mines, new miners without previous experience can't work on face equipment or high-voltage electricity during their first 90 days in the mine, and "shall always work in sight and sound of another employee" during that period. A detailed section on training, also negotiated in 1974, spells out guidelines for new miners: training in the use of escape ways and emergency evacuation, instruction in the use of mine maps, explanations of roof control, ventilation, rock dusting, first aid, and methane detection.

By comparison, there is only a single paragraph in the Scotia contract on safety. It gives the Safety Committee the same power to close a section as in the UMWA contract, but forbids the committee from making any inspections without company permission, and provides for committeemen to be discharged if they act "arbitrarily and capriciously"---terms left open to interpretation by the company.

Other UMWA contract provisions protect the seniority rights of veteran miners and establish a new pension plan providing increasing credit for long years of service. Under this plan, a UMWA miner retiring this year at age 62 with 40 years of service will receive $510 a month. Scotia miners upon retirement receive a flat credit of $5 a month multiplied by years of service, so a man with 40 years of service would receive $200 a month.

UMWA miners now receiving a cost-of-living allowance providing scheduled adjustments based on inflation increases. The allowance currently pays $2.00 a day on top of the basic wage, thus cutting in half the pay gap between UMWA miners and Scotia Employees Association members.

"This is the part that made me think," Mullins says, turning to the section of the UMWA contract that deals with death benefits. If a UMWA miner is killed in a mine accident, his widow receives a standard death benefit of $7.000 to $10,000 (depending on the number of children) plus an additional $10,000 to help absorb the shock of the sudden loss of income, and finally a continuing payment of $100 a month until her death or remarriage---all provisions negotiated in1974. The Scotia agreement provides no death benefits at all, although a miner who wants life insurance can arrange to have the premiums deducted from his paycheck.

If you're going to work in the mines you might as well have something set aside like those death benefits, in case something happens," Mullins says. His wife frowns hard at the television set, pretending not to listen to him.

"We're mostly real young men in that mine," he continues. "You want the money when you're young." There was (sic) some good men in there," he says.

Mullins' poignant story could well have been the story of dozens of young Scotia miners who had tough decisions to make following the two disastrous explosions of March 9 and 11. Not only the very young miners but every miner employed there had to weight the cost and benefit of continuing to work in a mine and for a company where so many good men had lost their lives while just trying to make a living. Some serious soul-searching went on, publically and privately, among every miner and every miner's family.

One of the reasons I decided to accept a job at Scotia was because I actually considered the company to be a safe coal company to work for. I was aware of their reputation for hiring many young miners without experience but I considered this as a positive for the company, not a negative trait at all. After all, how could a miner possibly get the experience he or she needed if no one would hire them because they didn't have any experience?

Scotia itself was a relatively young company, having been producing coal only since 1962. I knew that a few miners had been killed in the short time Scotia had been in business, but everyone, including me, knew, and knows, that coal mining is one of the most dangerous occupations one can choose. Despite this knowledge of the risks, I chose to become a coal miner and accepted a job with Scotia Coal Company. They took a chance in hiring me, an inexperienced miner, and I didn't want to abandon them now, when they needed all the help they could get to "get back on their feet" after the tragic explosions had rocked the company, the communities, and so many families. I made a personal decision to continue working in the mines and doing so while still working at Scotia.

As far as safety goes, it's true that Scotia's health and safety procedures could have been much better than they proved to be, but I was never asked to put my life in danger by a Scotia foreman while producing coal on a working section. I WAS once asked by a Scotia Company foreman while doing "dead work" to go into an area of the mine where some timbers had taken a lot of weight and were bowed so badly that they resembled elbows, and to set a couple of new timbers to help hold the roof. I looked him in the eyes and said," No, I'm sorry, but I'm not going to work under those timbers that are clearly ready to break." To this day, I don't know if he was serious or joking, but it didn't really matter to me. At the time of the incident, I had my Kentucky and Virginia Certified Mine Foreman's papers and knew when to "stand my ground," although (as the reader is probably already thinking) it's not necessary to be certified to know danger when one sees it.

It's very easy to get complacent when it comes to safety habits, and take chances that go beyond the norm. I once worked on a 'pillaring' section where the section foreman was a very knowledgeable coal miner but once had a close call. Pillaring is the act of mining every block of coal, including the large 90'x90'pillars of coal, as the section retreats out of an area. This is also known as "retreat" mining.

I was a shuttle car operator and was backed up between the last two pillars of coal holding the rock around us up. The boss went by my operator's deck where I was sitting and said, "I believe I'll go to the edge of the break and see if the timbers are "giving" (bending) any yet." I cautioned him, "I've been sitting here listening to the drawrock falling all around those timbers, I wouldn't go there if I were you." He looked down at me as I peeped out from under my canopy, and assured me that, "Well you know I'm the boss and it wouldn't dare fall while a boss is near the danger." He then walked the 90ft to the edge of the break where the timbers were set to break the fall that was expected to come soon.

A rock fall in the area where the coal has been removed is necessary to relieve the pressure when retreat mining, so the fall was anticipated and needed because the pressure on the block of coal we were working around was tremendous, causing pieces of rock to dribble from the roof.

The boss hadn't been gone to stand at the timber line more than a minute or two when I heard the slow rumbling of the mountain above us releasing the rock where we had mined all the coal from. Finally it released its grip with a crash, boom, and an earthquake like shaking all around us. I was only about 100ft from the fall and it took several minutes to clear the atmosphere enough where I could see the intersection through the dust and debris.

I wondered where the boss was and if he had escaped the fall. I got out of the operator's deck and started towards the intersection when I saw him stumbling along in the dark towards me with his caplight dragging along behind him, still attached to his belt. His mining cap was gone and he was clearly addled and confused. No visible injuries were apparent and after a few seconds I saw he was alright. As I picked up his headpiece of his caplight I said, "I thought you said it wouldn't fall while you were in danger!" As we searched for his mining hat he replied, "You know, I had my hands on two of those timbers when it fell. I thought I was a goner." From that moment, every time we wanted a rock fall to hurry up so as to relieve the pressure on a block of coal, we would prompt the foreman to "go hold on to the timbers, we need a fall!"

On April 20 1976, some of the widows and relatives of the eleven men that were still sealed inside the mine organized a picket line at the entrance to the Scotia mine. As the miners showed up for the second shift, the women handed them flyers or leaflets and asked them not to work until the bodies of the eleven miners have been removed.

The women numbered about ten and didn't physically attempt to prevent the miners from going through. One member of the group spoke up and said, "We're not trying to put miners out of work. We depend on coal companies for jobs but we also know the mines don't have to be made unsafe like Scotia. We're willing to support whatever efforts the miners want to do to make a safe mine."

David McKnight, the Scotia Employees Association President, came down to the mine entrance near highway 119 to talk to the women pickets after the second shift miners had all pasted through the pickets. He told the women he had been up for the past day and a half "talking to every one of the men." He said he had been discussing a new safety program that the Employees Association had drafted for its membership to follow. McKnight also told the group of pickets that neither the Company nor the miners could do anything (at the time) to recover the bodies. "We need a professional to lift those seals, he said, pointing out that it could not be done until federal mining officials determined from air samples that the mine was safe to re-enter.

"The men have sympathy for you, but they've got families to feed, and even if they walk out, that mine won't get opened one day sooner."

One of the widows said she had thought the mine was safe to open since the methane had dropped to a level of one percent, but samples that were taken the week before by MESA showed methane concentration of more that 14 percent at one spot in the mine.

McKnight also told the group that that the Scotia Employees Association planned to file charges against "some Scotia management personnel" in connection with one or both of the explosions after "the results from the hearings" are known. McKnight declined to name any company officials who might be charged.

One interesting incident occurred just before the sealing of the Scotia #1 Mine entrances after the explosions had occurred. It seems that Letcher County Judge Estill Blair had requested and was granted a delay in the sealing of the mine to permit an expert "daredevil from Peever, South Dakota, Larry Bumpous, to try to recover the miners' bodies.

Blair cited the importance of recovering the bodies of the eleven victims still in the mine. He noted, "This community will be paralyzed until those men have been recovered."

Twenty two year old Bumpous had been very successful in recovering the remains of people in other similar disasters, including an Illinois River accident.

Bumpous arrived in Letcher County in the early morning hours of March 17 1976, and was scheduled to have a briefing with Federal and County officials before making a determination if it would be possible to recover the miners.

His efforts, if even attempted, were without success.

CHAPTER SIXTEEN

Still Waiting

The hearings held at the Whitesburg Courthouse extended to the end of April, into the causes of the march 9 and 11 explosions at the Scotia Mine in Ovenfork.

During those hearings, some of the widows of the men who had been killed in the explosions issued a formal statement criticizing Scotia management and their husbands' fellow miners who "have not come forward with information they have about safety conditions at the mine."

Mrs. Geraldine McKnight, the widow of miner Roy McKnight, read the statement into the hearing record as Mrs. Jennifer Boggs, the widow of miner Dennis Boggs, stood by her side.

Mrs. McKnight's remarks, which she said were read "by request of some of the women whose husbands were killed at Scotia," follow:

We cannot understand why this disaster happened at Scotia. We cannot see why Scotia management allowed it to happen. We believe there had been no management at Scotia.

We are ashamed that men who worked side by side with our husbands have not come forward with information they have about how Scotia was run in regard to the lives of the men. To the ones who have come forward and shown respect to their dead friends, we extend our grateful thanks.

To the others, we feel the friendships our husbands held for them should mean more than their jobs at Scotia. We respect the fact that these men have families to provide for. However, we ask them to respect the fact that our husbands can no longer provide for us.

We are concerned that if these men do not stand up for the 26 dead men and themselves, they too may be in such a disaster as we have suffered. The only possible way that we can see to force Scotia to improve must come from the men themselves.

We have sat here day after day listening to obvious lies. During these hearings there have been times we have wanted to stand up and scream. It has been hard to hold back our feelings. These men were not numbers--they were our husbands, our children's fathers. They were our whole lives.

We refuse to allow our husbands to be filed away and forgotten. When our husbands were trapped and killed in Scotia mines we were not extended the courtesy as their wives to be told by Scotia that they were in there.

We have heard repeated many times in this courtroom how "overwhelmed" Scotia management is by this disaster. We wish to state, we too are overwhelmed. But if we can bear up under our loss and be concerned for the safety of the miners who are left at Scotia, cannot the management do the same? We suggest if the time spent asking advice of their attorneys was instead devoted to the welfare of the miners employed by them---perhaps their grief would be less.

To the members of the panel we wish to say "thank you." Mr. Barrett, as a coal miner and in such a position as head of MESA, we feel you will do all in your power to uncover what caused these terrible disasters at Scotia. We have every confidence in you.

To all men and women who helped recover our husbands---words alone cannot express our feelings in saying thank you.

To all the rescue teams who risked their lives going into Scotia mines, our husbands cannot say "thank you," but for them, we do say "thank you."

Members of the investigating panel that listened to these grieving ladies' statement that day in Whitesburg would have to have had hearts of stone to not be moved by those heartfelt words. To be sure, those of us who had worked in the upper two mines that Scotia operated had no knowledge of conditions in the Scotia#1 bottom mine, other than the rumor that it was a gassy mine that emitted lots of methane ever since it had been in operation. Few of us knew of any ventilation problems at any of the mines that Scotia operated, especially since the two newer upper mines were barely punched into the mountain and had excellent ventilation on the sections to the best of my knowledge. None of us from those two mines were asked to testify at the hearings held in Whitesburg, Ky., or anywhere else, again to the best of my knowledge.

I don't believe I ever saw or heard of anyone ever taking a methane test and having even a trace of methane to register on the monitor in the two Scotia upper mines. The only common deficiency in safety I observed before the explosions was in not monitoring the methane by testing for it every 20 minutes when a piece of equipment was working inby the last open break. After the explosions this regulation was meticulously observed, particularly in the Scotia Imboden Seam, where I worked for the last 16 years I was employed at Scotia.

In April, 1976, the two Clinchfield Coal Company Mine Rescue teams that participated in rescue operations after the explosions donated the $2,000 dollars they received for their work to relatives of the 26 victims. Although the work was done voluntarily, the Scotia Coal Company presented Joseph Hicks, Captain of the Wilder Mine team, and Allen Howell, Captain of the Chaney Creek team, with a check for $1,000 each. The teams turned the checks over to the Bank of Whitesburg, which handled the distribution of the money to the 26 families.

On Sunday evening, June 20 1976, relatives of the eleven men killed in the second explosion again picketed the entrance to the Scotia mine in an attempt to speed up the process to re-open the Scotia mine and recover the bodies.

They managed to stop the production of coal in the two Scotia mines that were still open and producing coal in Middle and Upper Taggart putting around 450 men out of work.

The coal miners honored the picket lines for two days, then decided to confront the 20 or 25 pickets on Tuesday afternoon. When confronted, the pickets, consisting of both men and women relatives of the eleven miners still trapped in the Scotia mine, relented and allowed the men through to go to work.

The picket line was set up despite MESA's announcement on June 18 that the Scotia mine would be unsealed in July and that it would perhaps take months to recover the bodies after the opening of the seals of the mine. The relatives were determined to close Scotia until the company or MESA submitted a plan that would quicken the recovery. Continuous negotiations between the relatives, Scotia Employees Association President

David McKnight, and company officials produced no such change in the plans.

The first reaction of those who came to work Sunday night or Monday morning, only to be turned away by the pickets, was a good-natured understanding, but by Tuesday the mood had changed. The relatives stood alone on the picket line and a group of still working miners and some of their wives stood just down the road, wondering why they were out of work because of a decision made by the company and MESA officials.

"I only had two more weeks of training," said a man who was training to re-enter the mine. Now that we get the (rescue) teams, they (the relatives) throw up a picket line. They sure put a cork in it." A miner's wife added, "These men don't have anything to do with it."

The group complained that the relatives were keeping them from making a living. They said the widows on the picket line were well taken care of with food stamps and death benefits and didn't have to worry with such things."One woman said she got $80,000," a miner's wife repeated. She ought to be home taking care of her house and children."

Another miner drove up and said, "Something has got to bleed or blister. I'm not fooling with this bunch in the morning."

It didn't take that long. An hour before the second shift was due to enter the mine at 2:00 p.m. some 40 women and men walked down the road and stood in front of the pickets. The anger that had built up on both sides now came together; the accusations were made.

"Whoever doesn't have a heart, go get your dinner buckets and go to work," a picket said after a few minutes of discussion. Within minutes, a green Chevy truck drove to the picket line, three men jumped in on the bed, and the vehicle went across the bridge and up the hill to the mines.

"They volunteered for the work,' a miner's wife yelled. "That's the chance they take." The widow's asked for understanding.

"Let'em go," a picket said as another truck with three more in the back drove through. "We'll remember you," the pickets yelled at each passing car or truck. By late afternoon, the Scotia Coal Co. had called its men back to work. The pickets remained. [*]

About a month before the widows and relatives set up their picket lines, the 450 men that were still working at Scotia were called out on strike by their union representatives after a vote authorizing the strike.

---

[*] *The Mountain Eagle*, Whitesburg, Ky., June 24, 1976.

After the second shift had finished their shift at 10:00 P.M., Monday, May 17 1976, the mines were declared closed by the Scotia Employees Association, although the final vote to strike didn't take place until Tuesday afternoon. According to SEA President David McKnight, over half the employees voted to go out on strike. Tuesday evening at 4:00 P.M., a car was parked crossways in the road leading to Scotia and the miners had been assigned time schedules to walk the picket line.

The firing by the company of two miners who had allegedly been caught smoking in the mine was the act that brought on the strike. At least one of the men had denied having been smoking at all.

SEA President McKnight stated that the strike was called because the company had not followed proper dismissal procedures as called for in the contract between the company and the union. He said that the two men had been fired by Superintendent Freddie Maggard before any discussion could happen between a union committee and company officials. McKnight contended that the conference should have been called before the firing of the men, and also stated that no written notice of dismissal was ever given to the two men.

Around 24 hours after the union had voted to strike the Scotia mines, the men voted to return back to work after discussions with the company. Scotia company officials insisted that the men were fired at a meeting held on Wednesday between company officials and the Scotia Employees Association. It was agreed that the case concerning the two men accused of smoking underground would be submitted to the Federal National Labor Relations Board for arbitration. The miners returned to work that afternoon, Wednesday, May, 19, 1976.

Author's note: I don't remember the outcome of the arbitration in this case and it's likely that this case was settled quietly in order not to stir things up if the union lost the case. I didn't personally know either of the men involved in the accusation, and have therefore chosen to omit their names at this late date.

In the 16 years I worked in Scotia's gassy #1 Imboden Seam Mine, I never once saw anyone even think about smoking in that mine. In the nearly two years I spent at Middle and Upper Taggart it happened infrequently, but not after the explosions, to the best of my knowledge. If someone had attempted to smoke in the bottom mine, their own best friend would have likely knocked the smoker in the head, as I heard expressed from many miners, many times in that mine. They were well aware of the possible consequences of breaking that regulation and weren't inclined to try their luck.

Many readers might be surprised to learn that while it's against the law to smoke in the mines, it's legal (or was in the 1960's-90's) to use a torch to cut and weld steel rails and mining equipment, or a canister of butane to shrink wrap a rubber sleeve around a spliced cable as long as the proper amount (in those days 250lb) of rock dust is nearby to put out any fire or flame-up that might occur.

When compared to these two producers of large flames, a puny match to light a cigarette seems straining at the gnat while swallowing an elephant, but there's logic in the impermissibility of smoking in the mines. A cigarette flung into a pile of coal dust and smoldering there could easily cause an explosion, as could lighting one up in the return entry of a mine where the methane is being carried out of the working face by the air flow. Also the very act of striking a match or a lighter could cause an explosion if methane is present in the atmosphere with the right mixture of both oxygen and methane (CH_4). There is a reason the law is on the books and the law against smoking has saved countless lives since its enactment.

Mine foremen, especially non-smokers, could be relentless when it came to the effort to stop miners from smoking in the mine. Two of the bosses I worked for when I was a classified motorman made it a habit to try to catch the guilty party or parties when they suspected that the men on a section might be breaking the rules on smoking.

In order to fire a man for smoking, he had to be caught in the act by two witnesses. This rule caused me some discomfort, because sometimes these two bosses would have me or the other motorman take them to a coal-producing section of the mine and have us accompany them in case someone was caught smoking. Thankfully, our trips never resulted in actually catching anyone smoking, although one boss said he could smell smoke "a mile away" because he hated smoking in the mine. There was a story or rumor that a boss came up on a miner smoking at the dinner hole and when the smoker saw the foreman coming he quickly handed his cigarette to the nearest miner while saying, "Here hold this for me." Without thinking, the poor non-smoker was holding the cigarette in his fingers when the boss walked up. Luckily, he knew the man with the cigarette didn't smoke and had never smoked, so he didn't fire him. He was aware of whose cigarette it actually was, but he couldn't prove it.

The following is an interview conducted by Jim Cornett in the Whitesburg, Ky. *Mountain Eagle* of March 10 1977,with an anonymous former Scotia miner whose brother was killed instantly in the first explosion on March 9, 1976. I'll not mention his name, (wrote Cornett) and I'm not trying to fix blame with this article. This is telling it like it is, from the viewpoint of one who was there.

Question. How long did you work at Scotia
Answer. I worked there six months.
Question. Did you know the mine was gassy?
Answer. Yes, my brother told me before I went to work there.
Question. Why would anyone want to work in a gassy mine?
Answer. For the money. I made about $62 a day there, the best money I ever made in my life.
Question. How could you tell when methane was present?
Answer. At least one man in your area had a methane detector. But, you had to stop working to look at them. You could tell when you were "gassed off." The air is usually cold in the mine, and when methane was present, it would get real hot. Sometimes it would feel like it was 110 degrees in there. My brother could tell by stirring up some dust. If the dust just hung in the air, he knew that we were gassed off.
Question. What did you do when methane was detected?
Answer. We stopped working until our work area was ventilated.
Question. Didn't you leave the mine, or at least the working area?
Answer. No, we just sat down and stopped working. Sometimes, I spent an entire shift just setting there, talking or sleeping, and still got paid for it.
Question. Weren't you afraid to work in a gassy place?
Answer. I was, at first. But then I got used to it, and it didn't bother me. You can't stay afraid all the time in a mine. You just go on working and hope it doesn't explode.
Question. You mean that sometimes you kept right on working, when you knew that methane was present?
Answer. That's right.
Question. Why weren't you asked to leave the mine, or at least leave your work area?
Answer. I guess the foreman just didn't want to scare us. If everyone got scared and ran out, someone might get hurt. Besides, if it was going to explode, there wasn't anything we could do about it anyway.

Question. Did you receive any safety training?

Answer. The others may have but I didn't the first six months I was there except for the one time they showed me how to use the self-rescuer.

Question. What do you think caused the explosion that killed your brother?

Answer. Not enough air. They had probably gassed off the area and didn't tell them about it. That happened a lot. There just wasn't enough ventilation in that area.

Question. At this time, or always?

Answer. Always. There never was enough air in there. I've worked in that area many times, and it was always gassy.

Question. What do you think could have been done to prevent the explosion?

Answer. That section could have been ventilated more. They were drilling a borehole in there, but they were taking their time about it, only working on it when they wanted to. It should have been well ventilated before letting those men work in there.

Question. Are you bitter about what happened?

Answer. No, not really. It was the workers' fault as much as it was the mine's. They shouldn't have been working in the gas, and the mine should have pulled them out when gas was detected.

Question. Would you work there again?

Answer. Yes, I believe I would. (At this point, his wife interrupted and said, "NO YOU WOULDN'T!")

Question. Did you notice any defective equipment?

Answer. Yes. The compressor was always throwing sparks. It was always shut down when methane was detected.

Question. Anything else?

Answer. The roof bolts were always popping out. I can't see how they held anything up anyhow. But, they said they worked, and I'm not an expert, so I didn't argue with them.

Question. What was done by Scotia to help your brother's wife?

Answer. Not much. They gave her Blue Cross and Blue Shield for one year---which is nothing. They also gave her his workman's compensation, and she didn't even have to sign up for it.

Question. Did the mine have any insurance on him?

Answer. No. Scotia offered her $30,000 if she would drop her suit against them. Her lawyer told her to take the money and deposit it, and the suit is still pending.

Question. Did he have any life insurance?

Answer. Yes. Luckily he had about $80,000 in life insurance.

Question. Did your brother have black lung?

Answer. We don't know. His wife wouldn't let them do an autopsy on him.

Question. What about the second explosion on March 11,1976? Do you think it could have been prevented?

Answer. Yes. By that time, all the curtains had been blown down, allowing the methane to build up again, Those men should have known better. That place should have been ventilated before they went in.

Question. Some of the men in the first explosion had on their self-rescuers. Why didn't they walk out after the explosion?

Answer. They probably thought the whole mine had blown up and caved in. If they had walked out, they probably would have made it. I also believe that the rescue teams could have made it to them before their air gave out, clearing the tracks as they went.

Question. *Is an hour enough time to get that far into the mine?*

Answer. It's more than enough. They should have made it out of there.

Question. *They had enough air in their self-rescuer for an hour---*

Answer. An hour! Not the ones they gave us! Ours lasted anywhere from five to forty five minutes. Forty five minutes at the most. They were lucky if they had enough air to last an hour!

Question. *Was the mine inspected often?*

Answer. Often enough. We could tell when the inspector was coming. The air would suddenly get better. They were probably robbing air from another section and sending it right along with the inspector. When he left, the air would get bad again.

Question. *Why did you like working there?*

Answer. Because I could take off anytime I wanted to. I can't do that with the job I've got now. If I wanted to, I could take 2 or 3 days off at a time, and nothing was said about it. The work wasn't really hard, and it was the easiest money I ever made, especially when we were gassed off, and just sat down our whole shift. Sometimes, I worked 2 or 3 days and nights in a row, without coming out of the mine, and I made an awful lot of money there. When we worked over like that, they would bring us in steaks to eat. If my job here ever gives out, I'll go back to Scotia or Lynch and try to get back in the mines. I liked the work and the people I worked with. We were all young men. I only wish they would ventilate Scotia better. It would be hard, but they could do it, if they wanted to. It's hard to pump air uphill to where my brother and I were working, but if the borehole had been completed, it would have been ok in there.

Question. Didn't the mine care about working conditions?

Answer. If they had, they would have given them more air. What does it matter to them if a few men get killed? They can get all the men they want to work. All the mines care about is selling the coal, and to heck with the little man back in that dark hole. If he dies, there is another man waiting to take his place. That bottom mine is just a big bomb, waiting for a spark to set it off. The only way they'll ever work it again is to increase the airflow to that area.

Question. Did you know any of the men who were killed with your brother?

Answer. Yes. I knew and worked with most of them. One of those men who was killed with my brother had a methane detector. He always carried it. One more may have had one, at least he should have had one.

Question. What about the men in the second explosion?

Answer. I knew some of them. There is another thing I can't understand. Why didn't they bring those bodies out? They could have got them. They could have gone in, ventilating and hanging curtains as they went, and worked their way right up to them. The only reason they didn't get them was that they were all scared to go in there. I would have gone in with anyone else and brought them all out. I think they were planning on going in, because someone brought an awful lot of plastic (for curtains) to the portal after the first explosion.

Question. In your opinion, who or what caused your brother's death?

Answer. The mine owners. All the safety violations should have been cleared up, and that area should have been well ventilated before those men were allowed to start and to keep working in there. It was probably gassed off and no air going in, just setting the stage for an explosion. That happened a lot while I was there.

Shortly after the two explosions, the UMWA began to consider organizing the Scotia miners. The UMWA organizing director, Tom Pysell, told the <u>Mountain Eagle</u>, "We have every intention of organizing every major non-union mine in Eastern Kentucky, but I don't want anyone thinking that we're trying to capitalize on the deaths of 26 miners. I won't say this couldn't have happened at a UMWA mine, because it could. But I do say we could provide the Scotia miners better safety protections and better job security."

He went on to say that UMWA miners and organizers had been talking informally with Scotia miners "and there's no question that some of them are serious about wanting us to represent them. Anyone who's serious about wanting protection, we want to talk with," Pysell said.

Scotia's contract with the Scotia Employees Association was set to expire on July 14, 1976, and under National Labor Relation Board regulations a union may only file for a representation election within 60 days prior to a contract's expiration.

On April 29 1976, Scotia's contract with the SEA was within the 60 day period when the UMWA legally made a move to offer Scotia employees the chance to move under their protection banner by posting this ad in the Whitesburg *Mountain Eagle*:

Attention

Scotia Coal Miners

The UMWA wants to be sure that each of you is provided the accurate answers to any questions you might have about UMWA contract protection. The UMWA representatives at Scotia are:------- , of Neon, -------, of Totz, -------, of Benham. You can reach them by phone by calling the ------ -- Motel and asking for the United Mine Workers.[+]

These organizers are authorized to represent the UMWA in the current organizing effort and can answer any questions you might have about membership in the UMWA. Feel free to contact them about any problem or question you might have. Other individuals who may appear at Scotia claiming to represent the UMWA do not speak for the UMWA unless they are UMWA elected officials or employee.

Remember, UMWA contract provisions offers you and your family such benefits and protection as:

- Individual right to withdraw from unsafe workplace
- Elected safety committee with power to shut down unsafe place

---

[+] Names redacted by author.

- Full pension and medical coverage after retirement
- Ten paid holidays and five paid personal or sick days
- Cost of living raises, shift differential pay, reporting pay, temporary assignment pay PLUS regular wages
- Full company paid medical coverage for entire family-no deductibles
- Lifetime pension and medical coverage for disabled miners or widows
- Contract protection against unfair firings or discipline
- Twelve regular vacation days, two floating vacation days, up to 13 graduated vacation days
- Neutral arbitration of dispute between labor and management
- $100 a week sickness and accident benefits
- Full time helpers on continuous miners and roof bolters for additional protection
- $75 yearly clothing allowance
- Overtime after 71/4 hours for outside workers
- Job bidding and job posting
- Lay-off according to seniority
- Paid safety inspections and training

Despite the push by the UMWA to organize the Scotia workers, a new contract was signed between the Scotia Coal Company and the Scotia Employees Association on July 14, 1976:

Scotia Coal Company
By: James Burley Williams (Superintendent)

Scotia Employees Association
By: David T. McKnight; President

By: Kenneth Goins; Secretary

By: James Powell; Mine Committeeman

By: Benny Adams; Mine Committeeman

By: Denver Sturgill; Mine Committeeman

The UMWA's failure to garner enough interest to even have a vote among the Scotia employees likely stemmed from at least two or three major factors.The first factor was that the contract that the Scotia Union had with the company was at least as good as the UMWA offered, and in some ways even better. The other factor that likely came into play was that some of the older Scotia workers had become disillusioned with the UMWA after the attempt to organize Scotia workers in the 1960's. I heard one of those men complain that the UMWA didn't support them in the strike like they should have, causing a majority of the men to cross the picket lines and go back to work at that time.

Regardless of the reason or reasons, there was little interest in not continuing our contract with the company as it was, except for an increase in pay rates each year over the next three years. The top pay rate went from $54.00 in 1975 to $77.00 in July, 1976. My own pay rate as a motorman went from $51.44 for an 8 hour shift in November, 1975, to $64.44 in July, 1976.

Sometimes negotiating with Scotia during contract time took on an informal nature between the company and the miners. I recall one incident where a strike had been called, either formally or informally, and the men, including myself, were standing a picket line at the Scotia entrance road. The reason for the strike has been lost in my memory, but I know that a Scotia official had driven to the picket line to see if he could talk to the men about the situation. As the miners and the company official talked, it became clear that a compromise could be quickly reached when one miner shouted out a question or complaint about the company not wanting to pay for a certain medication. The company official then caused a ripple of laughter from the picketing miners when he replied to the miner's medical question, "I tell you what; if you all will go on to work this evening we'll not only pay for that medication, but we'll pay for your bottles of aspirin!" That confrontation broke the ice and the men went to work with only a promise to fix whatever it was that caused the strike.

The company must have kept its word, as no following strike was called. Scotia always seemed willing to compromise when they could and always seemed to want good relations with the men. Of course, that's my impression of them and my opinion. I'm sure others may have had other impressions of the company. They weren't a perfect company by any means and the explosions revealed some glaring deficiencies, but in their relationships with the men on a personal level they tried to address any concerns expressed to them.

In late May 1976, MESA officials gathered at the Whitesburg MESA office with the widows and relatives of the eleven men still entombed in Scotia mine, for a briefing on the mine conditions. Charles Luxmore, Chief of the MESA safety staff, told a group of 20 relatives that "the danger of another explosion is too great to take a chance at this time." The relatives had expected that the briefing would instead be held to inform them of the date the mine would be unsealed.

Luxmore informed them that samples taken from the area where the two explosions originated showed the mine's atmosphere "has turned in the last week favorably." Luxmore said carbon monoxide levels have "decreased by one-fifth in the last few days." He continued that methane levels had increased to more than 30 percent (a level which would cause it to be unlikely to explode) and oxygen had been steadily dropping, he said.

He said he could not predict when the mine would be reopened. When the decision to seal the mine was made on March 13, MESA predicted it would be reopened in 60 to 90 days.

"It's strange to me," Lena Kiser, the mother of Kenneth Kiser, a MESA inspector killed in the second blast, bitterly commented, "they can put a man on the moon and they can't get those men out of there (the mine)."

Several of the group told Luxmore after the briefing that they would enter the mine themselves on June 9---three months after the first blast---if MESA had not reopened it by then. Luxmore said MESA would only allow trained rescue teams to first reenter the mine.

John Kiser, the brother of Kenneth Kiser and a Scotia miner, told Luxmore he knew of unsafe practices at the mine, but added he did "not blame MESA (for not correcting them) because one inspector couldn't take care of that mine.

He recounted one incident when he had his brother come on the section where he worked to check what he considered was inadequate ventilation.

"Kenneth shut it (the section) down, Kiser said, but air was diverted from other parts of the mine and ventilation was brought up to standard. That left other sections with inadequate ventilation "and the other men (in other parts of the mine) started hollering 'no air' he said.

Kiser also said that portal buses or jeeps miners rode underground habitually caught ablaze. "At least two or three of them would catch on fire every day," he said.

Referring to the unsafe conditions at the mine, Kiser warned. "They (the mine management) are going to go back doing the same things (when the mine is reopened) for production. They'll get by with what they can...unless something is done.[±]

On June 17 1976, Friends and relatives of the eight Scotia miners and three federal inspectors still entombed in the Scotia Mine learned that the mine was going to be unsealed July 14. The announcement, long awaited by the grieving families of the miners, was made by federal, state, company, and union officials. They stated that recovery teams planned to enter the mine by the belt-line driftmouth located near the bathhouse and that it would likely take months to reach the bodies.

The relatives were upset to hear that recovery might take so long to achieve and were quick to express their disapproval of the plan. They claimed that the bodies could be recovered quicker by going through the 386ft deep borehole at Frank's Creek, which would shorten the distance to the bodies to about 4,000ft, instead of the 4 to 4½ miles that the driftmouth route would have to traverse.

Robert Barrett, MESA's Administrator, and Jasper Cornett, vice-president for operations for Blue Diamond Coal Company, told the group that both points of entry were discussed at a Knoxville meeting earlier this month, but that the driftmouth entry was decided upon for safety and logistical reasons. Both acknowledged that if the driftmouth plan failed or became too difficult that the borehole route would be taken.

After the decision had been made that the Scotia mine would be unsealed on July 14, preparations for the unsealing were being made to have three shifts of volunteer miners to back up the three Scotia Mine Rescue teams that would work their way through the mine to recover the bodies.

While the mine rescue teams would have to work under oxygen to explore the mine areas and build seals every 500 ft or so as the teams advanced into the mine, the "fresh air crew" would come in afterwards and build backup seals to provide a double seal to assure that no toxic gases would leak from the seals.

Because the mine had been sealed for four months, the water in some entries would have to be pumped out of the mine, some block brattices would have to undergo minor repairs, (although the explosions hadn't reached anywhere near the portals of the mine,) and the fresh air would have to be restored to every part of the mine.

[±] The Whitesburg, Ky., *Mountain Eagle*, May 20, 1976.

When the mine rescue teams advanced under oxygen into the mine, they constantly monitored for methane and oxygen levels and were tethered to each other by a rope so that each man was accounted for at all times. They had to have a couple of men waiting in fresh air at the track seal where man doors were installed, to monitor the progress of the team as it advanced ahead to build more seals. This took lots of preparation, time, caution, and sweat to accomplish. This was the reason that it would take several months to ventilate the mine and to recover the bodies. Scotia couldn't afford to lose any more men than had already lost their lives. The advance through the mine would necessarily be a slow process.

A few days after the announcement that the mine would be reopened, our mine foreman at New (Upper) Taggart passed the word that volunteers were needed to help recover the bodies of the eleven men still trapped in the 2 Southeast Mains intersection.

I was still working as a motorman and really liked my job at the Upper mine and had heard so many tall tales about the Imboden Seam that I had some hesitation about volunteering to work on the "Bull Crew" as the fresh air crew was sometimes called. Very few others on the second shift volunteered at first, even though as an inducement, and because of the dangers involved, the company was offering a flat rate of pay of $120.00 per 8 hour shift plus time and a half for all over 8 hours of work performed.

This was nearly double the pay I was then earning for an 8 hour shift as a motorman. The money wasn't as important to the workers (including myself) at Scotia as was the knowledge that the families desperately wanted to have some closure to the tragic losses they had suffered, and they could only do that when the bodies were brought out of the#1 mine.

I didn't volunteer the first day the call for volunteers went out, as I wanted to first talk to Wanda to see how she felt about me working in the bottom mine. After all, she had saved my life once already when she kept me from volunteering to go in with the work crew that was in the second explosion. I superstitiously wondered if I might be pressing my luck if I decided to volunteer after once coming so close to being one of the eleven men still lying at 2 Southeast Mains.

When I went home the night that volunteers had been asked for, I mentioned to Wanda that I was thinking of volunteering to help recover the mine. "Surely you can't be serious," she said. "After you barely escaped the second explosion you want to try it again?"

Her logic was hard to argue with but I gave it my best shot and after convincing her (and myself) that the bottom mine would be very safe because inspectors, both state and federal, would be with us every step of the way, she finally said, "Well, do whatever you want to do, it's your life."

I had finally convinced my wife but I hadn't yet fully convinced myself that I was making the right move. I went to work the next day and still hadn't made up my own mind if I really wanted to leave my motorman job at New Taggart for an unknown and dangerous one in the bottom mine.

Each day that went by, a man or two would walk into the office and tell the mine foreman that he wanted to volunteer to help recover the Imboden mine. I knew that the number of men needed for the recovery crew wasn't yet known, so I expected that any day the cut-off would come. I was still having reservations about leaving my motorman job.

In June 1976, a new mine foreman took over the reins on the second shift at New Taggart. Jimmy Adams, from Craft's Colly, Letcher County, was a foreman at Middle Taggart when he received a promotion to mine foreman and became Wayne Morgan's and my boss.

Like all the Scotia foremen I had worked for, he was fair to his crew and treated us all alike. I explained to him that I was considering volunteering for the fresh air crew in the bottom mine but hadn't yet made up my mind. He said he understood and that all I would have to do was tell him if and when I decided to volunteer and he would see that I could transfer to the second shift fresh air crew. The second shift promise was important to me, as I had been on that shift since I started working at Scotia and liked it very much. I was still hesitant to make the move although the announced date of the mine's unsealing was drawing nearer.

CHAPTER SEVENTEEN

The Mine is Unsealed

When MESA officials, Scotia Company officials, and the Scotia Employees Association announced on June 17 that the Scotia mine would be unsealed on July 14, the first thought I had was that I hoped the families and friends of the eleven miners still in the mine wouldn't get their hopes up too much that the announced date would be the actual day of the unsealing. Much to my surprise, on that very date the process of knocking down the concrete seals was begun in earnest.

As of July 14, it had been 124 days since the bodies of the eleven miners had last been seen lying at the mouth of 2 Southeast Mains, 122 days since the decision had been made to seal the mine, and 117 days since the last seal was completed on March 19, 1976.

Officials estimated that recovery operations would take about 60 days to reach the bodies, depending on the conditions encountered as the mine rescue teams advanced into the mine. The accumulation of water was expected to be a major hindrance, especially in some areas of the mine where water had been a problem in the past.

Ventilation would have to be re-established by repairing any damaged brattices and building the seals every 500 feet would take time and much hard and dangerous labor as the teams advanced into the mine. Each seal had to be dug into a solid rib, meaning that all the loose coal on each rib would have to be dug out with a pick and shovel and a clean foundation in the mine floor prepared for each seal. All supplies needed to build a seal would have to be carried the 500 or 1,000 ft from the fresh air base to the location where the seal would be built.

Each move by the rescue teams would mean having to build from 4 to 8, and maybe even 12 seals, depending of the number of entries that

185

had to be closed off, and depending on other conditions encountered. This building of the seals had to be done while rescue team members carried a 30lb Drager breathing apparatus on their backs.

Even though the official plan called for the entry into the mine to start at the driftmouth, Blue Diamond officials admitted that once water was pumped out of the lowest point in the mine, their driftmouth entry plan might have to be abandoned.

To have to abandon the original plan would mean that the entry into the mine would have to be accomplished by going through the borehole located at Frank's Creek. That was the plan that was favored by the families of the eleven miners still in the mine, because the distance to the bodies would only be 3,000 to 4,000 ft from the borehole.

MESA's Assistant Administrator, Jack Crawford, described the rescue teams that would have to recover the mine as combined "rescue, recovery, and modified construction teams." Crawford was the man responsible for rescue and recovery operations in the nation's coal mines. When asked how long recovery operations would take, he said, "I don't know, this has turned out to be a lot slower than we anticipated."

Although the unsealing was begun on July 14 as planned, things didn't go as planned at first. Breaking through the double rows of concrete blocks with the fill in the middle was discovered to be too much of a job to conquer with sledge hammers, so drilling through the two walls of concrete was found to be necessary. Even drilling couldn't be utilized in the normal way. The workers doing the drilling had to wear their breathing apparatus and use soft bits at the seals even they were outside the mine, due to the possibility of encountering "black damp," (deficiency of oxygen) "afterdamp," (atmosphere following an explosion) or "firedamp," (an explosive mixture of methane and air.)

The unsealing turned out to be a much more difficult job than had been anticipated by anyone involved in the planning. The three Scotia rescue teams barely managed to make a dent in the first seal by the end of the first day, and the second day didn't see much more progress.

Although the breaking of the first seal was expected to take only a few hours, it was actually on the third day of drilling, July 16, that the first few small holes were drilled through the first seal. Discovering that the methane level at the seal was only two-tenths of one percent enabled the rest of the seals to be torn away with heavier equipment and complete the job.

On July14, the day the first attempt was made to tear out the first mine seal, the company invited relatives of the miners to come for the mine opening, but only relatives of two of the miners came to the mine. Shirley Barker, whose husband Glenn Barker was killed in the second explosion, and her sister-in-law Joyce Barker Polson and mother-in-law Loretta Barker came. Mrs. Lena Kiser, whose son, Kenneth Ray Kiser was one of the inspectors killed in the second explosion, and Kenneth Ray's brother Johnny and friend also came.

Scotia officials allowed the relatives to pass through the new front gate which had been recently put up just a few hundred feet from the main highway, Ky. 119. The new gate was 8ft high and was installed to keep anyone from driving onto Scotia property unless allowed access by the guard stationed there.

The relatives of the eleven men still trapped inside the mine had picketed the entrance to the mine access road twice before and the new gate was designed to limit or prevent any more like demonstrations. The last picket line the relatives set up to try to make the officials hurry their efforts to re-open the mine had shut down Scotia's three upper mining operations and caused the miners to lose three days of work.

When the relatives passed through the gate, they were directed to go to a safety trailer near the miners' bathhouse to monitor the progress of the mine's unsealing. While there, a company official, Alan Blevins, informed the relatives that they could come to the mine every week for a progress report, or the company could call them each week and report to them. Both Mrs. Kiser and Loretta Barker said they preferred to have the company call them.

When the rescue teams finally broke the seals after two days of frustrating drilling, they were able to unexpectedly able to explore about 2,000 ft into the mine where they built a set of seals in preparation to ventilate the section they had already explored.

Dow Phillips, Mesa's District 6 Manager, said the miners were very pleased at having finally entered the mine successfully after two days of chipping away at the concrete seals that they had expected to breach in half a day or less. He also said the mine appeared to be in good shape in the 2,000ft section that the mine rescue team had explored, with no problems with the mine roof or floor.

The same day that the three Scotia Mine Rescue teams began drilling into the concrete seals, July 14, I mentioned to the mine foreman, Jimmy Adams, that I was now ready to volunteer for the fresh air crew that would be backing up the rescue teams. I was encouraged to do so because I felt that by joining the crew at the outset would be much better than waiting until later, when a third shift was added. For now day shift and second shift volunteers were all they were asking for.

Several miners had already left New Taggart for the bottom mine during the week and I was a little concerned that I might have waited too late, but upon my arrival at the mine the next day, (Thursday) Jimmy Adams informed me he had spoken to the "powers that be" and I was to report to the bottom mine on the second shift, Monday, July 19, 1976.

Having asked for the job I couldn't back out now, even though I still wondered if I had made the right choice in volunteering. I had spent one year and ten months at New Taggart (the extent of my whole mining career at that time) and I knew every nook and cranny of the mine. I was also convinced that I had the best job at Scotia Coal Company as a motorman. A motorman was fortunate in that we spent at least half our time on the outside of the mine, stacking and storing supplies, keeping the track motors and jeeps in shape, and keeping the office and light- house swept, cleaned, and straightened up.

When we didn't have rock dusting on the track or belt to do, we sometimes could finish our supplying to the working sections and our housekeeping duties around lunch time. Then we could spend the rest of the shift doing maintenance work on our motors until time to pull the mantrips just before quitting time.

Motormen were privileged to get to see a lot of beautiful sunsets from the mountain top, especially during the summertime. Miners who worked on section sometimes ribbed us motormen by saying, "Boy, I sure wish I could watch the sunset every night. How do I get a job like that?" Of course we denied the accusation and offered to trade places with them if they thought our "pie job" was so easy. Thankfully, no one ever took us up on it. All joking aside, there were a lot of rough times and we had to stay busy like every other miner, but being outside was much better than being underground and we appreciated our jobs.

In the wintertime we paid for the privilege of working on the outside, in spades. One can imagine how cold it gets high on a mountain with the wind blowing almost continuously and the temps hovering in the low teens or sometimes at or near below zero. Gloves are very little help in loading supplies when you can't feel your hands and when the roof bolts are frozen solid to the steel sides of the supply cars. Occasionally we had to use the prongs of a forklift to pry the bolts apart after they had been in the cold weather awhile.

During the winter we stayed inside the mine as long as possible, and sometimes volunteered to (continuous) miner help or to help bolt the top on a section just to be out of the cold for a spell.

My motorman buddy always made sure he had his "airplane hat" (with ear flaps) with him when we worked outside for any period of time. I never did have the nerve to wear one on account of the possible ridicule from the section crews that the hat might elicit. I preferred to freeze instead.

I was giving this all up for an unknown situation in the bottom mine. I had never seen the inside of that mine and only heard others describe what it was like. Almost all miners who had worked there repeated the same stories;

"It's got the worst top you've ever seen." "There's water everywhere." "You have to really watch the gas!" "That high coal will get you killed, just a small rock falling from that height will kill you!" "I never wanted to work anywhere else but there." "Stay out of that mine if you can." "That slope is a killer in wintertime!" "There's not much ventilation in that mine, never has been." "I'll never work there again." "I can't wait to get back down there."

I had heard it all but I was about to find out for myself. I knew in my heart that no matter how depressing and awful the conditions in that mine might be, that I would at least be in "high top" down there, and that was worth a lot to me.

On Monday, July 19, at 1:30 p.m., I reported to the Scotia bathhouse where the mine foreman's office for the recovery crew was located. I was very pleased to discover that Bruce Jones, my former boss at New Taggart, was the second shift "Bull Crew" foreman. I felt immediately right at home, as I had always enjoyed working with and for Jones.

He had only a skeleton crew before the ten or so of us reported to him that evening. I believe Kenneth Sturgill, James Miles, Stephen Miles, and Hargus Maggard were the only members of the crew when I reported in, besides second shift foreman Jones, that had reported in to the bottom mine earlier in the week.

They had worked in the bottom mine prior to the explosions and most of them had testified about the explosions before the MESA hearings held in Whitesburg, April 5 through April 30, 1976. After the explosions they had worked at New Taggart until the unsealing of the bottom mine. I was already acquainted with them, having worked with them in and around the outside and sometimes inside New Taggart. They had the advantage of knowing the No. 1 mine from top to bottom and would make adjusting to the new mine much easier for those of us that had never worked in that mine.

When the mine was unsealed and the rescue teams explored the first 2,000 ft of the mine, it wasn't clear to me or anyone else who was exactly in charge of the recovery effort at the beginning. When asked about who was in charge, Ralph Dye, Public Information officer for Blue Diamond Coal Company and Scotia Coal Company, said, "I don't know who is really in charge. Ask Jack Crawford (MESA Assistant Administrator). Dye continued, The federal people are having a lot of input....they are more supervisory than advisory."

Jack Crawford explained, "The captain of the rescue team which is underground has final authority, but MESA will have people at the last fresh air base at all times. Crawford's assistant added, "MESA is monitoring the company during the operation." No one ever discussed what role the Kentucky Department of Mines and Minerals would play, if any, in the recovery operations at the mine.

Other members of our second shift crew included Wayne Wilson, Mike Halcomb, Tommy Gross, Paul Kemplin, Charlie Davidson, Brad Whitaker, and Mike "Greenie" Sullivan. A couple of other miners would later join our crew as we advanced into the mine. There might have been one or two others that I have missed but if so, I have forgotten their names after over forty years have passed. Bruce Jones assigned Tommy Gross and myself to be the motormen for the second shift crew. I had been his motorman at New Taggart for a few months as I have already mentioned in a previous chapter. I was already classified as a motorman but Tommy Gross was of a different classification.

I had never worked with Tommy before and met him for the first time when I reported to the Bull Crew, but I found him to be one of the best workers and one of the finest people I had ever known. He was one of those people who could do any job assigned to him and do it well, no matter the difficulties encountered. I always found him to be a real friend and a pleasure to work with.

Our first assignment was to take in a load of supplies for our second shift crew to build back-up seals after the rescue teams had built the first set of seals and the area had been ventilated. The set of seals we would build would provide an "air lock" for the Scotia mine rescue teams to enter to start another exploration of 500ft of the mine under oxygen.

The advancing rescue/exploration teams would be monitored in fresh air in front of the back-up seals that we would build. The two seals in the track entry were the ones we used to install metal doors in them to allow the rescue teams ingress and egress.

All the seals being built as the rescue teams advanced were temporary structures that had to be torn down as each 500 or 1,000 ft move-up was made. Then the area that had been explored could be ventilated to sweep out any remaining gases before anyone entered the area without breathing apparatuses. This was the procedure carried out throughout the whole process of exploring and ventilating the whole mine, a slow process which would take over four months to reach the bodies of the miners. Even after the bodies were reached, the ventilation and exploration of some areas of the mine would extend into 1977.

After we reported in on the first day, Tommy and I began loading our supplies into one of the same supply cars used to help carry the bodies of the first 15 miners killed to the outside in March. I had watched from the bridge spanning the slope track entry as those cars were pulled slowly out of the mine with yellow brattice cloth covering the bodies. Luckily, we were too busy loading our supplies to have time to think about the irony of now loading our supplies into one of those same cars.

We loaded several rolls of yellow brattice cloth, some 1"x4"x12' lumber, some rock dust, shovels, picks, mattocks, and several cases of two large canisters each, containing polyurethane "mine foam" which when sprayed on the edges of the seals we were to build would seal them tight against the top, sides, and floor of the mine. The boxes of foam had "Danger" marked on the cases and warnings about breathing the foam particles when spraying the seals, but as there was no air stirring when a seal was completed, we breathed lots of the material into our lungs.

After loading our supplies we coupled our one supply car to our motors and headed down the slope. It was my first trip into the mine and I was anxious to see for myself how this mine differed from the two mines that were located on the mountain above the No.1 Scotia mine.

We made sure our sanders were working properly before we started inside in case we lost control on the way down. Just before we entered the mine portal we had to stop on the steep slope to throw the run-away switch to the straight, then throw it back after we passed through it to divert any potential run-away vehicle into the side of the hill.

After we passed through the drift-mouth I saw that the track entered into a gradual right hand curvature and then straightened out again just before we encountered another run-away switch on the steepest grade of the slope. We again had to stop and throw this switch to the straight before passing through, then throw it back again after going through it. This was something we had never encountered as motormen in the upper mine and would take some getting used to before becoming comfortable with it. I was somewhat intimidated by the thought of possibly having to let a motor or jeep be stopped by going into the run-away switch. The timbers and solid block of coal at the end of the switch would mean a very hard jolt if one had to experience such an event. The fact that the track was several feet off the bottom and leaning to the left because of the steep angle of the run-away would be a tough situation for anyone aboard a run-away vehicle.

The slope entry was surrounded by solid blocks of coal for the first 500 ft or so, then encountered entries that had been mined when the mine first opened. The steep grade then continued for another 500 ft before leveling out, but one always had the impression or feeling that the track was on a downward grade when going deep into the mine. This sensation persisted until reaching the point where the Northeast Main switch intersects with the South Mains track, about 3½ miles into the mine.

After easing into the mine for about 2,000 feet we came to the area where we were going to build our first seals to back up the ones already completed by the rescue teams. No signs of the destruction that had taken place deeper in the mine were visible. There was not any sign of the water I had expected to see after the mine had been closed for so long, although there was plenty of moisture hanging on the roof and ribs. The coal ribs were still white with rock dust and no loose draw-rock was present. I was pleased to observe that the height of the mine was no where lower than 6ft. in the areas we had passed through on our way in the mine.

The miners who told of some places where the roof had collapsed and been cleaned up and re-bolted were telling the truth. Some entries near the mainline track had suffered rock falls, leaving a height of 10-20 ft to reach the roof. I'm sure some men were deterred from staying around very long when they saw those high entries. Later on in the mine recovery process I would get plenty of experience helping bolt some of those high and dangerous roofs.

Bruce Jones teamed Tommy Gross and I up with Hargas Maggard, James Miles, and Kenneth Sturgill to cut the track outby the seal built by the rescue teams earlier that day. Maggard was a maintenance foreman and would be in charge of our team. My first job was to take the track bolts loose from the fish-plates so we could take two rails loose and lay them beside the track. This was done to break the track connection from the outside, in case of a possible lightening strike on an outside steel rail being conducted all the way into the mine and setting off another methane explosion.

After taking the track apart we also disconnected the six inch metal waterline that led outside the mine from deeper inside the mine. This eliminated another possible source of an explosion should a bolt of lightning strike the outside pipe and be conducted to the inside. A new 6in. waterline made of pvc pipe was installed as we advanced instead of using the outdated and dilapidated metal waterline.

After we cut the track and waterline, I helped build my first seal there in the track entry. We first shoveled all the loose coal and debris from the mine floor, then dug into both ribs of the block of coal with our picks and mattocks until we came to solid coal to anchor out frame against. The work was brutal, as no air was stirring beyond the last open break to speak of, and we raised loads of dust with our shoveling and digging. We had the added "inspiration and motivation" of not only having our boss watching us but also a federal mine inspector was with us every minute. We felt that no time was to be wasted in the effort to recover the bodies, and it is my belief that the federal, state, company, and Scotia Union workers felt that way also.

The safety meeting we all attended before coming into the mine emphasized that we were expected to work safely and to work very hard in the effort to recover the bodies of the eleven miners as soon as we could so their families could have some closure. After all, they had been through a living nightmare over the past few months. Not only would our crew be working many hours of overtime, but we were expected to work seven days a week until the bodies were recovered from the mouth of 2 Southeast Mains. We could have a day or days off in the event of a family emergency, but otherwise we would be expected to work every day with no exceptions. After all, they continued, we had volunteered for this job and would be making big money to more than compensate us for the extra effort we were expected to make. We were given the option of going back to our regular job at any time if we decided the work was too hard or too dangerous for our liking. I'm proud to say that no one opted out at that first safety meeting, then or later.

The seals were fairly simple affairs but were very strong when they were built right. We started the building of the air-tight seal by building a sturdy frame to stretch our yellow brattice cloth across. Two posts or legs were cut to fit and wedged against the mine top and the 1"x4'x12' boards were cut to fit in a cross pattern to achieve greater strength, then the brattice cloth was nailed to the boards and stretched tightly against the rib on each side. To finish the seal, the polyurethane mine foam canisters were mixed and sprayed in every conceivable crack and corner to assure no leaks were left in the seal. This was harder work than it sounds like and each seal took about 2-3 hours to build from start to finish, with usually three men working on each seal at a time.

Our second shift crew of 10-15 men usually built 4 to 8 seals after a move forward by the rescue teams. Of course we had other work to do, such as building concrete brattices, pumping water, bolting loose top, re-installing rails that had been disconnected from the last move, repairing equipment, keeping the 6 ton motors, jeeps, and buses in running order, and doing anything else we could to achieve our goal.

On one occasion, Harvey Creech, (a Scotia staff mine foreman that worked with the fresh air crew,) and I were setting in the operator's deck of the jeep we were riding down the slope,when he looked at me and said, "Eddie, how do you feel about the possibility that you might have to be the one who brings the bodies outside?" I replied, "Harvey, I would consider it a privilege to be the one that did that." "That's what I wanted to hear. We (our crew) may be the ones that have to do that job." At the time of his question we were a little over the half-way point of recovering the mine and reaching the bodies. I assume he was just preparing me for that possibility and responsibility.

Shortly after the mine was unsealed and we had advanced 3 or 4,000 feet into the mine our second shift crew was assigned a permanent MESA inspector to observe our work and safety habits as we recovered the mine. His name was Inspector Charles Cruny, an experienced MESA employee from Pennsylvania.

He had already worked another disastrous explosion, the Consol No. 9 mine explosion in Farmington, West Virginia that occurred on November 20, 1968, in which 78 miners lost their lives. He told us several stories and incidents involving the recovery of that mine after the accident. When he was assigned to our crew permanently, he said that all the miners had eventually been recovered after that accident except one. We told Cruny that we hoped that in our recovery efforts we could recover every man, leaving no one behind. He assured us that was his goal also.

Cruny was a stickler for safety, especially strict concerning the wearing of safety glasses while building seals and using tools of any kind. This made our shoveling, hammering, and sledge hammer work difficult when sweat would be pouring down our faces and clouding our safety glasses. Knocking out a damaged block brattice while working in low oxygen could play havoc on the wearing of glasses, but Cruny made no exceptions. If you were using a tool you would be wearing safety glasses. He had a job to do and we had a job to do, so no one complained. (At least no one complained around him.)

Working seven days a week under so much stress on all of us was bound to cause some flare ups, most of which were minor events. One exception involved Inspector Cruny when he had been continuously with our crew for about three months.

We had been cautioned to turn over to the federal mine officials any unusual item or items we might happen upon while building seals. One of our crew had found a pocketknife while building a seal a few hundred feet from where the last explosion had come out of 2 Southeast Mains. He was busy shoveling, so he stuck the knife in his pocket while waiting until the federal inspector came back around to turn the knife in to him. Meanwhile a crew member mentioned to Inspector Cruny that his buddy had found the knife and stuck it in his pocket. Cruny rushed back to where the seal was being built and demanded to know where the knife was that he had found. This brought on a row between them that escalated into a shouting match which took some time for both men to calm down. The next day when we reported for work in the evening we learned that Inspector Cruny had been reassigned.

The stress that was associated with the dangers involved and with no days off caused everyone to be on edge after awhile. One night, the dispatcher sounded the alarm that a mine fan reading on the outside was showing a much higher reading than was normal so we were told to evacuate the mine immediately. We loaded up our buses and Tommy Gross and I hopped on our motors and two supply cars and headed outside as instructed. When we reached the bottom of the slope, we came upon a scene that was worrisome. A jeep had run out of charge and a couple of the men were near the panic stage. "Hurry up you bastards, get that m.f. jeep out of the way," one man shouted. Another shouted, "Push that s.o.b. out of the mine if he can't make it!"

At that moment I discovered for the first time since we started the recovery of the mine that one or two of our crew likely couldn't be counted on in an emergency. It was an eye opener for sure and it wasn't a comfortable feeling. It turned out that it was a false alarm, that the reading at the fan was due to the malfunction of an instrument, and there was no emergency. Whether it was actually a false alarm or just a test to see how long it would take us to evacuate the mine in the event of a disaster, is unknown to me even today.

In late September I took my first day off since the mine was reopened in July. It happened to be on Sunday when I decided after a rough week at work that I just had to have a day off to relax a little. I had not missed a day of recovery work and was just about worn out from lack of sleep and job stress. I felt guilty for even taking that one day off but I certainly wasn't the first one to do so, and some had missed multiple days of work.

I believe they allowed for the fact that we would need a little time to recuperate after a few months had passed. Anyway, nothing was ever said about any of us missing a day or so every now and then. That one day was all I missed during the more than four months it took to recover the bodies after the mine was re-opened.

CHAPTER EIGHTEEN

Nearing the End

I N October, 1976, Widows of the miners killed in the first explosion filed a suit against Blue Diamond Coal Company for $60 million dollars. The suit was filed in Knoxville Tennessee federal court, alleging that Blue Diamond failed to maintain proper ventilation in its Scotia Mine that would sweep explosive gas out of the mine, and that Blue Diamond did not follow acceptable safety procedures.

The suit was being handled by Washington attorney Gerald Stern, who successfully won a $13 ½ million settlement from Pittston Coal Company after one of its dams burst and killed 125 people in Buffalo Creek, West Virginia.

Stern and his colleague, George Framton Jr. was to be assisted by attorneys James Asher of Whitesburg, Eugent Goss of Harlan, and J.D. Lee of Knoxville.[*]

In late September Scotia rescue teams and the fresh air crews had reached nearly 8,500 feet into the mine. This was about the point where I had somewhat of a close call while helping complete the ventilation of an area that had just been explored and a move forward had been made by the rescue teams.

At the mouth of Northeast Main and Southeast Mains, the rescue teams had completed a set of seals near the intersection during the dayshift. That evening when our second shift crew came into the mine, we were accompanied by federal and state inspectors. When the switch area was tested, the methane test revealed a high amount of methane near the seal that had just been constructed by the rescue teams. We (myself and another member of the fresh air team) were directed to take some large

---

[*] The Whitesburg, Ky. *Mountain Eagle* Article by Bill Bishop, Oct. 28,1976

pieces of cardboard and fan the methane out into the entry where fresh air was sweeping the area. I grabbed the piece of cardboard and advanced into the area where I was directed and the next thing I knew I was falling to my knees and blacking out. I was out only a few seconds because the low oxygen I had encountered was located in a large recess in the mine ceiling where I had gone to fan the methane into an area where a piece of yellow brattice cloth was hung to direct the airflow. After I became fully conscious, the state inspector that had me moving the methane took another oxygen reading where I stood while fanning the dangerous gas, and found only 12 % oxygen in the atmosphere. Just a few feet away the reading was 19%. A minimum of 14% oxygen is needed maintain consciousness.

The members of my crew were used to working in 16-17% of oxygen, because some of the old works where Woods Tallman, the Scotia mine recovery expert, had us knocking out concrete brattices were almost always not receiving enough ventilation to keep oxygen levels up. Part of this was due to being in the old works part of Scotia mine where the ventilation was poor. The brattices had to be knocked out or repaired, according to how Mr. Tallman wanted the air to flow and we were getting paid well to do it. We were required to use brass tools always during the recovery because of the spark hazard.

When the oxygen level was found to be low at a brattice line we would take turns with the brass sledge hammer, only managing to hit a few licks with the sledge hammer in 16% oxygen before heading for fresh air behind us while someone else took a turn at the sledge hammer. I wonder today if the air would even reach 12% in some breaks. How we all managed to survive those conditions while recovering the mine is beyond me.

The stress that the miners were feeling as they advanced into the mine not only affected the miners themselves, but extended to the families of the miners. I know that my own wife and children worried constantly about what could happen and the worry only intensified the closer we got to the location of the miners' bodies. I realize it's difficult for those reading these words to understand the level of stress we were under, but nevertheless it was real and we were all feeling it.

I'm sure our stress never came close to what the grieving families themselves were going through though. I know that the company and the miners were motivated to work day and night to give them some relief from their ordeal. Company officials tried to stay out of our way so that we wouldn't be hindered in our work, but their words, looks, and actions let us know that we needed to push and push hard to reach our goal as quickly as possible.

Skeptics might say that sure they were in a hurry alright, in a hurry to get the mine in shape to run coal. That might have been part of the thinking, but I'm convinced in my own mind that they were sincerely concerned about the families also. Even human nature itself tells us that they weren't at all satisfied with what had happened at Scotia. They were also humiliated, embarrassed, and yes, even devastated by what had happened in March 1976. The stress that the recovery crews, their families, the company officials, and the families of the eleven miners suffered during this period was a common virtue.

As a member of the recovery crew, I decided to keep a journal for a few days so that I could maybe somehow tell my grandchildren a little of the kind of work we did during the recovery of Scotia. I've always loved studying history and I realize that what is of no interest to us today might be of great interest to others someday. With that in mind, I will reproduce what few words I wrote in my "journal" at that time. I also included these passages in one of my other books, _Six Years to Live_. There's nothing dramatic or of particular value or interest in what I wrote but they might be of some little interest to the reader:

Tuesday, September 21, 1976; 3:00 P.M. Started working on the motors and buses, cleaning the sand boxes and checking and filling the batteries with distilled water (in preparation to go inside the mine.)

3:20 P.M. Started inside the mine as a passenger in the second man-trip. The first bus (mantrip) that left in front of us is headed to the fresh air base. Ours is going to 18th crosscut to timber some bad top. We had two new men to join our crew today, Ellis Hill and Ed Wells. Also along with us was Paul Kemplin, Wayne Wilson, myself, and Merle Rhodes, boss. Arriving there, we carried and measured and sawed, then timbered some bad top in the 18th and 19th crosscuts.

5:P.M. Our crew had to leave for the outside so the ventilation crew could begin ventilating the 1-East return. Only the ventilation crew is allowed inside during this time.

5:30 P.M. Reached the outside, worked on buses and motors again. Repaired the lights on the motors and changed the charging batteries on one motor.

7:30 P.M. The ventilation of 1-East is completed, we again left for the inside of the mine to go to work.

8:00 P.M. We reached the 1-East area to begin our work there. We uncoupled and laid aside two joints of track. Our crew included Hargus Maggard, (boss) Kenneth Sturgill, and James Miles. We broke the water-line, capped the waterline, and cut the 7200 power cable.

10:00 P.M. We knocked out a concrete block stopping near the seal on the track entry with the same crew.

10:20 P.M. We walked to the track, nine of us crowded on the jeep mantrip and started outside after calling the dispatcher for track clearance.

10:40 P.M. We reached outside safely.

Wednesday, Sept. 22nd, 1976. 3:00 P.M. Wayne Wilson and I changed batteries in the (6 ton) motor.

3:30 P.M. We loaded a supply carload of timbers, header boards, and cap wedges to take inside.

5:00 P.M. We started inside. We picked up 700ft of plastic 3" water line at 1-East switch, and dragged it to the return entry. We also set a water pump in the 74th crosscut.

7:00 P.M. We dragged more plastic 3" water line into the return entry.

7;30 P.M. Wayne and I went to the 1-East seals to pick up "Regi Paks" (spray mine foam sealant) and loaded a load of garbage into the supply car.

10:00 P.M. We started outside with our motor and supply car, loaded with 27 empty Regi Paks and our load of garbage. Merle Rhodes (boss) was with us and got him to start the pump at 6J seal as it had a "Do not energize" tag on it and I wouldn't touch it. Besides, I didn't have a methane detector with me.

10:20 P.M. We reached outside and unloaded our carload of garbage, then worked on the motor until quit time. (11:00 P.M.)

Friday, Sept. 24, 1976. 3:00 P.M. Changed batteries in the motor. Loaded D.C. (direct current) bolting machine on "low boy" equipment hauler.

4:30 P.M. Started down the slope to inside with the bolting machine. Hargus Maggard and James Miles were along to help me.

5:00 P.M. We arrived at 2 East switch with roof bolter and low boy. Federal Inspector Cruny rejected the bolting machine. It needs a breaker box for the trailing cable. We had to turn around and take the bolting machine back to the outside to have the machine shop to correct deficiency.

5;30 P.M. We reached outside with the bolter. Backed the bolter and low boy into the shop and helped restock bolter cable and helped weld guide. After the repairs, I secured the bolter to low boy with chain and safety chain.

7:30 P.M. Started back down the slope with the low boy and bolter.

8:00 P.M. Cruny conducts another inspection and this time accepts the fixes. Only problem, bolting machine fails to run. It seems that newly installed breaker box is too small for bolter. (100 amp.) Need instead 2 lead 150 amp box. Crossed it over to unload it from low boy. Bolter badly needed to bolt bad roof on main line.

9:45 P.M. Started back outside with now empty low boy.

Sun., Sept. 26, 1976. Took day off! My first day off since we started recovery on July 22. Rest of crew scheduled to rock dust.

While the recovery crews were working towards the recovery of the eleven miners, the two other Scotia mines were still producing coal and undergoing inspections from federal and state inspectors. It was no secret that the two mines were working under increased scrutiny because of the events of March, 1976. In October, the two mines were cited four times by MESA for failure to provide adequate ventilation to the working areas. In all the two mines were cited 52 times for various violations of federal law in around 10 days of inspection during late September and early October.

The ventilation violations were especially troubling, given that they were similar to the ventilation violations that occurred frequently in the Scotia No.1 mine before the explosions. The ventilation violations at the upper mines included failure to check the calibration of a methane monitor on a continuous mining machine, two instances where escapeways were not posted or were access was blocked by mud and water, and three pieces of mining equipment were found to not have been kept in permissible condition. After the violations were cited by MESA inspectors, they were later corrected.

These inspections were part of a "Blitz" inspection that sent federal inspectors to all five of Upper (New) Taggart sections at the same time. During these inspections, 30 citations were issued by the seven MESA inspectors, including four closure orders issued for loose coal and coal dust in every working section of the mine.

Blue Diamond spokesman Ralph Dye at first said that he would not comment (about the violations) but later he labeled them "frivolous violations, like not having a pin in a fire extinguisher."

After being informed of the closure orders and continuous violations of ventilation regulations, Dye amended his statement to say that "they certainly need corrective action."

On November 1st 1976, Kentucky State Department of Mines and Minerals Commissioner H.N. Kirkpatrick announced that the work and rescue crews were within about 1,000 feet of the miners' bodies lying at the mouth of 2 Southeast Mains. "If nothing happens," he said, "the recovery team can go in and get the bodies two weeks from today. That is what we are planning, but you don't know what this last thousand feet is...."

On that same day, Blue Diamond Coal Company officials called a meeting between the company and the families of the eleven men to tell them that the bodies of the miners would be recovered in a matter of weeks. He also told them that rescue teams reopening the mine were working in the "most explosive range of gas you can find."

Jasper Cornett, a Blue Diamond vice-president, said that no exact date could be given for when the eleven bodies would be recovered. He said that the bodies could be reached in two to three weeks if no further obstacles were encountered. Cornett also mentioned that the teams were now advancing in eight percent methane and 17 percent oxygen.

(Both were in the range needed for an explosion to be possible. Only a 1200 degree spark was needed to set it off. This is why both the rescue teams and the fresh air teams carried brass tools to work with.)

Cornett also said that six or seven representatives from the eleven families would be allowed to accompany the final recovery teams. That group will (said Cornett) include federal, state, company, and employee representatives, funeral home employees and a representative of the Letcher County Coroner.

Cornett said that the recovery teams would ventilate the area before an attempt was made to retrieve the bodies. Bodies will be identified by the numbers on the batteries the men had carried and check-off numbers on their belts.

On Monday, (Nov. 1st) said Cornett, the recovery team made up of Kentucky mine inspectors split up and accompanied the five Blue Diamond teams. (Three Scotia teams and two Leatherwood Mines teams.) Wednesday, (Nov. 3rd)Federal Mining Enforcement and Safety Administration teams joined the other teams. This was done, said Cornett, "to make sure none of the evidence (of the cause of the two explosions) is destroyed or covered up."

Cornett also said that three or four members of the original Blue Diamond teams using back packs (breathing apparatuses) in the recovery effort have been removed because of "tension" or oxygen toxicity in their blood caused by the use of the breathing apparatus

Around the middle of the month of November the five rescue teams that had been engaged in advancing into the mine 500 to 1,000 feet at a time, and their day, evening, and night shift fresh air crew buddies had advanced to a point just over 500 feet of the mouth of 2 Southeast Mains.

To our crew we seemed so close, yet so far away from our goal but the process we were engaged in would have be done slowly and correctly, just as we had been doing since we started the recovery back in July. No matter how anxious we all were, things couldn't be hurried along.

The nearer we got to the bodies, the more anxious we had become, which was sensed and felt by everyone, including officials of the company and our immediate bosses, who continuously cautioned us to not forget that safety was still the No.1 priority in the rush to complete our task. No one wanted to see an act of carelessness cost someone to be injured or even killed when we were so close to the end of our mission.

When we reached what we all knew would be the next to last move-up we were motivated and anxious to get moving on to the next phase, which would be the move-up that would result in the recovery of the bodies.

The week we reached the next to last move, Dow Phillips, MESA's Pikeville, Kentucky District Manager predicted that "the recovery should be made in the latter part of next week." He was right on the money with his estimation.

CHAPTER NINETEEN

Recovery

A S we made our last move up and built four seals to back up the ones constructed by the rescue teams, we were within 500-1,000 ft of the bodies lying in the mouth of 2 Southeast Main. Each time we advanced into the mine it took about one week or more to get an area ventilated correctly, track rails cut, water line installed, rock dusting completed, and all the loose roof supported. As I stated in the last chapter, this work couldn't be hurried, as safety first was still the rule in our recovery efforts.

After the rescue teams had explored the next to last 1,000 ft. before reaching the mouth of 2 Southeast Mains, they constructed their four seals to seal off the area to be ventilated, then we went in on the second shift to construct our usual back-up seals. As we arrived in the area in our buses and Tommy and I with our motors and supplies, we began to see for the first time, signs of the second explosion. The ribs, roof and bottom was scorched in spots, but it was obvious that the brunt of the explosion hadn't reached more than 1,000 ft towards the Northeast Main-South Main intersection. This was about what we had expected to see, as the explosion naturally spent its fury down the straight at the mouth of 2 Southeast Mains and on down into the old works south of there.

Very little rock dust was left anywhere around the area where we were working and the blackness made it very difficult to see, even with our exceptionally bright caplights. Only the point at which the light beam was focused could be seen clearly. There was nothing to reflect the light off of, due to all the blackness around us.

The ventilation was always very poor after a move had been made and this one was no exception. All the digging, shoveling, and the stirring of the fine coal dust made breathing difficult and the sweat drained off us like rivulets once we started working in earnest. Fortunately, the cases of 8 ounce plastic bottles of water we had brought in with us was ice cold, thanks to the winter weather we left outside the mine.

After just a few minutes of hard labor, we couldn't tell by looking at each other's faces whose boys we were, since everyone's face was completely covered with coal dust, made worse by the sweat that was wiped frequently with the back of the hand. If we had been in a different situation things like that would have been comical but we were all serious in our actions at that moment.

After we finished building the four seals, cutting the track and removing a joint of waterline and capping it, we spent some time timbering and cleaning up garbage to load into the supply car we had brought in with us. No rock dusting was done for the length of the move up, due to the fact that federal inspectors, state inspectors, employees representatives, and company officials had more investigating of the area to do. We had brought in a bunch of officials with us who were there to observe and explore while we did the work we needed to do. We had state and federal inspectors with us all the time but as I failed to write their names down in my scribbling, I no longer remember who they were. They were there though, with us every step of the way.

That night, at around 10:30 P.M. we were preparing to leave the section and walking towards the mouth of Northeast Main to get to the man-trips. As I have related, the floor of the mine and everything else was pitch black which made for poor vision as we walked along beside the track. One of our crew struck with his boot an object lying in the deep coal dust and accidently kicked it out of the dust and against one of the track rails. Bending over and picking it up off the mine floor, he found that he was holding a damaged black mining cap. The blackened and scorched coal ribs made it almost impossible to see anything unless one had found an object in the very way our crew member had. Dozens of miners had walked in that very path all night without discovering the hard-hat.

I think I actually remember the man's name that was on the hat but since I can't be sure at this late date, I don't think I should reveal his name here because I could be completely wrong.

It doesn't really matter who found it nor whose it was because the point is that this was the first object we found that more than likely was blown along the track by the force of the explosion. We were a little more than 500 ft. from the bodies and yet here was probably one of their mining hats, blown so far from the area where they were located. For the first time, our crew could now get an idea of the power of the blasts that had ripped through the mine those eight months ago.

The member of our team that found the hat immediately turned it over to the boss with us. As I said, I don't remember for sure the owner's name that was on the hat, but most Scotia miners did mark their hard-hats with their name tape as a habit. I never heard if the hat was turned over to the family of the miner or not. As it happened, this hat was evidence of the kind that the investigators were looking for.

By Monday, Nov. 15, we were nearly ready for another move-up. This would be the last one we would have to make and we were all looking forward to bringing the tragic nightmare to a close. We spent the time waiting by rock dusting and bolting some of the bad roof just off the South Main track entry. Here is where I helped Wayne Wilson and Ed Wells take time-about bolting some very high roof that had fallen. We had first cleaned the fallen rock up with an EMCO scoop and dumped the rock in an unused break.

We had to have the shop people make up drill steel for drilling the holes to a length of about 12-15 feet. The drill steel itself was heavy and unwieldy and very difficult to get started into the roof. I had to stand on the top of the bolting machine canopy to hold the steel to get it started.

Each hole took several minutes to drill and after the hole had been drilled to the desired depth, I had to get the bolting machine operator to let me stand on the head of the drill steel holder and lift the head as high as he could before I could insert the two sticks of glue and the 10 ft roof bolt into the drilled hole. You are probably thinking, "was that safe?" I would say that it certainly didn't seem safe at the time but there was no other possible way to do the job and support the top.

We did have an inspector drop by once and watch our efforts, but he soon wondered off without any comment. Another one stopped by later in the day as Ed Wells was having all kinds of trouble while trying to drill the bolt hole, and I could see that he was about to blow up. He began to get various kinds of advice from the inspector, and it was obvious that Ed was getting more frustrated by the minute as the inspector advised him.

Finally after a round of suggestions and comments, Ed stopped the drill and stared directly at the inspector for what seemed like several minutes until the inspector took the hint and left the area, whistling as he went. It took us a couple of days to bolt that one intersection due to the height of the roof we had to contend with.

On November 18 1976, the Scotia rescue teams made the last move – up and built seals all around the intersection of 2 Southeast Mains where the bodies had been lying since March 11,[th] 1976. They were still working on the seals when we went inside to relieve them and to build the back-up seals. As they left, it was obvious to us that they had been working like brutes to finish the seals before we came in.

While waiting to come inside we were warned that we would have to work harder than we ever had in our lives to finish all the back-up seals that needed to be built before the bodies could be removed. (Eight or ten seals I believe was the number to be built.) Company officials also cautioned us that we would be working directly in the area where the bodies were lying, and that we were not to approach them in any manner closer than the 50 ft or so that separated them from us and the seals we would be building around them. We were told that there would be no ribbing and jawing each other like normally was carried on when we were working, and in fact we were warned not to talk above a whisper. Even the noise of our shovels, hammers, and mattocks would have to be muffled.

We understood what they were trying to accomplish and while their instructions were not necessary, they helped to remind us of the dignity, respect, and honor we needed to show our fallen fellow miners that we would be working around all night.

As we piled off our mantrips and walked into the area around the 2 Southeast Mains intersection, we had our first glimpse of the terrible destruction the second explosion had wrought. Everything was as black and dark as midnight and like the last move-up we could only see the point at which the beam of our caplight was shining. We weren't allowed within 50 ft of the bodies which could barely be discerned in the blackness of the soot blackened intersection.

The silence which engulfed that scene that night will never be forgotten; almost no one uttered a sound as we constructed our seals. The only sounds heard were from the necessary hammering of the nails into the boards of the seal frame.

While we were all very conscious of the bodies around us, no one spoke of them as we worked. I felt like we were really at a funeral and in a sense we were. The only time I really took notice of the scene was when holding a piece of brattice cloth over a frame of a seal, my light shined on a reflective object lying below the switch and realized that I had seen the reflective tape on a MESA jacket or pants.

There were so many seals to be built that we had no choice but to work through the night to get them all finished. As we built the last seal in the track entry leading to the mouth of Northeast Mains I caught another glimpse of three bodies that were lying closest to us. They were indistinguishable from their surroundings, but two mounds were clearly there. It looked as though at least these three miners had managed to run 15 or 20 feet before the force of the explosion hit the area. This would confirm that the two survivors did in fact hear the explosion as it first exploded in either the 2 Left or 2Southeast Mains area, then continued to blast down those entries and out the mouth of 2 Southeast Mains where the March 11 work crew was preparing to leave for the outside.

Our seal building efforts of November 18 took on a frenzied pace, as many state and federal officials were all around the explosion area, urging us to work at all possible speed because medical people, the coroner, pathologists, and some federal and state big shots were gathering on the outside of the mine to come inside to do some preliminary investigation of the scene and area where the bodies were located. The bodies themselves would also undergo an examination before they would be removed. At midnight, November 18 changed into Novernber 19, and we were still rushing to finish the seals so that the medical people could safely do the job they were waiting to do.

Eleven hearses/ ambulances were also gathered once again outside the mine to take the bodies to various area funeral homes. It was a full repeat of the aftermath of the first explosion. The only difference was that this time the wait for the bodies to be removed from the mine had taken much longer to come about.

The men of our work crew, including the bosses, were frantically digging, leveling, shoveling, nailing and spraying the seals that had to be done before any recovery of the bodies could take place. At one point I doubted that we could finish the job any sooner than several hours after the day shift was scheduled to start at 7:00 A.M. The blackened explosion site made the work much more difficult than it would have been if some rock dust had been scattered around the area. Rock dust tends make to make one's vision much better because the whiteness of the rock dust gives a nice contrast in comparison to the eerie darkness of a mine that is without any dust on the ribs, top, and floor. The investigators wanted the site to stay exactly how it was until their investigations were complete, and that was an understandable point that they made.

Finally, shortly after 5:00 A.M. the last seal was sprayed with mine foam sealant and our job was completed. Two man doors had been installed in two separate seals (in the track entries leading to 2 Southeast Mains and the mouth of Northeast Main) to allow access to the area where the bodies were located. Our job was completed. We had entered the mine nearly 15 hours ago, but it seemed more like 50 hours, we were so tired. We loaded on the mantrips very tired, sleepy, worn out in fact, and very jubilant with the knowledge that the bodies of the miners could now be turned over to their waiting families.

As our locomotives and mantrips emerged from the slope portal, we observed that some people were already waiting on the over-head pedestrian bridge, even though it was still dark at that hour.(Around 6:00 a.m.) As we climbed out of the buses, jeeps, and motors, we saw the waiting hearses and many people milling around the mine office, shop, and bathhouse. Some family members of the eleven miners were already arriving at the mine in order to be on hand when their loved ones were brought out of the mine.

At 7:00 A.M., the Kentucky State Mining Commissioner, Harrold Kirkpatrick, MESA chief Robert Barrett, three pathologists, and representatives from five area funeral homes went into the mine to begin the process to recover the bodies. The three pathologists, including Dr. George Nichols, the pathologist that had been present when the 15 miners killed in the first explosion were brought out of the mine, went along to examine the bodies before they were picked up off the mine floor. In total, 27 men would be included in the actual recovering crew.

When they arrived at the mouth of 2 Southeast Mains, inspectors from the Mining Enforcement and Safety Administration (MESA) mapped the area where the eleven bodies lay and took photos of the scene. The miners' personal effects were also gathered up and secured. Barrett and Kirkpatrick returned to the surface to brief the family members, then spoke to newsmen that were gathered just outside Scotia property.

Both Barrett and Kirkpatrick said that it appeared that all eleven men died from the initial force of the explosion, but later in the day, Joe Cook, Assistant Administrator of MESA, reported that as many as three or four of the dead miners had removed their self-rescuers from their belts. He said it wasn't clear if they had removed them after they heard the blast of the explosion or after a few seconds had passed.

Author's note: I never knew of a self rescuer being removed from one's belt at any time unless either they were changing mining belts, or they were going to use the rescuer. The two or three bodies I had observed a little ways ahead of the majority of the bodies were obviously (to me) starting to run away from the blast, but managed to only get about 20 ft before the blast roared through the intersection where they were.

Shortly after the jeeps and buses headed inside with the recovery crew, two locomotives (track motors) headed down the slope coupled to two supply cars with their bottoms covered with the familiar yellow brattice cloth. This would again be the mode of transportation with which the deceased miners were to be brought out of the mine.

After we arrived back on the surface, myself and members our fresh air recovery crew were met by company officials and were handed a pink business-card sized name tag (which I still have) to pin to the front of our shirts that read:

Official Business; Eddie Nickels
Signature   *Eddie Nickels*
Authorized *Jasper K Cornett*

This authorization would allow us to stay around until the bodies were actually brought out of the mine.

After the pathologists and funeral home workers had been in the mine for a couple of hours, members of the day shift fresh air crew brought them to the surface in the buses and jeeps they had rode inside the mine. We that were waiting outside knew that the bodies of the miners were probably going to be close behind them.

Family members and other visitors were still trickling in when at around 10:00 a.m. someone passed the word that if we wanted to watch the recovered miners as they came out of the mine, we needed to go to the pedestrian bridge over the slope right then.

About two or three dozen people were gathered on the bridge, and many others were watching the mine portal from the parking lot and the banks of the gorge, probably over a hundred people in total, when sometime after 11:30 a.m., first one locomotive, then the two supply cars and the rear locomotive pulled slowly out of the drift-mouth.

When the procession emerged from the portal, I once again witnessed the scene of supply cars loaded with the bodies of fallen miners covered by bright yellow brattice cloth crawling slowly up the slope entry. Bennett Adams and Dusty Banks were the motor operators and they were traveling very slowly up the slope in respect to the miners and all those others who were watching the scene from the banks of the hillsides.

My thoughts went back to just over eight months ago when I watched as a different load of fallen miners who had been in the first explosion had been brought slowly up those same tracks. For a coal miner to witness such a scene once in a lifetime when he works in the mines might be thought possible, but having to witness such tragedy twice in less than a year was heartbreaking and difficult to absorb.

As the supply cars emerged into the light of day, several family members and other observers burst into tears and moans; others were loudly crying and sobbing as other voices rang out with "Oh Lord God!, Oh Lord Jesus,"as the two motors with their precious cargo rumbled slowly up the hill and around the 180 degree curve to the bathhouse and mining office. "I hope you're Happy," shouted one woman to Scotia officials standing nearby. "I hope you rot in hell!"

I continued to stand on the bridge, transfixed with the sights and sounds I had just witnessed, not expecting as much emotion as had transpired, although I surely understood it.

I thought back at that moment to the day eight months before, when I stood on the hill above where I was standing now, and listened as a miner told me the day after the first explosion that he would probably never go back in the bottom mine again. He was wrong, and was destined to spend eight months lying at the mouth of 2 Southeast Mains because of a second explosion. He had volunteered to go back in one more time and now he was being carried out in a supply car, after having changed his mind and volunteering to help bolt some loose rock in 2 Southeast Mains on March 11, 1976. After 243 days underground, the eleven miners were back on the surface.

After arriving on the surface with the bodies, the two supply cars were backed into the mine shop and the doors were closed to allow the pathologists and Letcher County Coroner Charles Day to make one last examination of the eleven bodies before they were released to the funeral homes. Some of the relatives were also allowed to view the bodies in the mine shop before the funeral directors took charge of them.

The funeral homes that would be handling the arrangements for the eleven miners were as follows:

Don Polly, J,B. Holbrook, and Monroe Sturgill, the Blair Funeral Home in Whitesburg;

John Hackworth, Don Creech Sr. and Glenn Barker, the Parker Funeral Home in Cumberland;

James O. Williams, the Hindman Funeral Home in Hindman;

Kenneth Kiser, the Sturgill Funeral Home in Wise, Va.;

Richard Sammons and Grover Tussy, the Hall Brothers Funeral Home in Martin;

James Sturgill, the Polly and Craft Funeral Home in Jenkins.

After the bodies were brought out of the mine and had been taken to the funeral homes, Scotia officials announced a one week moratorium would be taken by all Scotia employees in honor of the 26 men who had lost their lives in the two explosions of March 9 and 11,1976. Scotia workers returned to their jobs Monday, Nov. 29.

The Scotia Mine Portal Courtesy of the *Mountain Eagle* (photo by Greg Edwards, Coalfield Progress, Norton, Va.)

CHAPTER TWENTY

Mine Recovery Continues

After the one week moratorium honoring the 26 deceased miners, Jasper Cornett, Scotia Vice-President for operations, announced that teams were now preparing to renew efforts to ventilate Northeast Main, the mine corridor out from the panel where the two explosions originated.

Cornett did not rule out the possibility that teams could be working to ventilate the sections of the mine sealed off by the recovery teams as they made their way to the bodies.

On Sunday November 21 1976, eight of the miners' funerals were conducted and three more funerals were scheduled for Monday 22, 1976.

When our second shift Bull Crew returned to work after the week's moratorium in late November, instead of now having to follow the rescue teams and building seals establishing ventilation, we were put to work in South Main cleaning up the intake entries in preparation for a new section to be designated South Main Parallel. This new section would be located about three miles from the bathhouse slope portal, about ½ mile from the 1-West section.

On the first day back Bruce Jones and I walked the entry where the new section would be turned off and mounds of coal and rock were piled in the area, which was obviously used in the past to store the rock and coal cleaned up from previous falls on South Main. Not only would the stored material have to be moved to start the new section, but cleaning it up would greatly improve ventilation to the whole mine.

Jones asked me where the coal and muck could, in my opinion, be stored more easily and be out of the way at the same time. After looking it over, I showed him where I thought would be the best place for me to put it, and he agreed and informed me I would be left alone to clean it up at my leisure and that he would leave another man with me for safety purposes.

I estimated the job would take about one week to finish, even with the big Eimco scoop that I would be using. While my buddy and I were doing this (I have forgotten who he was) the rest of the crew would be doing some ventilation repairs of block brattices, setting timbers, and bolting the roof where falls had occurred.

Our work was observed by company, state, and federal officials from time to time, as the mine still hadn't been released from extra scrutiny for coal production. We made sure we took our methane checks every 20 minutes, even though we would be in fresh air the majority of the time.

On February 14, 1977, mine rescue teams began ventilating the 2 Southeast Mains Section where the two explosions occurred, in preparation for the government's final investigation of the cause of the blasts.

Ronald Franks, a supervisor for the Mine Enforcement and Safety Administration (MESA), said the rescue teams ...composed of state and federal mining officials and company and employee representatives, began constructing air seals inby the mouth of 2 Southeast Mains on Monday, (the 14th.)

The investigation teams would be following the rescue teams as the section was ventilated. The process was estimated to take two weeks, and was not expected to be completed before the first anniversary of the explosions, federal mining officials said.

Final recovery of the 2 Southeast Mains Section had been delayed by rock dusting and by the abnormally cold weather, officials said

January and February were brutally cold and caused an untold number of delays in the ventilation and clean-up of the mine. Several times during those two months our crew had to dress like we were in Alaska, using several layers of clothing, several coats, and cover our faces completely because of having to use picks and shovels to clear the ice from the slope track to enable buses and motors to get into the mine. The ice had to be chipped little by little and was as hard as concrete. We used our old reliable supply cars to throw the ice chunks into when we managed to chip out a chunk of hard-as-stone ice.

Experienced coal miners who read these words will know how cold the driftmouth area gets in winter and how cold it was just inside the driftmouth can only be imagined when I tell you that a couple of times we were chipping ice when the outside temp was 21 below zero at night. I would think it was probably 30-35 below zero where we were, just inside the portal. We worked 10 minutes at a time, then ducked into a line of breaks for 10 minutes. I hope never to see it get that cold again.

One of the major objects in ventilating the 2 Southeast Mains Section was to allow the investigating of the 6 ton Goodman locomotive that had an air brake compressor that was thought to be the cause of the two explosions. The Goodman motor was approximately 2,800 feet from the mouth of the section, (where the eleven miners were killed.)

The ventilating teams planned to build seals to approach the motors in fresh air. The seals were projected to be built about 800 to 1,000 feet apart.

Around February 28th, 1977, the two locomotives at the end of the track in 2 Southeast Mains were finally reached. Ronnie Franks, of MESA, said that two electricians accompanying the rescue teams disconnected the batteries that operated the Goodman locomotive and insulated the leads. The 2 Southeast Section is 40 crosscuts, or 3,800 ft deep, Franks said , and a fresh air base had been established at the 19th crosscut, with the last seals at the 28th and 29th crosscuts.

Family members said that no group memorial services were planned, although some individual families would hold private services on the anniversary of the disaster.

The Scotia Employees Association also planned to place flowers on the graves of the miners who died in the blasts, and the company itself had designated March 9 and 10 as Commemoration Days when the mine would be closed.[*]

On March 10, A memorial service for the 26 miners was held at the Scotia new bathhouse at 11:00 a.m. Jennifer Boggs, whose husband Dennis was killed in the first explosion, obtained permission from the company to hold a service at the Ovenfork mine.

The Reverend Bill Mackey, Pastor of the Whitesburg First Baptist Church conducted the service. [+]

In late February, 1977, the Fresh Air crews made the transition from a mine recovery crew to a coal production crew. Like other coal production shifts, the day shift and second shift would be producing coal on the new section, while the third shift would do the maintenance work. Some of the third shift transferred to the production crews.

My classification when I came to the bottom mine was motorman, but in the production crew I worked as a shuttle car driver. The transition was fairly easy for me due to the greater height of the bottom mine and

[*] The *Whitesburg Mountain Eagle*, March 3, 1977.
[+] ibid March 10, 1977

the fact that although the shuttle cars were much bigger in the bottom mine, the older Torque cars were a cinch and great fun to operate. The shuttle car operators at the upper mines were bored because of repetition most of the time, but in the bottom mine the Torque cars had three gears, first, second, and third, which I called fast, faster, and fastest, because of the speed at which they could be operated. I really learned to love those shuttle cars and would have been pleased to have spent many years operating them.

The only drawback to being a shuttle car operator came five or six years later, when someone had a brainstorm and decided to install solid rubber tires on the SC 10 shuttle cars we had recently changed to. The solid tires would rattle the operator's teeth when a small bump was encountered. Kidneys and hemorrhoids were also affected and the backs of the operators hurt constantly, at home and at work.

Complaining did no good, even though all car drivers protested the tire change. We were told that the company put a lot of money into the change and we would have to live with it. I'm certain there were fewer flats (actually none of course) with the solid tires, but what was saved in time lost in fixing flats was miniscule in comparison with the production lost because of sick car operators and the fact that human beings couldn't run with those tires at the speed they did with air inflated tires.

At some point in time someone in a high position had mercy on us poor shaken shuttle car operators and installed our old air inflated tires on the 10 SC's. I imagine the medical bills were an indication that something was wrong with this picture, or maybe that person in a high position drove those solid tired back-breakers for a test drive. Either way, the change back to the old tires was a life-saver.

On Thursday, March 10, 1977, the last 900 ft. of the fatal 2 Southeast Mains Section was ventilated. The area was then investigated following the memorial period for the 26 miners of March 9 and 10.

Two months later, in May 1977, Harreld Kirkpatrick, Commissioner, Kentucky Department of Mines and Minerals, stated:

"Two locomotives had been going up a grade, pushing a load of steel and the wheels could have made a spark, plus they ran over a cable. All indications from what we have on paper are the first explosion did start around the locomotives, although what actually started it could have been quite a few things."

Kirkpatrick said the position of the two locomotives led his investigatory team to surmise that one (locomotive) had caused the first explosion.

Author's Note: Having worked on the recovery crew and seeing the area and observing both locomotives as they sat on the end of the track, one thing is perfectly clear to my eyes and others who worked with me. The steel cable that was dragged along with the wheel of the Goodman motor could not possibly have caused the explosion. In my opinion, and remember, I saw the motors sitting on the end of the track, the motors had already reached the end of the track and the parking brakes were set. The explosion happened while the motors were sitting still. I believe that if the steel cable had caused the explosion it would have happened before they reached the end of the track, not after they were parked there. So my conclusion #1 is that the first explosion was caused by the Goodman 6 ton locomotive with the brake compressor that kicked on every few minutes to build up pressure to the brakes.

Now about the second explosion; I was part of the crew that visited the 2 Left Section after the second explosion and the section had been ventilated. The official version of the cause of the second explosion was that a rock had fallen from the roof onto a bolting machine and caused a spark which set off the explosion. I, along with my co-workers, studied the scene on 2 Left. Nothing had been touched when we observed the surroundings on that section. We saw where the six miners had barricaded themselves inside a very small section of the mine. We saw how the corner of the barricade wasn't tight enough to keep the noxious gases outside the barricade. We saw where the infamous rock had fallen and was in fact, still lying on the bolting machine when we made our observations. The rock was, (to the best of my memory) about 4'x 6' and was in thickness about 6 to 8 inches, and had fallen about 4' from the roof onto the bolting machine. I thought at the time and still believe, even after the passage of over 40 years, that there was no way that rock had caused the second explosion. If the rock had been composed of sandstone or some other substance subject to cause sparking against metal, I might think differently, but slate is more akin to chalk that any other substance. Could the reader imagine a chalk-like rock as being the cause of a spark with a temperature of 1,200 degrees, which is the minimum heat needed to cause an explosion? I can't either. It's hardly possible that slate could spark to a temperature of 1,200 degrees, and it would have to fall from a greater distance that the 4' between the bolting machine and the roof (in my opinion.)

What else could account for the fact that the area around the bolting machine showed no signs of disturbance, except for the slate rock that had fallen on top of it? Even the rock dust was undisturbed by the so-called "explosion caused by a rock falling on the bolting machine."

I was, of course, only a Scotia recovery worker and not an official observer or investigator and will state here that the official story of the cause of the explosion will need to stay the official story. I'm not trying to change that. I'm just relating my thoughts and experiences at the time as someone who saw the scene first hand those many years ago and I want people to know that some of us had a different take of the cause of the second explosion.

Just for the record, let me say here that just as I am convinced that the second explosion wasn't caused by a falling rock on the bolting machine in the face area of 2 Left off 2 Southeast Mains, I'm equally convinced that the first explosion <u>was</u> caused by the Goodman motor with the compressor. I have been on that motor, have operated it many times after the motor was recovered from the explosion area, and observed the bright spark emanating from the compressor as it kicked on to build pressure for the brakes. It's without doubt (in my mind at least) the cause of the first and *likely the cause of the second explosion*. We'll never know for sure at this late date but using common sense in the absence of other evidence is entirely appropriate at this stage.

After the 2 Southeast Mains Section was opened and ventilated, it had to be re-sealed in late 1977 due to the many roof falls that occurred after the opening of the idle section. In early 1979, air samples taken from behind the seals in Southeast Mains showed an average of 12-13 percent methane at the No. 1 seal and 1-2 percent at the No. 8 seal. The lower than expected methane levels were attributed to the absence of coal production on the section.

In March, 1979, Mine Health and Safety (MSHA) officials stated that Scotia was now "one of the safest mines in Letcher County." Two MSHA inspectors, one on each production shift, were assigned to inspect Scotia each day as part of the federal inspectors program. This program places federal mine inspectors full time in mines with a history of safety problems.

Rehabilitation of the mine to improve the ventilation had been going on in stages since the explosions. The first part of the plan called for driving parallel airways from the 1-West section of the mine parallel to the South Main. This project was begun in November,1977. (The author worked on this section.)

The second stage called for a continuation of the ventilation passageways toward the (idle) Southeast sections of the mine. On August 10, 1978, Scotia miners began cutting from the inside out to connect with the passageways started in 1977.

Although Scotia was producing coal while driving the panels, Lawrence Phillips, MESA District Director, said, "The airways are being driven for a specific purpose and are not laid out for high coal production." At the time the airways were being driven only two coal producing sections were actively producing coal.

On January 12 1979, Scotia and federal officials had approved a plan to drive from 2 Southeast to within 200 ft of the still sealed 2 Southeast Mains Section. Mining officials projected that this plan would take nine months to cut within 200 ft of the sealed area.

Hargis Ison, supervisor of coal mine inspectors in MESA's Whitesburg office, said that, "This would leave a 200 ft block of coal surrounding the sealed area," while plans were being made for entering the 2 Southeast Mains area. "When Southeast Mains is driven into, said Ison, creating additional ventilation, the mine will be opened for the first time since 1976."

"After this phase, all areas of the mine affected by the explosions will be ventilated and accessible," said Lawrence Phillips, MESA District Director. "It's logical to assume that there is a lot of methane in there (2 Southeast Mains. That is probably to our advantage since anything over 15 percent is not explosive," he said. "We hope the methane level is around 75 to 80 percent." ±

In 1978, Blue Diamond Coal Company, the parent company of Scotia Coal Company, made a tentative agreement with the Indiana Standard Oil Company to sell its assets for 2.6 million common shares of Indiana Standard stocks. Blue Diamond had mined slightly less than 2 million tons of coal the year before in its six mines located in Kentucky, Tennessee, and Virginia, with revenues of about $46 million.

The acquisition of Blue Diamond assets was subject to the approval of Blue Diamond stock holders and directors, with Blue Diamond president Gordon Bonneyman and members of his family believed to be the principle owners of Blue Diamond. The deal fell through.

In 1986, longwall mining was introduced at Scotia in an effort to increase production and achieve more profitability. The first three longwall

---

± ibid March 1, 1977

panels were developed in an older part of the mine, under about 1,000 feet of cover.

These three panels were of a conventional three entry, yield abutment pillar design on 48 and 120 ft centers. After leaving those panels the longwall was moved to a large area of coal reserves that were located under much greater cover than were the first three panels. In this large area of reserves, a series of panels, each measuring 700 ft wide and 7,000 ft long were projected to mine in sequence.

Longwall sections were capable of putting out a tremendous amount of coal in an 8 hour shift, and in like manner, took a lot of man-hours to set up to prepare for production of a panel. A move from one panel to the next required a small army to accomplish. Every shield and every piece of the longwall had to be moved by rail and took several weeks to complete each move. There were close to 100 shields (40 ton roof jacks) that had to be moved one at a time and set up in the new longwall panel during a move.

Enough timbers were required to be set in advance of the longwall likely took a good sized forest of trees to be made into 8"x8" x4' timbers for cribbing the return and intake entries of a longwall section. I spent several months helping timber ahead of Scotia's longwall machine and eating the dust the shear spewed. My respirator filter had to be changed every hour, but most of the dust came into the lungs via the rubber face seals which were in fact nearly useless in keeping the dust out.

Imagine if you can, having to climb up the side of a not-yet-tightened 10 or 12 ft high crib with a heavy 8"x8" on your shoulder that must be placed on the top rung of the crib while holding on to the unfinished crib blocks in order to keep from falling to the mine floor. This was the life of a crib man trying to stay ahead of a giant machine that is capable of cutting down over 1,000 tons of coal per hour. Ten hours of uninterrupted coal production would fill a 100 car unit train, which are statistics that boggle a coal miner's mind, almost.

The only drawback with such a coal producing monster is in the moving to a new panel. I remember once at Scotia where there was a major breakdown of something (don't remember what) during the moving of the shields and the move to a new panel took more than a month instead of the projected and normal two weeks it usually took to make a new move. Scotia officials were getting desperate after so long of a delay to get back into production. I wouldn't doubt but that hundreds of thousands of dollars were lost on that particular set-up.

In March 1979, three years after the two fatal explosions at Scotia, two Scotia miners lost their lives in a roof fall in the Upper Taggart seam of coal. Grant Sturgill, age 46, and Ernest Statzer, 38, were killed, while another miner, Larkin Napier, a continuous miner operator, managed to escape with his life due to the protection provided by the canopy on the machine. It took rescue teams six hours to tunnel through the rock in order to rescue him.

In August, 1980, Blue Diamond Coal Company, in an out-of-court settlement, settled the suit between themselves and the 13 widows and 22 children of the 15 men who died in the first explosion at Scotia for $5.9 million, but it could add up to $10 or 12 million in total damages to the survivors who chose the long-term deferred annuities benefit. The company also agreed to pay back $400,000 that the widows have received in worker's compensation benefits should those payments be successfully challenged as a result of the negligence settlement.

In June, 1981, the Federal Government settled the suit filed by the widows of the eight non-government employees of Scotia Coal Company that were killed in the second explosion for $2.1 million. The widows' attorney, Gerald Stern of Washington D.C., had sought $8 million in damages from the United States on behalf of the widows of the eight non-government employees who died in the explosion. The three Mine Enforcement and Safety Administration inspectors were covered by Government indemnity payments.

On Tuesday, July 13, 1982, the Scotia Employees Association went on strike. This is the letter that was sent to union members:

Scotia Employees Association

To All Members

As everyone is aware by now, our union is on strike, because of disputes in our contract talks. In order for our strike to be effective it is very important that each and every member participate. Our contract, (and equally so, our strike) effects not only the 221 Union members who were working as of 7/17/82, but also, the 225 who are on layoff panel.

Since it is hard to depend solely on volunteers to man the picket lines, we feel it necessary to set up a schedule by shifts. If each member does his part, it will only be necessary to be on picket duty once every three days. Surely, each of us can put in this minimum amount of time to try and insure our jobs.

A picket duty schedule will be posted at the Union Hall, so that each person can check to see which shift and mine he/she is scheduled to picket at. If you are scheduled for a particular shift, and cannot take part, it will be your duty to have someone in your place on the line.

If everyone does not participate, it will be necessary to put an assessment on each man not pulling his required duty. If you have questions about the picket schedule, you can call (the Union Hall.)

By participating in this picket duty, we have an opportunity, not only to make the union stronger, but we will also show the company that we are together, as a whole group for the first time, and that we are serious in our intentions.

Benny Adams, President
Mike Dingus, Secretary

Below is a letter I received from Blue Diamond Coal Company in May, 1983 while a few union employees still remained laid off:

Blue Diamond Coal Company

May 16, 1983

Dear Mr. Nickles: (sic)

This is to apprise you of the situation at the Scotia Mine. This week we plan to recall 21 contract employees in order to check out and ready the underground equipment in the Imboden Mine and the preparation plant for operation.

The issue confronting the Company and the Union is what level of sales can we capture in order to recall employees and keep them employed, and how soon can we increase the number of people working. Coal markets continue to be extremely soft and the level of production at which we would prefer to operate is greater than our present sales commitments, but we would like to commence operations at a higher level in order to be more efficient.

The only way of accomplishing our goal of higher production is to lower our cost of mining and gain a larger market share (by selling our coal cheaper). Accordingly, we have requested your mine committee to submit the following program for consideration at your May 21st meeting.

1. Delay the July 1983 wage increase to April 1, 1984.
2. Delay the July 1984 wage increase to January 1, 1985.
3. Blue Diamond will employ at least 100 contract employees from June 1, 1983 until the end of the contract to keep the delay in effect.

We have discussed in detail with your mine committee the Company's plans to reduce mining costs in order to gain more sales. These include the investment of $3 million in borrowed funds for a new mine and new equipment to improve productivity and lower costs. Mine management and the mine committee are familiar with the situation at Scotia and I urge you to discuss with them how the program above could help us achieve a higher level of employment.

Sincerely,
Ted B. Helms (Executive Vice President)

CHAPTER TWENTY ONE

Decisions and Fines

IN 1982, the demand for coal began a decline in one of those infamous "bust" cycles that have been a part of a coal miner's life ever since commercial coal mining began in the United States. This resulted in a partial lay-off for Scotia workers, who then numbered approximately 446 men and women hourly employees. The number laid off was 225, while employees remaining on the job numbered 221 union members.

A few laid-off workers at a time were called back to work after a few months, but the majority would be out of work for about nine months or more. When a call-back to work came for an individual miner, it was usually in a different classification, as the employee was called from the lay-off panel by seniority as per contract.

Although I was among those laid off for a few months I was fortunate enough to be called back in the same classification, (shuttle car operator). During this period of time and for the next 4-5 years, the section that I was on went through several section foremen, for a variety of reasons. Most of them were promoted into a better position, and some of them were transferred to a new mine or a new section.

So many years have passed since then that I have forgotten the different names of sections where our production crew worked, but most of us stayed together as a unit through the years. Of course there were always some that quit their job or changed their section or job classification from time to time, but on the whole, more section foremen left the section than hourly employees.

Some of the men I worked during this period included:
Mike Halcomb, Bill Kilbourne, Brad Whitaker, Doyle Perry, Wesley Rosenbaum, Tim Maggard, Paul Maggard, Joe Shelton, Tommy Gross, Clifford Smith, William "Bill" Blair, Wayne Wilson, Stephen Miles, James

Miles, Hargus Maggard, Charlie Davidson, Larry Childers, Steve Brock, Mack Brock, Roger Sturgill, Kenneth Sturgill, Mike Sullivan, William "Bill" Collier, Paul Fields, Frank Fields, Jerry Dixon, Walt Brown, "Preacher" Fleming, Jerry Kirk, Jerry Smith, James Sargent, Hershal Fields, Charlie Baker, Adean Adams, Bennett Adams, Larry Brock, Mike Dingus, Jimmy Nickels- (my brother), Philip Nickels,- (my brother), Danny Adams, Doug Arnett (killed in a roof fall), Johnny Breeding (killed in a roof fall), Bob Smith, Joe Collins, John Caudill, Wayne Day, Eddie Bentley, Connie McKnight, David Morris, Luther Halcomb, "Booty" Halcomb, Willie Perry, Johnny Adams, Gary Sexton, Steve Sturgill, James Sargent, Larry and Buddy Brock, and many others whose names I don't recall.

Some of the Section Foremen over the years include:
Wayne McDougal, Jerry Gilliam, John Fuller, Veril Boggs, Jack Begley, Bob Childers, Bruce Jones, Sonny Cornett. Jimmy Adams, Merle Rhodes, J.R. Ison, Ben Rose, Eddie Taylor, Carl Petry, Bill Baker, Jerry McCowan, John Dixon, David McKnight, John Richardson, and Jerry Herrin.

William "Bill" Blair was my neighbor who worked on my coal producing section at Scotia as a continuous miner helper. He had retired as a printer in Illinois, then he and his wife (Joy) moved back home to Letcher County when he retired. I was sitting in a cross-cut in my shuttle car waiting my turn to be loaded with coal from the continuous miner when I watched as the coal rib and drawrock broke off where he was standing and pinned his leg to the mine bottom, breaking it. The rock and coal was around 4' thick and I first feared that he was killed, but as I ran towards him, I saw his caplight shining against the roof, so I knew he wasn't covered completely up, but he was caught from his thigh to his foot. It took several of us to remove the rock and get him to the track, but he barely complained the whole time. He was a WWII veteran and never seemed to get excited no matter what happened. After a month or two, he came back to work in his miner helping job, as if nothing out of the ordinary had happened.

Bill was the only man I ever met who was present when my grandfather G. C.Sexton was killed in the mine at Thornton, Kentucky, in December, 1940. Bill said a loaded car of coal jumped the track (my grandfather was a brakeman) and pinned him against the coal rib. He lived just long enough to get on the surface and managed to say, "I just thank God that He allowed me to live this long." He was 53 years old when he was killed.

After the two explosions at Scotia, there were many repercussions, including heavy fines instituted against the Company. Below is the decision and order of the many violations written in the aftermath of the tragedies:

Federal Mine Safety and Health review Commission
Office of Administration Law Judge

Secretary of Labor,
Mine Safety and Health
Administration (MSHA,
Petitioner-Respondent

v.

Scotia Coal Company
Respondent-Applicant

Decision and Order

In the aftermath of the twin methane gas explosions of March 9& 11 1976, that took the lives of 23 miners and 3 mine inspectors at the Scotia Mine in Ovenfork, Letcher County, Kentucky, the Secretary of the Interior cited Scotia Coal Company, a wholly owned subsidiary of Blue Diamond Coal Company, Knoxville, Tennessee, for 71 violations of the Federal Coal Mine Health and Safety Act of 1969. (Footnote 1) –Footnotes are at end of the report). Two years later, civil penalties were assessed in the amount of $266,404.

The 43 less serious violations were settled in December 1980 for $33,400, subject to approval of the trial judge, with the consent of the parties, increased the settlement amount to $36,400 and dismissed these 43 charges.

The 28 captioned review-penalty proceedings cover the 15 conditions and practices believed by the Secretary to have contributed directly to the lethal accumulation of methane gas and the ignition that caused the first explosion, (see footnote 2) plus one combustible and 12 electrical violations uncovered during the course of the departmental investigation that were believed to be indicative of a pervasive indifference to safe mining practices.

These 28 unwarrantable failure to comply violations were initially assessed at $230,500. On Thursday, November 12, 1981, the parties entered into a settlement agreement under which Scotia offered to pay the lump sum of $200,000, or 87% of the amount initially assessed, which sum was allocated by the Secretary in accordance with his evaluation of the "individual meaning and collective significance of the violations" for the 1976 disaster. The sum offered in settlement will be the largest ever paid by a mine operator for civil penalties assessed as the result of a single coal mine disaster. (Footnote 3)

Except as other indicated, my (the Judge's) evaluation and allocation of the $200,000 accords with that recommended by the Secretary. (Footnote 4)

I fully concur in the Secretary's overall evaluation of the gravity of these evaluations, namely, that "When viewed in the light of the underlying mine practices and the events of March 9, 1976.... The violations, individually and collectively are seen as extremely grave, occurring through culpable negligence, the products of reckless management attitudes and a method of operation which demonstrated indifference to federal safety standards." (Footnote 5)

A.

For the contributory violations, which include the six violations covered by the pending criminal indictment, (Footnote 6) the Secretary assessed the maximum statutory amount of $10,000 each, finding that "The violations cannot be viewed in isolation, but must be considered within the context of mine management's attitude, which condoned and even fostered the simultaneous existence of so many serious, related violations. The deadly interaction of these violations produced the tragic results."

I (the Judge) concur in this finding and in the Secretary's further finding that:

The ultimate illustration of the destructive reinforcement of related violations occurred in the explosion area of 2 Southeast Main (s). To begin with, Scotia failed to comply with its approved Ventilation Plan when starting the 2 Left section off 2 Southeast Main (s). Ventilation in the area was questionable, at best, and had not received MESA approval, although Scotia knew that such approval was required. (The proposal, had it been submitted, would not have been approved.) Production in 2 Left Section should have proceeded only after positive, permanent ventilation controls had been installed. By using a makeshift temporary curtain before it completed construction of overcasts, Scotia ignored prudent ventilation methods, as well as federal standards, for the sake of a short-term production gain---a- gain as it turned out, achieved at a terrible price.

Even assuming (as Scotia claims) a check curtain was hung at the intersection of 2 Left Section with 2 Southeast Main (s), the lack of permanent ventilation controls at that point created the potential for a dangerous short-circuit of intake air and a ventilation "dead end" at the inby end of 2 Southeast Main (s). If the check curtain was installed, it was reportedly maintained in such a haphazard manner as to provide little, if any, ventilation control, thus enhancing the potential for a short-circuit of air. Then, the night before the explosion occurred, plastic curtains were hung in the Nos. 4 and 5 entries (the intake air courses) of 2 Southeast Main (s) inby the 2 Left Section, thus aggravating the risk of methane accumulation in the area.

Another violation of Scotia's ventilation plan, together with another ventilation dead end was found at the inby end of Northeast Main. The Secretary assessed maximum penalties for these violations as well as for a violation which charged that on March 1, 1976, Scotia knowingly submitted to MESA a mine map which concealed those conditions and compounded the hazards created by the violations of Scotia's Ventilation Plan. When considered in the context of Scotia's pattern of violations, I find this action fully warranted.

B.

To its hazardous ventilation practices, the Secretary found Scotia added a reckless indifference to its obligation to inspect and examine idle or dead end areas for explosive accumulations of methane gas. Another violation maximally assessed charged that on the morning of March 9, 1976, the dead end area of 2 Southeast Main (s), an area which had been idle since February 9, 1976, was not examined for a deadly methane accumulation prior to the time two miners were ordered to haul a load of steel rails into the area using two locomotives with electrical connections capable of causing an incendive (sic) spark. (Footnote 7) The Secretary's evaluation, in which I concur, states:

Scotia's failure to examine 2 Southeast Main (s) inby 2 Left Section on March 9, 1976, is particularly glaring since management knew that the entire 2 Southeast Main (s), including 2 Left Section, was being ventilated in violation of Scotia's approved Ventilation Plan, and the potential existed for a dangerous short-circuit of intake air and a ventilation "dead end."...

.....the management foreman who ordered the workmen to enter the area had a duty to verify that the area had been examined before the miners were to enter, or that the workmen were qualified and equipped to make such examinations. The failure to so verify or to have the examinations done constituted an un warrantable failure on the part of mine management to comply with the standards, especially in view of the specific knowledge of management that the ventilation system in the 2 Southeast Main (s) area posed a potential for methane accumulation inby 2 Left Section. When the violation of Order No. 4 LPD is viewed in context with other major violations also present, this management failure to grasp the last chance to avoid culmination of the hazards it had created, starkly illustrates Scotia's reckless indifference to federal safety standards.

Violations of the preshift examination (methane checks) requirement were found in three of the five working sections of the Scotia Mine. The Secretary's view, in which I concur, was that:

Taken together, and along with other examination violations, these violations reflect clear indifference to safety. Buttressing this disturbing conclusion is the evidence that Scotia employed only one regular fireboss to make the preshift examinations required to be performed in the widely-dispersed working sections within three hours before beginning the

7:00 a.m., day shift. This employee's normal work shift ended at 5:00 a.m., allowing only one hour of regular work time (between 4:00 a.m. and 5:00 a. m.) to perform all the examinations required before the day shift began.

C.

The constraints on the time and availability of a fireboss resulted in a charge that it was allegedly the practice of the fireboss to certify to pre-shift examinations that were not made or certainly not made by him. It was, of course the alleged failure to make preshift or onshift methane checks in the idled section (the dead end) of 2 Southeast Main (s) that set the stage for the explosion that occurred when the two locomotives came to a stop at the 31st crosscut at 11:45 a.m., Tuesday March 9, 1976.

The final ingredient of the lethal mix that resulted in the disaster of March 9 was introduced when the Scotia Mine's underground construction foreman arranged to have a motor crew pick up a load of rails with the Nos. 6 and 8 battery-powered locomotives for delivery to the dead end of 2 Southeast Main (s). This was the area in which ventilation had been totally blocked for six or seven hours on the evening shift the day before by the installation of check curtains across the Nos. 4 and 5 (intake air) entries. (Footnote 8)

Although ventilation of some sort was restored around midnight on March 8, it was inby this ventilation stoppage that an explosive concentration of methane occurred before 11;45 a.m., March 9. To my mind the intentional interruption of the air flow into an area known to liberate explosive concentrations of methane gas was an act of reckless endangerment that finds no excuse in the claimed negligence of MESA in failing to detect the action. For these reasons, I fully concur in the assessment of maximum penalties for these violations.

D.

When high enough concentrations of methane gas, 5 to 15 percent, in an underground coal mine are associated with inadequate ventilation and an ignition source, a violent coal mine explosion is very likely to occur. (Footnote 9)

According to the Secretary the "evidence is conclusive" that the ignition source in the case of the first explosion was on one of the battery-operated locomotives, and most likely the No. 6, (Goodman) locomotive. As the Secretary points out, "The evidence, which includes positive laboratory tests demonstrates that, on or within each locomotive, there were several potential ignition sources for an explosive methane-air mixture."

In the case of the No. 6 (Goodman), locomotive, the Secretary claims a "copper wire bridge" was deliberately inserted in order to reactivate the circuit after the fuse element had broken." In the case of the No. 8, (Westinghouse) locomotive the Secretary's representatives claimed they "observed that electrical connections to the terminals of the locomotive batteries and between the batteries themselves, were neither mechanically nor electrically efficient, a condition chiefly due to the absence of suitable connectors."

Neither of these violations, however, is believed by MESA's experts to have been "the actual cause of the spark which ignited the methane gas of March 9." What the experts hypothesize is "that the accumulated methane gas was ignited by the arcing created by the open-type controller on the No. 6 Goodman locomotive when the controller was turned to the "off" position by the locomotive operator after reaching his destination at the inby end of 2 Southeast Main (s)."

The controller, of course, is the device on electrically- powered locomotives that regulates speed and direction. Counsel for the Secretary suggests that the absence of a permissible, explosive proof controller on the No. 6 locomotive was not a violation because it was not taken inby the last open crosscut of 2 Southeast Main (s) on March 9. Recent decisions by the commission indicate that if the locomotives were manufactured as permissible equipment, as apparently they were, they may be deemed intended for use inby the last open crosscut and should, therefore, have been maintained in a permissible, i. e., explosion proof condition.

I concur in the maximum assessments for the two electrical violations on the locomotives because their presence (1) was indicative of a knowing disregard for voluntary compliance and (2) they or similar conditions completed the triad of circumstances that contributed directly to the explosion of March 9.

II

A

The Secretary allotted $42,500 of the proffered settlement sum among 12 electrical violations. These, while not believed to have contributed to the conditions which caused the explosion of March 9, 1976, created severe electrical shock hazards and potential sources for explosive ignitions. In his prehearing submission, the Secretary found these violations were "part of a pervasive failure" to comply and stated he believed,

......these violations were caused not only by a systemic failure in electrical maintenance, but also by the Coal Act and its standards. A close look at these violations demonstrates they did not result from mere happenstance. Most were clear, unmistakable breaches of the electrical protections of the standards, and ironic evidence of Scotia's "production at all costs" attitude; ironic because the investigation revealed that the mine electrical system, as originally purchased and installed, was high-grade.

While the $42,500 allocated amounted to a 42% reduction in the amount initially assessed for these 12 violations, I find that when viewed in the context of the total settlement (Footnote 10) the allocation made was reasonable.

B

The last violation covered by the proffered settlement involves an alleged excessive accumulation of float coal dust. Investigators found excessive float coal dust, which is highly explosive, deposited on rock-dusted surfaces for a distance of approximately 2,500 feet in the 1 West Main, running from the mouth of the main inby along the conveyor belt entry. The accumulation covered the layer of white rock dust to such an extent that the area appeared black in color. The belt roller, of course, provided a potential source of heat and ignition that could have caused a fire or explosion. The existence of this violation is another example of the operator's reckless disregard for voluntary compliance. The Secretary allocated $7,500 to the settlement of this violation which was the amount initially assessed by MESA. I concur in this action.

III

Had the result in these proceedings been achieved within two years after the Scotia disaster, it might have been cited as a triumph of effective enforcement. Coming as it does at this late date, in the context of new, multiple mine disasters, it may be further proof of the adage that laggardly enforcement and justice delayed is tragedy invited. (Footnote 11)

The enormity of the social and economic cost of these mine disasters compels I take note of the great and continuing hazards that both operators and miners face twelve years after enactment of the mandatory safety standards and almost six years after the Scotia Mine disaster. The latest news bulletins disclose that during the five-day period between December 3 and 8, 1981, 27 miners were killed in coal mine accidents and explosions and that deaths among underground coal miners in 1981 were the highest in seven years. Even as this is written a mine explosion at the R.F.H. Coal Company in Craynor, Kentucky is reported to have killed seven more miners for a total of 33 miners killed in less than two months.

Meanwhile, MSHA has indicated that it intends to comply with the administration's budget-cutting plans by projecting the elimination of up to 150 underground coal mine inspectors, reducing the number of enforcement personnel from 1,629 to 1,479. (Footnote 12) At least 153 miners were killed on the job in U.S. coal mines during 1981, compared with 133 in all of 1980. To reduce the enforcement effort by 10% when fatal accidents are up 15% represents the kind of callous illogic that few intimately engaged in coal mine health and safety can endorse.

I also take cognizance of the fact that for no discernable reason the 1982 budget for the Federal Mine Safety and Health Review Commission was slashed by 28%, from $4.3 million to $3.1 million, and that the commission, which is a vital link in the enforcement effort, suffered a 28% reduction in its support staff and administration law judges. This crippling blow to the prompt adjudication of enforcement cases will seriously disrupt the Commission's already limited ability to protect miners and to afford operators a forum for expedited determination of their challenges to erroneous closure orders and other enforcement actions.

In the face of the rising rate of institutional manslaughter, the calls for further deregulation and relaxation of the enforcement effort seem unreal, if not morally irresponsible. (Footnote 13) Several statistical studies have found that safety improves with the frequency of federal inspections. (Footnote 14) A study of 539 bituminous underground coal mines producing more than 100.000 tons annually indicated a 50% increase in federal inspection rates would result in 11 fewer fatalities, 2,400 fewer disabling injuries, and 3,800 fewer non--disabling injuries per year. (Footnote 15)

The staggering fact is that over 2,000 miners have been killed since Congress passed the Mine Safety Law in 1969. The statistics show this is the worst occupational safety record of any major industry and that laxity in the enforcement effort has resulted in a sharp reversal of the improvements of the last few years. It is time we stopped regarding the rising tide of deaths and disabling injuries with complacency. Something must be done and done quickly to correct the low level of morale at both the inspectorate and adjudicatory levels.

IV

..... Notwithstanding my misgivings and the absence of any assurance that corporate management's attitude toward mine safety has changed, (Footnote 16), an independent evaluation and de novo review of the entire administrative record including the MESA "Report of the Scotia Mine Disaster," (Footnote 17) the Secretary of Labor's Verified Statement to Judge Hermansdorfer concerning the same and the mine operators' comments thereon, leads me reluctantly to conclude the settlement proposed is in accord with the purposes and policy of the act.

Accordingly, it is ordered that the motions to approve settlement and to withdraw the challenges to the validity of the orders be, and hereby are, GRANTED. It is FURTHER ORDERED that the operator pay the amount of the settlement agreed upon, $200,000, on or before Monday March 1, 1982, and that subject to payment the captioned matters be dismissed.[*]

Joseph B. Kennedy
Administrative Law Judge

Footnote One
In March 1978, responsibility for enforcement was shifted from the Secretary of the Interior to the Secretary of Labor and from the Mining Enforcement and Safety Administration (MESA) to the Mine Safety and Health Administration (MSHA).

Footnote Two
Responsibility for the second explosion, at a time when the government was in control of the mine, is the subject of separate litigation between Blue Diamond and the Department of Justice. Claims brought by the survivors of the miners killed in the first explosion were settled for approx-

---

[*] https://wwwfmshrc.gov/decisions/alj/82010089.pdf (assessed 5-15-17)

imately 6 million dollars in 1980 and by survivors of the victims of the second explosion for approximately 2 million dollars in 1981. Boggs v. Blue Diamond Coal Company, 590 F. 2nd 655 (6th Cir. 1979). In the pending criminal case, the United States seeks the imposition of $240,000 in criminal penalties against the corporate mine operators. United States v. Blue Diamond Coal Company,---F. 2nd---, No. 80-5084, 6th Circuit, decided December 17, 1981.

Footnote Three
When the present settlement proposal, $200,000, is added to the sum already paid, $36,400, the mine operators will have paid a total of $236,400 in civil penalties which is 89% of MESA's initial assessment for the 71 violations charged.

Footnote Four
The Secretary's evaluation appears in counsel's motion to approve settlement which incorporated by reference counsel's earlier response to the trial judge's pretrial order of May 1, 1980. Counsel for the Secretary is to be commended for the clarity of expression and organization of these pleadings and for the diligence demonstrated in their preparation.

Footnote Five
It is the Secretary's position that both Blue Diamond Coal Company and Scotia Coal Company were responsible for the safety violations at the Scotia Mine.

Footnote Six
On June 25, 1979, a Federal Grand Jury in Pikeville, Kentucky handed down an indictment charging Blue Diamond and Scotia Coal Companies with six criminal violations of the Mine Safety Law. Four counts charge a willful failure to comply with the ventilation plan for the Scotia Mine and to make required inspections and examinations for potentially explosive concentrations of methane gas. The mine operators are also charged with two counts of making knowingly false statements in records required to be maintained with respect to its ventilation and examination practices.

On February 19, 1980, Judge Hermansdorfer of the United States District Court for the Eastern District of Kentucky granted the mine operators motion to suppress evidentiary records on the ground that their seizure violated the mine operators' rights under the Search and Seizure Clause of the Fourth Amendment. The United States appealed the suppression order and on December 17, 1981, the Court of Appeals for the Sixth Circuit reversed the decision of the District Court finding that the warrantless seizure of statutorily required records from the office of a coal operator is not violative (sic)of the Fourth Amendment. United States v. Blue Diamond Coal Company, supra. The mine operators will reportedly petition the court for a rehearing and may seek a review of the matter by the Supreme Court. Past and prospective delays in the criminal proceeding vindicate the Commission's decision to deny the mine operators a stay of the civil penalty proceedings pending final resolution of the criminal proceedings. Scotia Coal Mining Company, 2 FMSHRC 622; 1 MSHC 2327 (1980)

Footnote Seven
An incendive (sic) spark is an electrical spark of sufficient intensity to ignite a gas or other flammable material.

Footnote Eight
This was done to achieve temporary compliance with a notice of violation issued by a MESA inspector between 3:30 and 4:00 o'clock that afternoon. This citation issued when the inspector found less than 9,000 cubic feet of air per minute was sweeping the last open crosscut of the 2 Left Section. The notice was terminated about two hours later when the inspector re-measured the air flow and found it to be 10,472 feet per minute. The inspector, who was on the section for approximately seven hours, never attempted to determine how the additional 2,360 feet of air flow was achieved. MESA and the Secretary claim he was not authorized to inspect any area of the mine other than the 2 Left Section and therefore did not concern himself with the adequacy of the ventilation controls or with the short-circuit of the ventilation into the dead end area of 2 Southeast Main (s). Had he done so he might have discovered that in order to achieve compliance with his citation the operator had robbed air from 2 Southeast Main (s) and that the entire section was being operated in violation of the approved Ventilation Plan. This arbitrary and somewhat incredible limitation on inspection activity deprived the miners of a last clear chance for the federal regulatory presence to intervene and to avert the disaster.

Footnote Nine

The legislative history of the Mine Safety Law reflects congressional concern for the danger of explosions resulting from ignition of undetected accumulations of methane in coal mines:

The most hazardous condition that can exist in a coal mine, and lead to disaster-type accidents, is the accumulation of methane gas in explosive amounts. Methane can be ignited with relatively little energy and there are, even under the best mining conditions, numerous potential sources always present. Men working in the face areas where coal is mined and where fresh methane can be emitted in large volumes due to the disturbance of the coal bed, are required to take numerous safety precautions to ensure that methane is not present in explosive amounts, All equipment inby the last open crosscut must be of a permissible type, and frequent examinations, both preshift and onshift, are made to determine methane concentrations. The present bill requires examinations for methane onshift at least once each coal producing shift, at the start of each coal producing shift before electrical equipment is energized, at least every 20 minutes during a shift when electrically operated equipment is energized, before intentional roof falls are made, before explosives are fired, and before welding is done. When, on examination, methane concentrations exceeds 1.5 volume per centum, the electricity must be shut off in the section affected, and men withdrawn from the section until the methane content is reduced. H.R. Rep. No. 91-563, 91st Cong., 1st Sess. 21.
Footnote 10

The average per violation for the 28 violations is $7, 142.85 which is the highest average ever paid for a comparable number of violations.

Footnote Eleven

Existing and prospective budgetary restrictions raise the specter of a de facto, if not a de jure, repeal of the act. Despite conventional political wisdom to the contrary, experience teaches that in the mining industry, and especially underground coal mining, voluntarism is no substitute for compulsory enforcement. The history of mine safety shows a federal regulatory presence is required to reduce disastrous accidents and achieve even a modicum of safety.

Footnote Twelve

Due to action of the Congress, another 210 metal and non-metal mine inspectors have been furloughed. (At that time.)

Footnote Thirteen

The importance of the federal enforcement effort is well recognized by the miners, especially the non-union miners. As one West Virginia miner put it, "The only thing keeping the rock off your back when you're two miles underground is Government regulations." See "Miners, Mr. President, Are not slag," Op. Ed. Page, N.Y. Times, Sunday, January 24, 1982.

Footnote Fourteen

Low productivity in American Coal Mining: Causes and Cures, GAO Rpt. EMD 81-17, March 3, 1981, at 55-56

Footnote Fifteen

The Direct Use of Coal, Office of Technology Assessment, Congress of the United States, (1979), at 283

Footnote Sixteen

Counsel for Scotia have always stoutly maintained that because MESA was in pari delicto, the operator culpability, if any, was extremely low. Counsel have made clear that the settlement is proffered solely in the interest of conserving their clients financial resources and not out of any sense of social remorse or responsibility.

Footnote Seventeen

This report was received in camera and has never been publicly released because of an outstanding suppression order issued by judge Hermansdorfer in January, 1978. Since the report is not admissible in the criminal case and most of the civil litigation has been settled, I strongly recommend the Department of Justice seek vacation of the suppression order. My independent review of the matter leads me to conclude that while the report, as supplemented, is not perfect, it is trustworthy. Furthermore, the conclusions reached at p. 57 are supported by a preponderance of the reliable, probative and substantial evidence in the administrative record considered as a whole. Thie is not to say that ventilation problems were not either undetected or ignored by MESA or could not have been, by the exercise of greater diligence or suspicion, discovered. Nevertheless, two wrongs do not make a right, nor is the public interest served by surpressing the report because a court arguably believed MESA tried to coverup its own wrong-doing at the expense of the mine operators. The law places primary responsibility for compliance on the mine operators. With all due deference to Judge Hermansdorfer, my independent review of the administrative record leads me to conclude that actors other than God and MESA were primarily responsible for the concentration of methane gas that exploded at the 31st crosscut of the 2 Southeast Main (s) Section of the Scotia Mine at 11:45 a.m., Tuesday March 9, 1976.

CHAPTER TWENTY TWO

Striving to Succeed

After the two mine explosions of March 9 and 11, 1976, some, if not many, people assumed that Scotia management would be not only penalized with heavy fines, but criminal charges would likely be filed against the Company. Their assumptions proved to be correct.

We have learned in chapter Twenty that Scotia paid $236,400 in civil penalties for the 71 violations cited after the two explosions, which was 89% of MESA's initial assessment for the violations. We learned also that the sum offered in settlement would be the largest ever paid by a coal mine operator for civil penalties assessed as the result of a single coal mine disaster.

On June 25 1979, a Federal Grand Jury in Pikeville, Kentucky handed down an indictment charging Blue Diamond and Scotia Coal Companies with six criminal violations of the Mine Safety Law. Four counts charge a willful failure to comply with the ventilation plan for the Scotia Mine and to make required inspections and examinations for potentially explosive concentrations of methane gas. Two counts were charges of making knowingly false statements in records required to be maintained with respect to its ventilation and examination practices.

In early April, 1983, the criminal charges were dropped against Blue Diamond and Scotia Coal Companies in a plea deal with federal prosecutors. In exchange for dropping all six criminal charges, Scotia agreed to plead guilty in two criminal counts and pleaded no contest to three other counts contained in the June 1979 indictment.

Under the agreement Scotia pleaded guilty to:

- Failing to train each of its miners in the use of self-rescuing devises, and
- Falsifying mine records about a pre-shift mine examination The company also pleaded no contest to charges that it,
- Knowingly falsified mine ventilation maps to show ventilation devices appearing in places where there were none.
- Did not follow the approved ventilation plans for the No. 1 Mine, or properly control levels of methane and coal dust in the mine.
- Did not have a certified person check or "fireboss" idle areas of the No. 1 Mine for methane and for oxygen deficiency shortly before miners went to work on March 9.

Blue Diamond claimed that the guilty pleas were not an admission of guilt on Scotia's part. Rather, said Blue Diamond vice president Herman Stallard, the agreement was reached to bring litigation stemming from the first explosion to an end. "This has been dragging on forever and ever and everything has got to come to an end," Stallard told reporters.

Blue Diamond attorney Robert I. Cusick of Louisville said the company does not "feel guilty." According to Cusick, Blue Diamond entered into the plea bargain arrangement because of the "tremendous displacement of money and attention that would occur in a trial that might last two to three weeks."

A spokesman for the U.S. Justice Department in Washington said the agreement represents, " a savings of time and money. It has been dragging on for a long time."

Some widows of the men killed in the Scotia explosions criticized the government for the plea-bargaining agreement.

"I'm surprised they (Scotia) admitted their guilt but I also can't understand why they dropped the charges," said a Cumberland woman who is the widow of a miner killed in the second explosion.

"All they are going to get is a little fine and I think more charges should be filed," said the widow, who asked that her name not be used. "I think they ought to lay it to them. Fifteen lives is a lot of people, but they don't seem to care."

"It's almost as if Scotia is taking a fall-guy position to let Blue Diamond get off," said Geraldine King, widow of Roy McKnight, a miner killed in the first explosion." "We had hoped with our case to make some of these parent firms more responsible," said Mrs. King, who has remarried and now lives in Louisville. "I'm amazed by it because we held that Blue Diamond was liable."

Another widow said she doesn't think the $95,000 in fines Scotia may have to pay is a large enough penalty.

"It's a small price to pay," said Libby Gibbs of Brodhead, the widow of Dennis Boggs. "That doesn't seem like very much to me."

More than a dozen lawsuits have been filed as a result of the Scotia disasters. [+]

The following is a poem by a former Scotia coal miner, Pat Pate. This poem was published in _The Mountain Eagle_ , Whitesburg, Kentucky, March 10, 1983:

Scotia Remembered

My Friend, the Coal Miner

There is no man on earth who is finer
Than you my friend, the coal miner
I was with you from two until ten
I was with you thru thick and thin
I was with you in sickness and health
I was with you, Oh What Wealth

You talked of your wife, your kids at home
You talked of bikes and lakes & mountains you roam
You talked of these mines, the machines you run
You laughed and joked, the work's not hard, Alas, it's fun

At the end of the shift the feeling we can't hide
Oh, Thank the Lord! It's good to be outside
A coal miner's life if you will study
Is that of love he has for his buddy

[+] _The Mountain Eagle,_ Thursday, April 7, 1983.

Scotia-Coal Mine of Doom

I have had many friends since the year '49
And all these miners at Scotia were friends of mine
Twenty six lives, Oh! What a loss
These men were my friends, Yes, one my boss
My friends lived in different places
As long as I live I'll remember their faces
My friends are at rest beneath the sod
One could have been me, But for the Grace of God

It's been seven years and what a shame
A miner is killed and we don't know his name
Seven years have passed and I am so sad
To think of the orphans who have lost a dad
Coal miners will work, Coal miners will die
And as in the past, We all wonder why?

Written by Scotia Miner, Pat Pate, Gulston, Kentucky

Pat Pate worked at Scotia in 1976.

In February, 1985, Scotia officials approached the Scotia Employees Association representatives concerning a proposal to change the contract from a 5 day, 8 hours per day work-cycle, to a, 4 days on 4 days off, 10 hours per day work cycle. On February 22, the Employees Association sent each union hourly employee a notice of a "Special Called Meeting" to discuss the proposed change:

There will be a "Special Called Meeting," Saturday, March 2, 1985 at 9:00 a.m. at the Union hall.

The primary purpose of the meeting is to <u>*DISCUSS*</u> *the proposed 4 day work week offered by the Company.*

At the Union meeting of Feb. 16, 1985 the Executive Board of the Union was requested, by majority vote; to approach the Company for a written copy of their proposal and if they felt the proposal had merit, each member was to be sent a copy, and a "<u>Special Meeting</u>" was to be called, to vote on whether to enter into contract negotiations at this time. The_Executive Board has voted Unanimously to veto this proposal, as *authorized at the last meeting. We do, however, feel that each member should be informed as to the contents of the proposal.*

The matter concerning whether or not we want to enter into negotiations at this time, for a new short term contract, until July, needs to be finalized at this meeting.

Each member of the Union should make every effort to attend this meeting, as decisions made in the Union Hall are binding on the Union Membership as a whole.

Whether it was accepted at this special meeting or at a subsequent meeting, the four day work cycle was soon accepted and approved by the Scotia Employees Association membership. In time, most of us came to like the four day work schedule, which gave the workers time to accomplish the many odds and ends of life at home without having to take a day off through the week.

The Company also apparently liked the way the change turned out too, as those two extra hours provided a lot of time to run a few extra cuts of coal each shift. I believe that most of the Scotia workers were aware that the best hours of production were at the end of a shift, because everyone seemed to "pick it up a notch" when quit time was nearing.

This was especially relevant when the longwall mining system was adopted by Scotia in 1986. When one considers that a longwall crew can produce around 1,000 tons per hour or better, those extra two hours of a shift can provide enough coal to load 20 railroad cars with 100 tons each.

The fact that Scotia Coal Co. produced approximately 1, 315,000 tons of coal in 1989 while employing only 300 workers is another confirmation of the difference a longwall section can make in increasing coal production. Even with 500 workers employed in other years, Scotia had been producing, on average, about 850,000 tons of coal per year before the advent of the longwall section at the mine.

The following letter from the Blue Diamond Coal Company was mailed to Scotia employees just after the four day work-week had been approved by the Scotia workers. The letter is dated May 13, 1988:

Dear Fellow Employee:

As you know, we recently closed our Justice Mine because the coal contract with Georgia Power Company was terminated under a buy-out agreement. This mine could not produce coal at a competitive cost in to-

day's market. As a result, Blue Diamond lost its investment in the mine and the Stearns community will lose 228 jobs. It was difficult for me to be involved in this situation because of the adverse impact on so many people's livelihood and the effect on their families. I am writing so that each of you will understand what happened and to discuss our future.

We have negotiated a new coal supply contract from Georgia Power beginning in 1989, with shipments to reach 750,000 tons per year in 1991. This contract, in addition to our Orlando Utilities and Central Illinois Light contracts, will give us about 2.25 million tons per year sold under long-term contract that can be shipped from either Leatherwood or Scotia. Having two operations with large reserves has been a strong selling point for us in getting these contracts. However, all three sales agreements have provisions during their terms for market price reviews and termination if we cannot be competitive.

In order to hold these contracts and sell the remainder of our tonnage, we must maintain a production cost that is competitive on today's market. Our task is the following:

*1. **Work Safely**—This is your most important responsibility, not only to co-workers, but to your family.*

*2. **Be Productive**- Each person must maximize the amount of coal produced on his section or in his mine through teamwork.*

*3. **Spend Wisely**- We need to spend only what is necessary and get the maximum use out of our supplies by eliminating waste.*

Over capacity in the coal industry and the aggressiveness of our competitors will keep coal markets weak for the foreseeable future. In order to produce coal as cheaply as possible, we plan to keep investing in the most modern plants and mining equipment. However, this continuing investment is only justified by profitable operations, and profits come from safety, productivity and wise spending. Attention to these three goals is necessary for our job security.

A good effort by all employees, along with new equipment, primarily the Scotia longwall, helped us achieve a dramatic increase in productivity last year. We are the smallest independent producer to successfully install a longwall system. With the cooperation of all employees at Leatherwood and in response to adverse circumstances, we completely changed our work schedule and the way we operate. We did not have a fatal accident last year and reduced our lost time accident rate. You should take pride in these accomplishments!

Where do we go from here? I am negotiating now with two land companies in the Leatherwood Area to acquire additional reserves. We are also studying the applicability of longwalling in the Leatherwood Area. These studies and reserve acquisitions are not because of faith in coal markets, but because of faith in the people of Blue Diamond. We can work safer, we can be more productive, and we can make our supply dollars go further! We can meet the challenge with **BLUE PRIDE!**

Sincerely,
Ted B. Helms

This letter confirms the increased productivity associated with the acquisition of the longwall system at Scotia in 1986. The new equipment mentioned in the letter included new diesel shuttle cars for the bottom mine sometime between 1988 and 1990. I was fortunate enough to be a shuttle car operator on a section that received these new diesels, and, in fact, at one time, we actually operated three diesel cars at the same time on the section for awhile.

I was not a regular on the section, as my classification had been changed to trackman in 1987, due to a reduction in working force that had taken place in that year. When our railroad steel laying was caught up, I was usually assigned to the diesel section to operate one of the three diesel shuttle cars. I thought it was one of the best jobs Scotia had.

They were much faster than shuttle cars powered by electricity and their load capacity was greater than the SC 10's and the older Torque cars we had used in the past in the bottom mine. Even the ride was smoother and the operator's deck was roomier and more comfortable. Even the operator's vision of his surroundings was better due to the higher position of the seats, even though we still had our canopies over our heads. Of course all this was complimented by having 6ft or better height of the coal we were mining. Usually there was 24in. or more drawrock on top of the coal seam, making the height of the section even higher for the workers to enjoy.

The one thing that slowed production a little, but was entirely necessary, was the testing for carbon monoxide, hydrogen sulfide, and carbon dioxide every 15 or 20 minutes while operating one of those cars. I also usually carried a methane monitor with me when I could get one, as usually only the continuous miner operator had one to check for methane in the face area.

When I received my Kentucky Assistant Mine Foreman certificate in 1978, I sometimes bossed a production section when a boss was off, so I was first assigned a methane monitor (spotter) at that time. In January, 1980, after I had enough experience as a miner (over 5 years) I received my Kentucky Mine Foreman certificate, and in the late 1980's my Virginia Mine Foreman certificate. The Virginia certification was reciprocal with my Kentucky certificate, so no testing for the Virginia papers was required at that time.

With Scotia's production increasing so much by 1989, and with the added production of the Leatherwood Mine, it appeared at first glance that things were finally going good for the Blue Diamond Coal Company, but as we shall see in the next chapter, things weren't so rosy as they seemed.

During the period that I was still classified as a motorman, Tommy Gross and I had an opportunity to move some equipment we wished we had never had to move, after the terrible incident that had caused the equipment to be there. I'm speaking of the locomotives (motors) and supply cars that were in the second explosion and that were still sitting on the track at the mouth of 2 Southeast Mains.

Our second shift fresh air crew had drawn the assignment of taking the two supply cars and two motors to the outside after the area had been completely opened up and ventilated.

It was an eerie feeling to stand in the spot where so many of our friends and co-workers had lost their lives. I couldn't help but think about what the explosion must have sounded like as it roared down the grade from 2 Southeast Mains. I walked to the spot to revisit where I had observed the reflective clothing of one of the federal inspectors the night we built so many seals around them in preparation for their recovery.

I observed the infamous "hanging slab of roof" that had caused the eleven victims and the two survivors to have been there the night of March 11. From looking at it, I couldn't tell that it was much worse than many other places in the mine, except for the fact that the roof was so low there to begin with. The entry where the rock was located would vie for the lowest spot in the mine I thought, as I studied it for awhile.

I walked to the spot where the two repairmen had been crouched behind the 7200 volt power box when the blast came booming down the 2 SEM entries and wondered how in the world they had managed to escape the force of the blast, as they were only a few feet from the open break. The whole area was still as black as the blackest midnight, and the yellow 7200 box was barely able to break up the distortion of the blackness all around it. Like the area where the rock needed bolting, the area around the intersection and the power box was very low (about 50 inches) which made the escape of the two survivors much more difficult than had the roof been higher here.

I next walked to the area outby the motors and supply cars where I had observed the two or three bodies of the miners who had made an attempt to run when they heard the explosion coming, but managed to run only about 20 ft. before the force of the blast caught them. One miner was ahead of the other two by about five feet, and the two behind him were lying side by side if my observations were correct on the night we built the seals. Also the fact that our seal line was between 50 to 100 ft. from where the bodies were lying made our observations difficult. We honored the prohibition to not get any nearer than that needed to build the seals. The fact that the bodies were so difficult to make out in the blackness of the residue that was left by the blast, caused me to be unsure exactly how many miners were in the act of running, but I believe three was the correct number of men that managed to run a few feet.

The oddity is that the two survivors who were closer to the edge of the break they were in survived, while those men that were running were deeper inside the break and still lost their lives. The only contributing factor in the survival of the two repairmen must have been that they were protected by a very small pile of gob they were crouched behind.

While our crew was making their observations and commenting on what happened here, we couldn't help but notice the pungent smell of formaldehyde, which had been liberally used by the pathologists and other medical people when they recovered the bodies of the miners. Forever after, from November, 1976, until the mine closed in December, 1991, the smell of that disinfectant lingered strongly in the area where the miners were recovered. Nearly every new miner or visitor, when passing through that area would invariably ask, "What's that smelling so strong?" When someone would explain what happened at that spot, most would then exclaim, "That explosion happened years ago, why is the smell still here?" None of us who had been there could answer that question.

Gross and I hitched our motors to the two supply cars, with me operating the front motor, and Gross the rear motor, we left for the mine surface. Bruce Jones, the boss, and several men climbed in a jeep motor behind us and brought up the rear of the convoy. Since I was in front I was headed into the fresh air as we went towards the surface, but Tommy Gross and the jeep occupants were in a bad spot as I found out when we reached the outside. Gross got off his motor as soon as we stopped beside the maintenance shop and was gagging and trying to retch as were some of the men in the jeep who were following us.

When he caught his breath Gross hollowed at me that the smell of the formaldehyde and other fluids that were in the bottom of the supply cars had affected nearly everyone behind the cars by causing them to feel nauseated for the whole 4½ miles to the surface of the mine. Since I was in front I didn't have a clue that those behind me were in misery until we got outside, due to the noise generated by the locomotives and the supply cars.

CHAPTER TWENTY THREE

The End of Scotia

A t the beginning of 1990 I was still a member of the Bottom Mine track crew, doing the same type of work that the two motormen who died in the first explosion were doing when they pushed a load of rails into 2 Southeast Mains on March 9,1976. We still used the old No. 6 Goodman and the No. 8 Westinghouse locomotives to pull 33ft. long, 80 lb steel rails into and out of the mine. The Goodman still operated with the same compressor that was highly suspected as the cause of the first, and probably the cause of the second explosions. As long as the Goodman didn't go past the last open crosscut,(which was highly improbable to occur anyway), it was still permissible and therefore still an efficient and legal piece of mining equipment.

Jerry McCown was the track boss and Eddie "Jack" Roberts, Dale Jackson, Don Caudill, Patrick Fouts, and Danny Roberts made up the rest of the crew. Sometimes another man or two would be assigned temporarily to help us out. If all five were allowed to work together the work wasn't too harsh, but usually one or more of us were sent to help with another project somewhere in the mine, leaving us with a man short to install 25-30 steel rails or to take up the same number of rails from an idle or abandoned section to store on the surface.

Out track crew was assigned to the third shift so that we could stay out of the way of coal production while installing our steel rails. We certainly didn't want to block a mantrip that was required to be at the end of the track to be used as an emergency vehicle when miners were working on the section.

Normally it was fairly easy to keep the track moved up on a section as they advanced, but the habit that management had of using our crew for other things sometimes caused us to get behind and have to either "double back" to catch up or start work early. We were already working 10 hour shifts since 1988, and after 10 hours of hard work, any overtime hours worked just added to the misery of back-breaking work that track laying entailed. It didn't help that I was the lightest and smallest man on the track crew at 6' 1" and 205 lbs. Every other man was both taller and at least 25 lb heavier than I, and looking at them made me feel like a runt.

Considering that each 33 ft steel rail weighed 830 lbs, I was probably too light for the job. We used "rail dogs" to carry and lift the rails, which meant I had to carry a load equal to my own weight when we installed a rail. (The rail dogs were like a giant set of tongs that clamped the rail tightly when you lifted it about thigh high.)

Each member of the crew had a "lifting buddy" and mine just happened to be big Don Caudill, who was at least 6' 7" and 250lbs. When he and I lifted our end of the rail, to get the rail even with his thigh meant that I had to lift it above my waist to balance the rail. I don't believe I went even one day without excruciating back pain the whole time I spent on the track crew, which was over five years.

Every time we worked near the 2 Southeast Mains or the 2 Left Section I thought of what had happened there, and how I never expected to work in the same area after all the damage that was done by the explosions. But by that time everything was cleaned up and parallel sections had been driven for airways which greatly improved ventilation. (I had worked as a shuttle car operator on some of those parallel sections after the mine was recovered.)

As was mentioned in the last chapter, everything pointed to long-term security as Blue Diamond and Scotia employees. It was obvious to the workforce that production was up at Scotia since the acquisition of the longwall system and some new equipment, such as the new diesel shuttle cars, and a new continuous miner or two.

The change in the work schedule in 1988 had also been a success, both with the Company because of increased productivity, and with the men because of the time off the new schedule provided. But even with the increased production and a positive mine-set of the workers and the Company that a corner had been turned, rumors began circulating early in 1990 that Blue Diamond was considering selling Scotia Coal Company.

Most of us thought they were just a re-hash of the same rumors that had been circulating among the workforce for years, that Blue Diamond wanted to "get rid of Scotia."

Whether the rumors of that time were true or not, it was obvious that all the changes that had been instituted over the past two years were not sufficient enough to allow the Company to "turn the corner," in their effort to become a profitable enterprise. The first confirmation that their goal had not been reached was when Scotia employees received the following letter from Blue Diamond Coal Company July 5, 1990:

Dear Fellow Employee:

Blue Diamond Coal Company has lost over $12.0 million the last two years. The three prior to that, we were profitable but not at a satisfactory level. During this five year period we have bought a longwall, a new preparation plant, and a new coal mine. Our reserve base has expanded to 185 million tons, but we are producing like we are running out of reserves. We need to begin replacing continuous miners, but cannot because out debt over this period has risen to $55 million. We are in a strong reserve position, but a weak financial situation.

How can we improve our situation? Because of the unpredictability of coal markets, we should not count on better prices. Our efforts must focus on how we can reduce costs to make our operations more competitive. Our long-term sales contracts put us in a favorable position to move our production. We can sell all the tonnage our present workforce can produce. The problem we face is not lack of reserves, nor lack of sales, nor plant and equipment—the problem is our lack of production.

To identify what our opportunities are to lower cost and increase production, I want each employee to think about the attached list. During the next two weeks, each section foreman or supervisor should schedule a one hour meeting with his crew to discuss the attached list. This meeting should be scheduled so that it disrupts production as little as possible. Hersh Hayden, along with the Superintendent, will then meet with all supervisors in small groups to discuss your ideas. I will keep you informed of our cost reduction progress. By communicating with each other, by better teamwork and by getting back to basics, we can assure our future.

Sincerely,
Ted Helms

Back to Basics
Blue Diamond Coal Company

1. **Safety** – Our accident rate for 1989 went above the national average. With our experienced workforce, surely we are better than average!

2. **Teamwork** – Do we have it? How can we get people working together better?

3. **Downtime** –What can we do to prevent loss of motors, wheel units, belts, etc. that cost money to fix and disrupt production?

4. **Production Goals** – This affects cost more than anything. Do we have goals? Are they too low?

5. **Supplies** – Are we using wisely? Do we have waste or recover things that can be used again?

6. **Use of Time** – Are you getting enough direction or information to use your time in a productive manner? Do we have unnecessary overtime? Do we have people standing around?

7. **Mine Plans** – Are we cutting rock for machinery clearance or for people? What can we change to improve safety and production?

    The letter above, along with the list of ideals to "help us get back to basics," was what might be called the "swan song" or "last gasp" for Blue Diamond management's effort to cut costs at the Scotia Mine. They didn't have the option of furloughing any more workers to try to achieve their cost- cutting goals, as the work force of 300 was about as low as it could go and still hold production levels to the increased levels it had reached.
    As events would bring out, Blue Diamond was likely already in talks to sale the Scotia Mine and assets, confirming the rumors that had been circulating for the past several months. The increased production had

been so obvious to the Union workers that they themselves came to discount the possibility of the rumors of being remotely truthful. The next letter from Blue Diamond to the employees of Scotia would finally convince them that more change was in store for Scotia.

On August 14, 1990, this notice was sent to each employee of Scotia Coal Company:

To the Employees of
The Scotia Operation:

This is to advise you that Blue Diamond has entered into an agreement to sell the Scotia Operation to Arch Mineral Corporation. The changeover is expected to occur about the end of August or early September. A subsidiary of Arch has committed to me that they will offer employment to all active employees at Scotia. They have contractually committed to assume the Scotia Employees Association Contract.

As you are aware, this is a difficult and competitive period for the coal industry. Because of your efforts and the planned move of the longwall into better mining conditions, I expect that costs at Scotia will continue to improve. Employee suggestions and communication resulting from our "Back to Basics" program has been especially encouraging to me. I appreciate your support on this effort and hope that he pending transaction will not affect your enthusiasm.

Arch Mineral is headquartered in St. Louis, Missouri, and produces approximately 25 million tons of coal per year. Their philosophy is to let each operation stand on its own from an economic standpoint. Scotia would be independent of the Lynch operation, with each having its own management,equipment, facilities and labor policy. They plan to expand production at Scotia in the future, which should create opportunities for each of you. As more information is available, we will keep you informed. Thank you for your efforts.

Sincerely,
Ted Helms

When reading the notice above it is clear that Blue Diamond did receive an agreement from Arch Mineral to keep the keep the Scotia work-force that they inherited with the purchase of the Scotia Mine. This helped the selling of the Company to be accepted a little more easily.

Scotia management had always been fairly accommodating to the workers of Scotia when they had a disagreement of one kind or another, and we hoped that Arch would be the same way. Almost always a buy-out of another company means a reduction in work-force, as the new company expects to pare the help down to the barest necessity needed to more quickly re-coup their investment in the new business. Blue Diamond had managed to spare Scotia Employees from this tradition by insisting that all the current employees keep their jobs. For that, I and other employees were grateful.

On November 12, 1990, Scotia Employees received this letter in the mail:

Cumberland River Coal Company
Cumberland, Kentucky

Dear Employee:

As of September 9, 1990, you became a member of the KYVA Coal Company team. I would like to give you a brief sketch of our organization and point out my impressions, some general goals and what's in store for KYVA.

The most fundamental question is what is KYVA? KYVA is a wholly owned subsidiary of Arch Mineral Corporation which is based in St. Louis, Missouri. KYVA controls several companies, including your company, Cumberland River Coal Company. As for the name KYVA, it is taken from the abbreviation for Kentucky (KY) and Virginia (VA).

My impression of Cumberland River Coal is an organization of people who have reacted to some very basic changes in a constructive and dedicated way. This attitude is important and essential as we move from the "old way" to new and different methods to make Cumberland River a key coal producer......

As for the future, we are strategically located with high quality reserves. If we can produce coal at a competitive price, we will be able to enter new markets and possibly open new mines.

The immediate future will be a transition period. We need to have a skilled, professional, safety conscious work force, who welcome change because they know that change is essential to survive in today's competitive coal market. We have all the ingredients to make a bright future. The key to that future is how we adapt to change.
Wishing you the best of success at KYVA.

Sincerely,
Gerald D. Peacock
President

After the acquisition of Scotia by Arch Mineral and the changing of the name from Scotia Coal Company to Cumberland River Coal Company, Arch began investing in new equipment and new facilities aimed at improving over-all operations at the mine. Arch invested over $13 million in improvements by May 1991, after paying Blue Diamond $30 million for the Scotia Mine and preparation plant. Arch reportedly also assumed $10 million of Blue Diamond's debt when the deal was finalized in September, 1990.
Some of the expenditures made include the following items:

Continuous Miner Units
- Two remanufactured Joy 14 CM10 continuous miners equipped with remote control and scrubber units replaced old 12 CM miners
- Six Simmons/Rand Unihaulers (shuttle cars) replace four 10SC22 shuttle cars.
- Steel matting in conjunction with tension roof bolts replaces straps and JOY fully –grouted resin bolts in critical areas.

Longwall Unit
- 42 Longwall shields reconditioned, 12 more to follow.

- Beam Support Technique used during longwall move. Future moves will include meshing in conjunction with beaming process.

Belt Conveyor System

- Slope Belt Drive Unit changing from 50's vintage wound rotor motors to standard squirrel cage motors with delay fill fluid coupling, giving a "softer" start, and meaning less maintenance/ less cost.
- 8,000 feet of new conveyor belt installed, replacing old belts.
- More than half of all underground belts have been vulcanized, eliminating mechanical belt fasteners and improving splice life/scraper life.
- Scraper and scavenger conveyor systems added.
- Transfer point design changed to improve loading capability

General Mine Items

- Office Trailer with six offices and one conference room installed to replace one office at Borehole.
- Both bathhouses refurbished.
- Old bathhouse converted to new mine office and new longwall office.
- Filtered/chlorinated water system installed.
- Elevator ropes replaced.

Preparation Plant

- Raw coal drag conveyor replaced with belt structure
- Structural painting
- High intensity lighting installed.
- Replacement of screen vibrators. Air springs replaced with steel springs.
- Feed belts modified.
- Coal washing baths rebuilt.
- Two newer model D-9L dozers added.
- Major clean-up program initiated.
- Loadout tracks cleaned, raised.

Surface Areas

- Old equipment, scrap metal, scrap belt and obsolete supplies (accumulated for more than 20 years) removed and sold.
- Area landscaping and reclamation.

- Buildings reconstructed, painted, re-plumbed.
- Adequate sewage installed.
- Removal of old buildings.
- Cut brush and cleared land.
- New guard shack constructed.
- Removal of old sawmill, power lines and telephone poles.
- Installation of dumpsters to place all scrap metal in.
- Mine garbage dumpster site moved from main yard to old rotary dumpster.[*]

These were just a few of the improvements made in the first eight months after Arch took over the mine. They not only improved the material assets but also made the improvement of safety and the reducing of safety violations a priority. President Gerald Peacock noted that in the first six months of 1990, Scotia received more Mine Health and Safety Administration (MSHA) violations than all of Arch Mineral Corporation subsidiaries combined over the past two years. (This was before Arch bought Scotia Coal Company.)Peacock made it clear that those statistics would not be tolerated by Arch Mineral.

Cumberland River Coal Company (CRCC) was budgeted to product over 2 million tons of coal in 1991 and had commitments for 931,000 tons. By the end of June 1991, production was 562,000 tons, with 520,000 sold on the spot market. [+]

KYVA Coal was a subsidiary of Arch Mineral, as has already been mentioned, and under the KYVA banner was Cumberland River Coal Company, of Cumberland, Kentucky, Arch on the North Fork, Jackson, Kentucky, Hawkeye, Pikeville, Kentucky, and Pine Mountain Coal, Big Stone Gap, Virginia. Arch on the North Fork ceased operations in October, 1990, and their last shipment of coal was shipped in November, 1990.

In June, 1990, KYVA Coal Company set up their headquarters in Norton, Virginia, in order to establish a central location from which to handle the functions of the different coal companies that were part of the Arch subsidiary.

---

[*] KYVA NEWS May, 1991.
[+] ibid

Arch revamped nearly all of the beltline leading out of the Oven-fork (old Scotia #1) mine, changing out over 9,000 feet of old belt and eliminating one belt drive. The number of belts leading out of the mine to the coal stockpile was reduced from 16 to 13 belts. The new belt was also of a higher quality.

The Cumberland Coal Company Mine Rescue Team (they had only one team in 1991) was a dandy, having won the state championship twice, once under Blue Diamond in 1987, and again in 1990 after KYVA Coal Company had taken over the reins at Scotia. The members of the 1991 Mine Rescue Team were:

Mike Sparks, Captain, Randy Watts, Map Man; John Richardson, Gas Man; Mike Holcomb, Gas Man; Dale Jackson, Rear Captain-Benchman; Bob Childers, Briefing Officer; Danny Wright, Alternate; Steve Sturgill, Alternate; Ronnie Biggerstaff, Trainer.±

Judging from all the money invested in improvements in the former Scotia Mine it was clear to me that Arch Mineral was serious about its efforts to turn the newly acquired mine into a profitable enterprise. The only downside to their efforts was the fact that they were relying on the "spot market" or short term sales of their coal which was a gamble at best and not very good news for the employees at Cumberland River Coal Company.

During that period of time (1991) some utilities were depending on buying their coal on the spot market so they wouldn't have to rely on long-term contracts which often entailed agreeing to a "mining costs" contract. That is, they would have to agree to whatever the costs were to mine the coal, plus a percentage over those costs. It was much simpler for them to buy their coal on the spot market and pass any increase of the price of coal on to their customers.

The message from KYVA marketing was also not very positive in nature; "KYVA is up against everybody when it comes to spot sales. Long term contracts are often too low for what coal companies' project their costs to be, so coal companies are often reluctant to sign long term agreements. Buyers are afraid to buy long term and sellers are afraid to sell long term—hence the growing spot market, where buyers and sellers can dispel their fears by "quick fix' coal sales....The

---

± KYVA News August, 1991.

outlook for selling spot market coal to utility companies in the immediate is bleak. If all the utility company coal deliveries stopped today, (1991) they would still have enough (coal) stockpiled to power the entire nation for six months!....Add to that the increased use of alternative energy sources such as, solar, nuclear, and hydroelectric and you begin to see the reason why the coal industry is facing some very difficult times.....Since it relies so heavily on short term sales, KYVA is particularly vulnerable. We will have to work together, keep our minds and actions focused, and make the best of the changes we have already made if we are going to be competitive in today's coal market." [≠]

A major player in KYVA's effort to increase production and lower costs was the longwall mining system. The longwall system had allowed Blue Diamond to see a profit the last three years of the 80's, but bad roof conditions kept the longwall from ever really reaching its full potential even after Arch took over the company in 1990.

As the KYVA News said, "Geologic conditions severely limited production and a fall prevented extraction of equipment from the tailgate area." (I remember well the frustration and disappointment with the condition of the roof during the move from that panel. In May of 1991 the move to a panel with much improved roof conditions was completed.)

During all this time our track crew helped on the longwall when we weren't laying rails or removing rails on other sections. We built hundreds, if not thousands of cribs to support the roof where the longwall was mining. On my very last shift on the longwall, my brother Jimmy and I worked all night in the atrociously dusty return side of the longwall building 10 ft high cribs with 8"x8"x4' timbers. We didn't know it then but our timbering days were over shortly after that shift.

The following letter was the beginning of the end of the Cumberland River Coal Company (Scotia) Mine:

Cumberland River Coal Company
Cumberland, Kentucky
November 12, 1991

[≠] ibid

Dear Eddie.

By letter dated September 13, 1991, notice was provided to the Scotia Employees Association of a mine closure for all employees of Cumberland River Coal Company. We regret to advise you that our company will proceed with the closure, effective November 12, 1991.

Effective that date, you will be placed on layoff status in accordance with Article XII, Sections 4, 5, 6, 7 and 8 of the "Seniority and Opportunity" provision per the Agreement between Scotia Employees Association and Cumberland River Coal Company.

Also, within five (5) days from the above date, you must fill out a Standardized Panel Form if you wish to be listed on the recall panel. The forms are in the Cumberland River Coal Company office and are available Monday through Friday between the hours of 8:00 a. m. and 5:00 p. m. each day.

Your benefits will remain in effect until <u>December 12, 1991</u>, at which time they will terminate. Attached is an outline of those benefits. Further information may be obtained by contacting KYVA Coal Company, Human Resource Department, xxx xxxx xxx, Norton, Virginia.

Finally, we regret that we are forced to take this action. As you know, Cumberland River Coal Company is attempting to develop and mine additional reserves. To date, these efforts have not been successful. We remain committed to mine our property. At the earliest, this will not happen until next year. We hope you will continue to support us in our efforts.

Sincerely
Dan Stickel
Mine Manager

CHAPTER TWENTY FOUR

Epilogue

The last day of work on the day shift at the Cumberland River Coal Company Scotia Mine felt more like attending a wake than going to work. As we boarded the elevator at the Bore Hole located on Frank's Creek, most of us knew that this day likely marked the end of coal production at the Scotia Mine for sure. The poor roof conditions were unlikely to improve while the mine was closed for the year or more that had been projected by Mine Manager Dan Stickel in his letter informing us of the mine closure.

We knew that common sense dictated that when that gigantic coal mining system called a "longwall" was brought out of the mine, it would never again be taken back inside. The layoff would be a long one, everyone felt it, and the mood of the workers as we exited the elevator and boarded the mantrips was one of total resignation that whatever would be, would be and there was nothing we could do to change it.

There was none of the usual horseplay or verbal ribbing of each other, only expressions of "I don't know what I'll do, I have a house and car to pay for and a family to feed." Others talked of going back to school and learning a trade or a profession. Some verbalized that, "This will give me a chance to get out of the mines for good, which I've been wanting to do!" The more positive ones in the group said, Oh, we'll be back here in a few months at most. I'm gonna rest up and wait for that!"

Some of us could see it coming just a short time after Arch took over the mine. They were open about the fact that production must increase or their attempt to revitalize the mine would be a failure and we would be out of a job. Blue Diamond had a lais-sez-faire attitude in dealing with the

263

Scotia workers, but Arch was more demanding in their relationships but understandably so, as they were trying to ramp up productivity in order to save the workers' jobs. Their system of demanding more from their workers would have likely been a success if the mining conditions had allowed the longwall to produce coal to the maximum tonnage that it was capable of producing under ideal conditions.

The competition from other coal mining concerns that were working under better geological conditions had too much of an advantage in a tight coal market to overcome. I feel that Arch had given it their best shot and there was no shame in failure if one has done their best. Arch had done their best and failed.

Arch laid off 293 hourly workers and about 100 salaried employees, leaving 18 hourly workers to close up the mine. Those 18 workers removed most of the equipment from the mine. It was only then that even the most positive of the workers knew for sure that the Scotia Mine was gone for good.

The Company's general counsel, Blair Gardner, said the company would help laid-off workers find new jobs. (That didn't materialize, to my knowledge, at least concerning those workers I have talked to along with myself and my brother.) No one helped us get a job.

"We're not proud that we failed to make it a financially successful operation," Mr. Gardner said. "We are proud of the fact that we've made this a much safer place for these people to work." *

The tragic explosions of March 9 and 11 1976, affected not only the families of the 23 Scotia miners and 3 MESA inspectors who lost their lives, but also affected the Company and all the workers at Scotia during that time. At least one miner committed suicide and another also attempted to end his own life but failed in the attempt. Another miner who was working on the recovery crew was killed on his way to work in an auto accident, and many suffered obvious symptoms of PTSD, although at the time of the explosions, no one complained of any symptoms, and likely knew very little about the condition.

For many of us, bad dreams and nightmares of being trapped in a dark coal mine and trying to run away while the rock was falling all around us became a common occurrence. I still have those dreams occa-

---

* http//www.nytimes.com/1991/11/30/us/infamous-mine-is-closed-amid-worries-about-jobs.html

sionally. I don't claim to have PTSD and believe it's overused in today's society but I doubt that anyone who has worked as a miner doesn't at one time or another have similar dreams and/or nightmares.

Anyone who has donned a miner's hat and caplight and worked in the mines for any length of time has their own stories of their brush with death while working underground. I had two separate occasions where my chance of living or dying was no better than 50/50 while working as a miner. Both times, I came mere inches from being crushed.

I tell this, not for sympathy, but to confirm that coal mining is a dangerous vocation, no matter how safe you think you are or how careful you work. Safety in a coal mine is a fleeting thing. No matter how hard you try, there are times you will have one of those 50/50 chances. That's why miners are paid so well. They begin earning their money the moment they step from the outside into the drift mouth.

Blue Diamond and Scotia never really recovered from the tragedy of losing the lives of 26 men in two days time. I believe that an incident or incidents like the explosions they suffered as operators of the mine has to affect any human being alive. No doubt, if they had it to do over they would do things much differently than they did in 1976, but that could be said for MESA and the employees of Scotia also.

MESA (today MSHA) would be much tougher with their inspections, Scotia would not deviate from the Ventilation Plan, and the workers would insist on better ventilation before mining one block of coal. But we can't change history. The tragedies happened and there were many lessons learned from them that likely saved many other lives through the years.

The explosions at Scotia Mine in 1976 resulted in the passage of the Federal Mine Safety and health Act of 1977. This legislation strengthened provisions of the 1969 Act and also incorporated new mandates for all non-coal mines. The Act also renamed MESA as MSHA and moved the agency from the U.S. Department of the Interior to the U.S. Department of Labor.

Below are some of the new provisions that were included in the 1977 Federal Mine Safety and Health Act:

- Placed coal mines, metal and nonmetal mines under a single law, with enforcement provisions similar to 1969 Act.(A separate safety and health standards were retained)

- Moved enforcement agency to Department of Labor, renamed it Mine Safety and Health Administration (MSHA)
- Requirement for four annual inspections at all underground mines, two at all surface mines.
- Advisory standards for metal and nonmetal mines eliminated
- State enforcement plans in metal and nonmetal sector discontinued.
- Provisions for mandatory miner training.
- Mine rescue teams required for all underground mines
- Increased involvement of miners and their representatives in health and safety activities. [+]

After a short time of idleness, Cumberland River Coal Company moved equipment to Virginia and began mining coal in the Pardee Mine located near Appalachia, in Wise County, Virginia. In later years, they opened another underground mine in Letcher County Kentucky, near the old Scotia complex.

On July 21, 2014, Arch Coal, Inc. announced that it was idling the Cumberland River Coal Company Complex located in Wise County, Virginia and Letcher County, Kentucky. The mining complex had previously shutdown two contract mines during the second quarter of 2013.

"With this move, we are actively responding to currently challenged metallurgical coal markets while striving to enhance our overall competitive cost position in Appalachia," said John W. Eaves, Arch's president and chief executive officer. "Our strategy is to increasingly shift our portfolio toward higher-margin, lower cost metallurgical coal operations, while retaining our valuable reserves for when market conditions strengthen in the future. We will continue to serve our customers here and abroad with the high level of quality they have come to expect from Arch."

In total, 213 full time positions will be eliminated by idling Cumberland River, and the company is taking steps to provide opportunities at other Arch subsidiaries where available.

"We deeply regret the need to take this action," said Eaves. "We thank the men and women at Cumberland River for their dedication, hard work and strong commitment to operating in a safe and responsible manner."[±]

[+] U.S. Department of Labor Mine Safety and Health Administration (MSHA)
[±] Arch Coal, Inc./Investors News Release

When Cumberland River Coal Company idled the Wise County, Virginia and Letcher County, Kentucky Complexes in 2014, the last four original Scotia workers were witnesses to, and a part of, the end of an era. It was left to Charlie Pease, Roger Yeary, Eddie Bentley, and Steve Brock to close the door on the history of the Scotia years.

Today, Scotia Coal Company consists of only of a name, an idea, an attempt to provide an energy source for the good of our nation, county, and state, and did so reasonably well for almost 30 years, with their attempt at providing good jobs and good pay overshadowed by the events of those two terrible days in March, 1976.

I have tried to show in this book how the fault for the explosions that changed so many lives lies not totally in the actions of one person, company, or organization, but that blame has to be shared by many, as the facts show. When a man- made disaster strikes any organization or company, the finger-pointing makes it very difficult to get at the truth. The Scotia tragedy was no different.

The hearings held in Washington D.C. and in Whitesburg brought out very little in the way of facts that could place the blame at the door of one individual, but placed the blame squarely on a series of misguided actions and non- actions by several individuals and officials who really should have known better.

For the explosions to have happened at Scotia, many different combinations had to come together with just the right ingredients and timing to cause the first explosion, and as we now know, the first explosion led directly to the second.

- The ventilation was diverted from 2 Southeast Mains to 2 Left
- This allowed the methane in 2 Southeast Mains to reach the 5-15% level needed to explode
- The oxygen level was still in the range needed to explode (12%) or above.
- There had to be an ignition source of 1200 % or better to set the explosion off.
- This ignition source was provided by the compressor on the #6 Goodman locomotive, which just happened to be pushing steel rails in to the 2 Southeast Mains Section . They could have been told to do it the next day (when the methane levels might have been too great to explode) but they were sent on the 9th.

- No overcasts had yet been built at the mouth of 2 Left. If they had been there, 2 SEM would be receiving enough ventilation to sweep out the methane emulating from the roof, coal and rock on the section. (and also from the methane "feeder" located near the track on the hill outby the 2 SEM Section, which was real, and which I observed with my own eyes.)
- The construction foreman decided to send the track crew to 2 SEM on this day, when the atmosphere would be inundated with just the right combination for an explosion and was just waiting for an ignition source to set it off. Who knew? Certainly he didn't know and can't be faulted for doing his job, but it might have had a different outcome if one of the motor operators had been equipped with a methane detector and had been trained to use it.
- The hearings brought out the fact that the section hadn't been fire-bossed before the two locomotives took the rails on the section. Would the examination for methane have found the amount that eventually caused the explosion and would the fire boss have prohibited the track crew from taking rails into the area? We'll never know.

What we do know is that if even if only one of the several incidents listed above had not come together perfectly the explosions would not have happened. They did happen and those of us who were there at the time will never be able to erase those terrible days from our minds. The hope is that other coal miners of the present and those of the future might benefit from the mistakes and lessons learned from the Scotia Mine disasters.

Scotia Miners-Charlie Pease,Roger Yeary,Eddie Bentley,Steve

Brock. (courtesy of Steve Brock) Last four Scotia retirees.

The photos on this page and on the following pages are courtesy of the Kenton County Public Library, Covington, Kentucky, unless otherwise noted.

Robert Barrett, MESA Administrator

Scotia RS2 1051
Oxen Fork, KY 6/7/79

Scotia yard engine-courtesy of Jay and Robert W Thompson

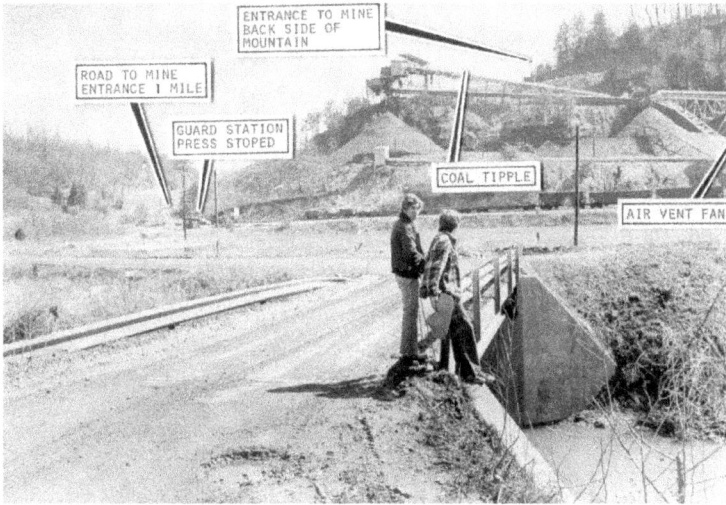

Scotia Mine Entrance

Press conference after explosions, 1976

U.S. Steel Mine Rescue Team

Friends and relatives gather at Scotia Mine After Explosions

Scotia bathhouse and tipple on left, main "bathhouse" portal on right.

Scotia tipple and loading facility

Family and friends at gravesite of Scotia Miner

Friends and family setting wreaths.

Funeral procession for deceased Miner

People gathering at Scotia after the explosions

Scotia yard engine, courtesy of The Railroad Photography of Jay and Robert W. Thompson.

Worst Mine Disaster in U.S., Monongah 6 & 8, Monongah, W. Va. 1907, 362 Dead. (MSHA Photo)

Scotia Mine Disaster Plaque

Photos courtesy of Dylan Nickels

Scotia Entrance 2017

Photo courtesy of Dylan Nickels

Brothers-Philip, Jimmy, Eddie Nickels, Scotia Miners
1976   (Author's photo collection.)

Foreman Harvey Creech checking newly built seal, 1976.
(Author's photo collection)

Second shift recovery crew and inspector, 1976.

(Author's photo collection.)
Eddie Nickels, Hargis Maggard, Jerry Smith, 2nd shift

Merle Rhodes and Hargis Maggard - Bosses

Scotia-Coal Mine of Doom

Ed Wells, Wayne Wilson, Eddie Nickels, Merle Rhodes,
Tommy Gross   (Author's photos)

Bosses-Bruce Jones, Hargis Maggard, Harvey Creech

(Author's photo collection.)
Near where the explosions took place

Memorial to Scotia Miners, Hemphill, Kentucky
Photo courtesy of Dylan Nickels

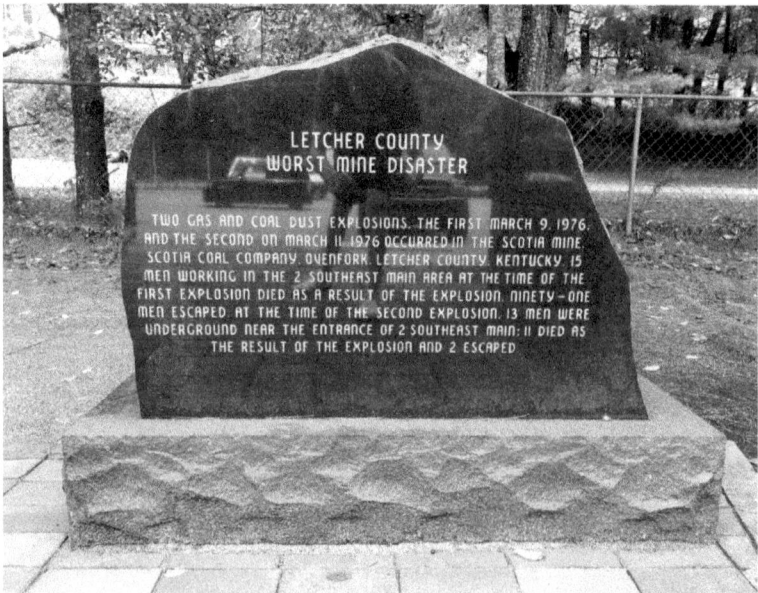

Memorial to Letcher County Miners
Photo courtesy of Dylan Nickels

1st Lieutenant Alexander "Sandy" Bonnyman
U.S. Marine Corps Reserves WWII

Medal of Honor Recipient

Public Domain Photo

Appendix A

Alexander "Sandy" Bonnyman Jr.

World War II—Medal of Honor Recipient

First Lieutenant, U.S. Marine Corps Reserves. For actions at Japanese-held Tarawa in the Gilbert Islands; November 23, 1943

Accredited to New Mexico, Sandy Bonnyman was born on May 2, 1910, in Atlanta, Georgia, but the family soon moved to Knoxville, Tennessee. His father was the president of Knoxville's Blue Diamond Coal Company, Which was one of the largest coal mining companies in the United States

Sandy Bonnyman was movie-star handsome, played on Princeton's football team and studied engineering. But he dropped out of college and began flight training with the Army Air Corps. He later washed out of flight school, reportedly for repeatedly buzzing control towers, and was honorably discharged September 19, 1932.

After his discharge, he went to work with his father, and married Josphine Bell at San Antonio, Texas in 1933. In 1938 he acquired his own copper mine in the mountains of New Mexico.

Exempt from the draft because of both his age and his vital industry, he nevertheless chose to enlist in the Marines as a private. He first distinguished himself at Guadalcanal, receiving a battlefield commission for his exceptional leadership.

On November 20, 1943, Bonnyman and his men were in Tarawa in the Gilbert Islands, attempting to come ashore under furious fire from Japanese shore batteries. Over three days, Bonnyman, who was supposed to be in a non-combat role directing operations, repeatedly braved overwhelming fire to lead men across the long, exposed Betio pier, organizing them into demolition teams to attack a bombproof Japanese emplacement that was raining fire on American troops. He (led his troops up) the sandy slope of the bunker and (directed) the calculated use of flame-(throwers) gunners, grenades, and rifle fire to destroy the bunker.

Bonnyman crawled 40 yards into enemy territory and placed demolitions in the opening of the heavily garrisoned installation. Withdrawing only for more ammunition, Bonnyman led his men in a renewed assault, repeatedly exposing himself to enemy fire as he stormed the bastion. He directed the placement of explosives in both entrances and stormed to the top of the installation. He flushed out more than 100 enemy soldiers, who were shot down instantly, and caused the death of another 150 Japanese troops inside the emplacement by dropping short-fused TNT charges down the air vents.

As the enemy poured out, he made a heroic stand atop the structure in the face of a fearless enemy charge, and killed three more before he fell. The final frames of the film show Bonnyman kneeling atop the bombproof, firing into the enemy, and turning to wave forward other marines before he fell, mortally wounded.

"By his dauntless fighting spirit, unrelenting aggressiveness and forceful leadership through three days of unremitting, violent battle, 1st Lieutenant Bonnyman inspired his men to heroic effort, enabling them to beat off the counterattack and break the back of hostile resistance."

James F. Forrestal, then Secretary of the Navy, presented the Medal of Honor to Bonnyman's teen-aged daughter, Frances, in Washington, D.C., January 22, 1947.

Bonnyman was declared Missing in Action or Buried at Sea, and his name appears on the Tablets of the Missing at the National Memorial Cemetery of the Pacific in Honolulu, Hawaii. In 2008, however just four days after families commemorated the 65th anniversary of the historic Battle of Tarawa, researchers announced that they had located the remains of 139 missing U.S. Marines killed there, with Bonnyman believed to be among them. *Lt. Bonnyman's remains were among those recovered. He was finally laid to rest in Knoxville, Tennessee on Sept. 27, 2015.

---

* Medal of Honor Convention

Appendix B

The President of the United States takes pride in presenting the MEDAL OF HONOR posthumously to:

First Lieutenant Alexander Bonnyman, Jr.
United States Marine Corps reserve

For service as set forth in the following
CITATION:

For conspicuous gallantry and intrepidity at the risk of his life above and beyond the call of duty as Executive Officer of the Second Battalion Shore Party, Eighth Marines, Second Marine Division, during the assault against enemy Japanese—held Tarawa in the Gilbert Islands, from 20 to 22 November 1943. Acting on his own imitative when assault troops were pinned down at the far end of Betio Pier by the overwhelming fire of Japanese shore batteries, First Lieutenant Bonnyman repeatedly defied the blasting fury of the enemy bombardment to organize and lead the besieged men over the long, open pier to the beach and then, voluntarily obtaining flame throwers and demolitions, organized his pioneer shore party into assault demolitions and directed the blowing of several hostile installations before the close of D-Day. Determined to affect an opening in the enemy's strongly organized defense line the following day, he voluntarily crawled approximately forty yards forward of our lines and placed demolitions in the entrance of a large Japanese emplacement as the initial move in his planned attack against the heavily garrisoned, bombproof installation which was stubbornly resisting despite the destruction early in the action of a large number of Japanese who had been inflicting heavy casualties on our forces and holding up our advance. Withdrawing only to replenish his ammunition, he led his men in a renewed assault, fearlessly exposing himself to the merciless slash of hostile fire as he stormed the formidable bastion, directed the placement of demolition charges in both entrances and seized the top of the bombproof position, flushing more than one hundred of the enemy who were instantly cut down and effecting the annihilation of approximately one and fifty troop inside the structure, defending his strategic position with indomitable determination in the face of the desperate

287

charge and killing three of the enemy before he fell, mortally wounded. By his dauntless fighting spirit, unrelenting aggressiveness and forceful leadership throughout three days of unremitting, violent battle, First Lieutenant Bonnyman had inspired his men to heroic, effort, enabling them to beat off the counterattack and break the back of hostile resistance in the sector for an immediate gain of four hundred yards with no further casualties to our forces in this zone. He gallantly gave his life for his country.

/S/Harry S. Truman

Appendix C

The following is the remembrance of a former Scotia Miner concerning the two explosions of March 9 and 11, 1976:

I had only been a miner a couple of years when the dreadful explosions happened. Being a young man of 22, mining was still fairly new to me.

As I prepared to go to work that day, March 9, 1976, it seemed to be just another 2nd shift work day. Little did I realize how wrong I was.

After my usual 15 minute drive across Pine Mountain, I arrived at the entrance of Scotia Coal Company. Something was different. Several strange vehicles were gathered there. As I drove up to the guard shack, instead of the usual wave from the guard, he flagged me down and nervously said, "There's been an explosion. We don't know yet how bad it is. You can go on in, but I don't know if there will be any work today."

I drove another ½ mile to the employee parking area. Co-workers were talking among themselves, trying to sort out what was going on. All we knew at that time was that there had been a huge underground explosion.

After an hour or so of confusion, and exchanging thoughts and rumors, the Company officials informed us there would be no work, and we should go home. Most of us left, but a few decided to stay a while longer, in case they were needed.

I drove back to the entrance. By this time, news of the explosion was beginning to spread throughout the county. There was a crowd starting to gather at the guard shack, mostly consisting of family members of coal miners. At that time, no one knew the extent of the accident, but it was easy to see the concern in their faces. My mom, dad, my Sister Kathy, and sister-in-law Wanda were among them. They were beyond relieved to see me, then quickly asked me if Eddie, my brother, was o.k. I explained to them that he was o.k., but had decided to stay at the mine site a while longer.

After getting home we listened intently to the news, to try and find out what had actually happened. As we began to learn just how serious it was, we were shocked and heartbroken.

Fifteen hard-working miners had lost their lives. But unfortunately, the mine wasn't yet finished with its devastation. Two days later when eleven brave men attempted a rescue or recovery mission, they too lost their lives in a second explosion.

Twenty six families' lives changed forever on those two terrible days.

I worked many years at Scotia after the twin explosions, but I was different afterward, as I believe everyone who worked there at that time was. The realization of mortality, and the importance of life, family, and friends were lessons we all learned and kept with us forever, along with the memory of that tragic time in our lives.

Jimmy D. Nickels,
Former Scotia Coal Miner

Appendix D

Dec. 4, 1976

Allen, Ky.

To the Rescue Teams or anyone who participated in the Recovery of the Eleven Bodies from the Scotia Mine:

Gentlemen:

I would like to thank each one of you who worked and took part in any way in the recovery. To me, one of those men was one of the greatest men on earth. He was Grover Tussey, my husband. I just wish that the bodies had been retrieved in the beginning. I am not acquainted with any of you, but I am sure that God knows each one of you by name. I wanted you to know that I am grateful for the recovery. May God richly bless each one of you and your family in my prayer.

Sincerely,

Mrs. Grover Tussey

BIBLIOGRAPHY

BOOKS

Caudill, Harry M., *Night Comes to the Cumberlands* , Little, Brown and Co. 1963

Clark-Kirkpatrick, *Exploring Kentucky*, 1960

Clark, Thomas D. , *Agrarian Kentucky*, The University Press of Kentucky, 1977

Clark, Thomas D., *A History of Kentucky*, The John Bradford Press, Lexington, Kentucky, 1960

Coal Mining Reference Book, Kentucky Mining Institute, 1973

Cornett, Terry, *Letcher County History*, 1967

Freese, Barbara, *Coal, A Human History*, Penguin Books, 2003

Guerrant, Edward O., *Blue Grass Confederate*, Edited by William C. Davis and Meredith L Swentor, Louisiana State University press, 1999.

Johnston, J Stoddard, *First Explorations of Kentucky*, Louisville, Kentucky, John P Morton and Company, 1898

McWhirter, Norris and Ross, *Guinness Book of World Records*, Bantam Books, 1974

Nickels, Eddie, *Six Years to Live*, Createspace, 2013

Warner, Ezra J., *Generals in Gray*, Louisiana State University Press, Baton Rouge, Louisiana,2013

Periodicals

United Mine Workers Journal, April, 1976

Mountain Life and Work, July, 1976

Pamphlets

Commonwealth of Kentucky, Department of Mines and Minerals; _Surface Mining Safety Standards_, Coal and Clay, 1975

Contracts, Scotia Employees Association, 1974-75-76; 1977-78-79; 1980-81-82; 1983-84-85; 1986-87-88; 1989-90-91

Federal Register/Vol. 76, No. 119/Tuesday June 21, 2011/ _Rules and Regulations_

Kravitz, Jeffrey H. _An Examination of Major Mine Disasters in the United States and a Historical Summary of MSHA's Mine Emergency Operations program._

Portable Methane Detector Instruction Manual, CSE Mine Service, Beckley, West Virginia

United States Department of the Interior, Mine Enforcement and Safety Administration, (MESA) _Entitlement of Miners_, 1969, The Federal Coal Mine Health and Safety Act of 1969.

United States Department of the Interior; _Investigations to determine the cause of the explosions March 9 and 11 at the Scotia Mine in Oven Fork, Kentucky; Whitesburg, Kentucky (public hearings)._

United States Department of Labor, Mine Safety and Health Administration; _Winter Alert Safety Manual,_ 1985

Unites States Department of Labor, Mine Safety and Health Administration Review Committee; _sol (MSHA) v. Scotia Coal_ , 1982

NEWSPAPERS
The Chicago Tribune, Chicago, Illinois, December 8, 1978

The Courier Journal, Louisville, Kentucky, March 14, 1976

The Letcher County Community Press, Cromona, Kentucky, March 18, 1976;

Lexington Herald –Leader, Lexington, Kentucky, November 13, 1991

The Mountain Eagle, Whitesburg, Letcher County, Kentucky; March 11, 18, 25, 1976; April 1, 8, 15, 22, 29, 1976; May 6, 13, 20, 27, 1976; June 24, 1976; July 15, 22, 1976; August 5, 12, 1976; September 23, 30, 1976; October 14, 28, 1976; November 4, 25, 1976, December 2, 9,30, 1976; March 10,1977; April 7, 1983

The New York Times, New York City, New York, June 20, 1981

Government Reports

Mine Disasters in the United States, The United States Mine Rescue Association.

Scotia Coal Mine Disaster, U.S. Government Printing Office, 1976; A Staff Report Prepared by the Staff of the House Committee on Education and Labor Standards, John H Dent, Chairman.

Index

E

F

G

H

I

J

K

L

M

S

T

U

V

W

About the Author

Eddie Nickels is a retired Scotia Coal Miner who is eminently qualified to write of the two devastating explosions of March 9 and 11, 1976. As a volunteer on the mine recovery team, he had occasion to visit the sites of both explosions and to observe the areas involved in some detail. He also helped to recover and ventilate the active sections of the mine in order for production of coal to resume. After retirement from Scotia he worked for and retired from a large insurance company as an Insurance Account Representative. He has three children, eight grandchildren, and five great-grandchildren, and lives in Mayking, Kentucky. He is the author of three other books; _Six Years to Live; Marine Corps Draftee; and Garfield versus Marshall._

www.ingramcontent.com/pod-product-compliance
Lightning Source LLC
Chambersburg PA
CBHW081323090426
42737CB00017B/3011